FLAT BROKE WITH TWO GOATS

FLAT BROKE WITH TWO GOATS

a memoir

JENNIFER McGAHA

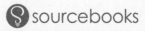

sourcebooks

Published by Sourcebooks, Inc.
P.O. Box 4410, Naperville, Illinois 60567-4410
(630) 961-3900
Fax: (630) 961-2168
sourcebooks.com

Library of Congress Cataloging-in-Publication Data

Names: McGaha, Jennifer, author.
Title: Flat broke with two goats : a memoir / Jennifer McGaha.
Description: Naperville, Illinois : Sourcebooks, [2018]
Identifiers: LCCN 2017015544 | (pbk. : alk. paper)
Subjects: LCSH: Farmers--Appalachian Region--Biography. | Autobiography.
Classification: LCC S417.M45 M34 2018 | DDC 630.9756/8--dc23 LC record
available at https://lccn.loc.gov/2017015544

Printed and bound in the United States of America.
VP 10 9 8 7 6 5 4 3 2 1

For my maternal grandparents, Hubert and Adeline Boyd,

whose love continues to sustain us all.

A mountain keeps an echo deep inside itself. That's how I hold your voice.

—RUMI

FLAT BROKE WITH TWO GOATS

Chapter One

I WAS UPSTAIRS FOLDING LAUNDRY when I heard the horn. From the wide porch window, I watched a blue car with a flashing yellow light on top ease around the bend—the mailman. Our mailbox stood next to the main road, almost a mile away from the house, and because our driveway was full of holes and bumps and sagging telephone wires, most delivery people left our packages there, wedged against the mailbox flag. In fact, since our move here to the woods, we had only had one other group of unexpected visitors, Jehovah's Witnesses who sprang from their car, stuck a leaflet on a window ledge, and were gone before I could get to the door.

So I knew the mailman's presence meant only one thing: certified mail. And I knew that certified mail meant only one thing: bad news. Still, I might as well get this over with. I threw down the towel in my hand and headed outside just as two of our five dogs, Hester, a yellow Lab mix, and Reba, a lanky Carolina dog, sprinted down the driveway. Yapping and snarling, they lunged at the mailman's tires.

"Man," the mailman said, surveying me, the snarling dogs, the ramshackle house, the old outhouse, the pieces of scrap metal and scrap lumber strewn everywhere. "I feel like I'm in a Chevy Chase film."

Don't we all, I wanted to say. *Don't we all.*

I supposed he meant *Funny Farm*, the 1988 film where Chevy plays a New Yorker who moves to rural Vermont in search of rest and solace and instead finds mayhem. At best, it was a generous interpretation of our circumstances. We had lived here, in this century-old cabin in the mountains of western North Carolina, for six months. Still, in that moment just after I woke in the mornings, before my conscious mind was fully engaged, I often pictured myself back in my sun-soaked bedroom in the spacious Cape Cod–style house just a few miles from here, the house we had lived in for eight years, the house with finished ceilings and floors, where I had not once seen a venomous snake, where mice were an occasional occurrence rather than an everyday hazard.

I signed for the letter the mailman handed me and noted the name on the return address, an attorney in Asheville. Of course, I knew what it was. I had been expecting it for weeks, so now that it had finally arrived, it was, in a way, a relief. No longer was the foreclosure something that was *going to* happen. It was something that was *currently happening*, something I was already getting through, which meant, somehow, I might emerge, perhaps not unscathed but stable, sane, not a total wreck of a person. So I took the fact that I shushed my dogs and helped the mailman turn around in the drive to be a good sign, an indication that I would survive this, that someday, we would refer to the time our house was foreclosed in the past tense. It would be something that happened long ago, something barely worth mentioning. *The house we lived in before the financial collapse*, we would say. *The home we lost just before things got better*.

I had experienced this same kind of numb acquiescence several years before when my grandfather was dying. For months, I had been so consumed with grief and worry over his failing health that when he was actually lying in his hospice bed, his breaths low and raspy, the air filled with strange, acrid scents, something in me released. All those months of trying to keep him alive, of holding out hope that he might suddenly spring up and walk out of the hospital vibrant, spirited, whole, were over. As I sat next to his bedside, talking to my children, eating the casseroles people brought, grading student papers while he oscillated in and out of consciousness, I had thought, *Maybe, just maybe, I can get through this*.

During the Great Recession, millions of Americans lost their jobs, and millions of families lost their homes, so David and I were hardly alone in our circumstances. The greatest financial calamity since the Great Depression, the recession had struck rural Appalachia particularly hard. Here, many of us remained only one or two generations removed from the sort of hand-to-mouth existence our forebears had experienced.

Though the recession officially lasted less than two years, the ramifications continued long after that time. Jobs were scarce. Unemployment and underemployment were rampant, and real estate sales were virtually nonexistent. Three years after the official end of the recession, the year our home was foreclosed, foreclosure notices continued to splatter the local newspaper. Somehow, though, knowing we were not alone did not make our situation any easier. Instead, the thought of all those empty homes—all those lives interrupted— compounded my loss, filled me with a greater sadness, the sum of all those broken parts.

Inside the cabin, I opened the envelope from the attorney. The papers outlined everything I already knew, skipping a few of the more salient points, such as how irresponsible and short-sighted we were for entering into a contract where our friends, Jeff and Denise, had owner-financed our home. Our kids—their daughter and son and our three children—had grown up together. Their daughter, Jacqueline, and our older son, Aaron, had been particularly close. They met in kinder-garten, back when Jeff and Denise still lived in the house we would later buy, and they had been good friends for the past fifteen years— three-quarters of their lives. Denise and I became friends too, in the way people do when their lives necessarily intersect, in that "it takes a village" sort of way people in small towns raise their kids. We emailed regularly, lunched sometimes, occasionally spent weekends with all of our kids at their summer cottage in nearby Montreat.

Together, Denise and I worried about Jacqueline's difficulty reading, my younger son's attention issues, our older children's crowd of friends. We shared carpool duties and recipes and jokes about the more eccentric members of the Episcopal church we both attended. We baked each other Christmas cookies and exchanged gifts. Our families celebrated special events together at their new home, a rambling, circular house in a gated golfing community. We consoled each other when the young daughter of a mutual friend died of brain cancer and again when our kids' fifteen-year-old classmate fatally shot himself in the face.

When David and I bought Jeff and Denise's house, the arrangement had seemed ideal. The Cape Cod–style house looked out over wide pastures and expansive cornfields. The two-acre property had at one time been an apple orchard, and from our front porch, we could look over the cabins and trailers and farmhouse and see where the fields ended and DuPont Forest began—dense woods of pines and hardwoods. The setting was rural, quiet, ideal for us, our three children, and our dogs, who were disturbing our next-door neighbor in town. Jeff and Denise built the house themselves, and it had already been on the market for a couple of years when we looked at it. One factor making the house hard to sell was that the water pipes were made of polybutylene, a type of material known to corrode. We knew this might pose a potential problem for us down the road, but at the time, we were ready for a change and willing to take the risk. We would deal with the pipes later, we said. *If* a problem occurred.

After we moved in, however, we soon realized the house had other issues. The upstairs bath leaked through the ceiling onto the kitchen counter. The porch wood had not been properly treated, and it soon rotted and fell apart. Within the first few years, we had to replace all of the wood outside—the back deck, the door frames. And then the roof began leaking in multiple places. One morning, I woke to find boxes of our family photos full of water. Eventually, we set a metal mixing bowl beneath the largest leak in our bedroom. At night, the pinging of the water was so loud, we folded a washcloth and tucked it into the bowl to mute the sound. We needed a new roof, but there never seemed to be enough money left over after paying our other expenses. We would make do until we had some extra cash, we thought. Surely, that would be soon.

Still, we enjoyed the abundant sunshine and the quiet pace of country life. I grew basil in pots on the front porch, tomatoes in a bed out front. We fenced in the spacious backyard for our dogs, and in the midst of the old apple grove, David grew peppers and okra and corn and squash. My favorite thing about the house, though, was the sunroom. It was large and full of windows, and we had all our special family dinners there. I loved cooking. I loved chopping onions, smashing garlic cloves, slicing peppers, sautéing spices to bring out their flavors. I loved the way the house filled with the scent of cumin and coriander and chilies, the way my kids, summoned by the smells, clustered around the kitchen island sneaking bites of tortillas, French bread, and pepper-jack cheese. And I loved that moment when dinner was finally ready and all five of us gathered at the long, wooden table in the sunroom. I loved the clamor and chaos of everyone reaching over and around and between everyone else, of our dogs barking and begging for food, of the incessant banter of my children.

I would do anything for those few moments a day, for that hour or half hour at the dinner table with my family, so I cooked with a sort of primal ferocity, as if the safety and sanctity of my family depended on it. In the winter, I made soups and stews and homemade bread, lasagna, tostadas, enchiladas, shrimp and grits, barbecued spare ribs, cream-cheese braids, fondue. In the summer, I made gazpacho, corn chowder, squash casserole, stuffed peppers, Thai lettuce wraps with three different sauces, homemade pesto. On hot summer nights, the neighbor's children Hula-Hooped on their roof, and while we lingered at the dinner table over wine and angel-hair pasta with fresh pesto, we watched the hoops spinning around and around, the effect both dizzying and exhilarating.

Pesto was simple to make, but something about it always felt extravagant, perhaps because we only ate it at the height of summer when we had our own crop of fresh basil, perhaps because it tasted so fresh and bright, like summer itself. Even today, the bright scent of basil, the evening sun slanting through the apple trees, and the sounds of my children's voices merge together in my mind, one seamless, three-dimensional snapshot.

When we bought Jeff and Denise's house, our children were still children, our sons, Eli and Aaron, ten and twelve, our daughter, Alex, fifteen, a freshman in high school. By the time the house was foreclosed, eight years later, Aaron and Alex were in college, and Eli was eighteen, a high school senior. My kids walked into that house one moment as children and left the next as adults. Maybe under other circumstances, it would have seemed different, a more natural letting go. As it was, when we lost the house, I was filled with a strange yet pressing sense that I was deserting my children, simply walking away and leaving them behind. Later, after we moved to the cabin, I would think back on those years at the Cape Cod house with a critic's eye, dissecting every moment, looking for affirmation that I had, in fact, been a decent mother, that my kids had had happy childhoods.

We had debt, even then, but David was making well over six figures a year as a private accountant and part-time real estate agent, and the house payments were manageable—so manageable, in fact, that we decided to send our kids to a private school in Asheville for middle school and high school. David and I had both gone to the local public schools, and our experiences there had not been good overall. We wanted better for our kids. Though the school in Asheville was pricey, our kids received generous amounts of financial aid, and we paid only a couple of thousand the first year our daughter went there. However, when our boys began attending as well, the total price tag got higher and higher until the amount we were paying for all three kids was about the cost of the average public college tuition. And then there was the cost of gas for the hour-and-a-half daily commute.

Still, we loved the school community, which was, in many ways, much more diverse than the public school in our own community. Maybe our kids would avoid some of the challenges David and I had faced in high school. Maybe the other kids would be more ambitious than many of our peers had been. Maybe their ambition would rub off on our children. Maybe our kids would be challenged more academically and, as a result, get into better colleges and secure better jobs. Maybe their lives would be easier than ours had been, their success more readily ensured. Our decision seemed logical enough at the time. Plus, we had every reason to believe our upward earning trend would continue. *When the kids are older, we'll start saving*, we said. *When the kids are older, we'll pay off our debts.*

Each year at the private school was more costly, however, and eventually, we needed to borrow more money to keep up with our expenses. We got a second mortgage, then a third until our monthly mortgage payments totaled over three thousand dollars. David worked long hours, sleeping little, drinking tons of coffee. Although at the time I assumed he preferred the calm chaos of his office to the outright chaos of a home full of kids and pets, I now know he was desperately trying to keep up. And then the country sank into the second greatest economic crisis in history, and, like millions of other Americans, we sank right along with it.

David's accounting business relied heavily on building contractors and other laborers who were soon out of work, and his real estate commissions came to a sudden and definitive halt. His income was quickly cut in half, then in half again, and my adjunct teaching positions contributed little to our family income. All those years of overspending, of thinking we would pay things off next month, next year, start a savings plan sometime in the future, finally caught up with us. Though David had been the eternal optimist, adept at always staying one step ahead—borrowing from A to pay B, borrowing from C to pay A—our lives had at last become one meandering, nonsensical equation. We were more than $350,000 in debt. Our credit cards were maxed out. Our cars were old and in desperate need of repairs. And, even worse, we had a tax problem. *A major tax problem.*

Nostalgia Pesto

For this recipe, I use a variety of types of basil leaves. Lemon is especially good.

- 2 cups fresh basil leaves
- 2 cloves garlic, roughly chopped
- ½ cup extra-virgin olive oil
- ¼ cup pine nuts or walnuts, toasted
- ¼ cup Parmesan or Romano cheese, shredded
- Sea salt, to taste

In a food processor, pulse the basil and garlic until combined. Add the nuts and cheese. Pulse a few more times. Gradually drizzle in the olive oil until the mixture is smooth. Season with sea salt. Serve over hot noodles to a wistful crowd in a cheerful, sunlit room.

Chapter Two

LATE ONE APRIL NIGHT, I woke to a strange, gasping sound. David lay beside me, his face buried in a pillow. For a moment, I was perfectly still, groggy, unsure of what to do, unsure even of what exactly was happening.

"What's wrong?" I finally asked. "Is something wrong?"

He was quiet for several minutes. And then he said, "Two IRS agents came to my office today."

For a long time, that was all he said. Still half-asleep, I struggled to figure out what he meant. David routinely dealt with the IRS through his job, so it didn't make sense that this was a problem, yet something told me not to ask questions, to just let him talk. So I waited. The room was still and dark, the only sound the whir of the fan on the dresser. Maybe he hadn't spoken after all. Maybe I had been dreaming. I was just drifting back off to sleep when he spoke again.

"We owe back taxes," he said.

Even now, years later, I can still feel the weight of the quiet that followed, the weight of everything I had ever thought or believed crashing down all at once. David and I had been married twenty years, and because he was an accountant, he had always been in charge of our finances, including our taxes. He had filled out the forms, then brought them to me to sign. My income information was simple, straightforward. I never made more than ten thousand dollars a year, and because I didn't know how much David made in any given year until I actually saw the return, there was not a lot to discuss. I just signed the forms he handed me, usually in a rush on April 15, after all his clients' taxes had been completed, when I was in between running the kids to school and soccer practice and play practice and choir and he was too exhausted to explain it all.

"Sign here," he would say.

And I did. Lying next to him now, I could not figure out how he could have made such a mistake. He was an accountant, for Christ's sake. He had been filing other people's taxes for almost twenty years. But of course, if we owed back taxes, we simply had to pay it—one hundred dollars, one thousand dollars, two thousand dollars—whatever it was. But even as I formulated those thoughts, I sensed that the problem was bigger than that.

"How much?" I finally asked.

In response, there were no words, only that strange gasping.

So I asked again. "How much?"

And that's when he told me. The whole saga unfolded in jerky sobs, in starts and stops and half-formed thoughts, David's voice odd and strained, a faraway echo. For the last several years, we had not filed tax returns. With the late penalties, we owed more than one hundred thousand dollars to the IRS, another eight thousand dollars to the state. Wide awake now, I both heard him and didn't hear him. What he was saying was not real. It was a dream. He was telling me there was a little green man on our roof, a unicorn in our yard. I wanted him to go back to sleep and stop dragging me into his nightmare.

"I just didn't have the money," he said, his voice fading like a distant train. "I'm sorry. I'm so, so sorry."

I struggled to remember. Hadn't I signed a return last year? Or the year before? Or two years before that? And if not, how could I possibly not have noticed? How does one not notice *four years* of missed tax returns? But even in the haze of shock and denial, in the aftermath of this seismic shift wherein my husband was not dead but was still, nonetheless, not the man I had known just hours before, I knew that everything he was telling me was true, that our lives had just been upended, that I had fallen asleep in one world—a world in which I believed that David would always work things out, *could* always work things out—and awoken in quite another world, one I had no clue how to navigate.

There had, of course, been signs that things were not going well, signs I should have seen but somehow didn't. When I was growing up, my parents had created for my brother and me the perfect upper-middle-class lifestyle. We had everything we needed and most things we wanted. We took piano lessons. We went to summer camp. We swam at the local country club. We had college funds. And while what

I should have learned from living a relatively privileged childhood was the value of hard work and frugality, what I learned instead was that money was not something with which I needed to be overly concerned. If and when I needed it, it would magically appear—like a genie.

It was this sort of head-in-the-clouds approach to finances that allowed me to ignore all the indications that something was very wrong with our finances—the stacks of unopened bills in David's home office, the telephone that rang incessantly but that we never answered unless we recognized the caller ID. That had been going on for years. More recently, though, there had been other, even more obvious indications. Twice, the phone had been disconnected. On more than one occasion, I had come home to find the power turned off. We had also been visited by a sheriff's deputy delivering a summons to appear in court for a bill that had not been paid. And then one day, I was sitting on a barstool at the island in the kitchen when there was a knock at the door. The front door was open, and the sun cast a large, yellow rectangle on the faux-wood floors.

A man about my age stood on the front porch. He wore jeans, a T-shirt, a baseball cap. *Thank God.* He was not with the sheriff's department, the power company, the phone company. He held in his hand a piece of paper, and I assumed he was trying to deliver a package to one of our neighbors. It happened often. The houses in our cul-de-sac were numbered from the right side of the road to the end and back down the left side, so even though our house was the first on the road, we were number twenty-three.

"Hi," I said, stepping onto the porch.

"Hey," he said.

My dogs barked furiously, all at the same deafening frequency, and while we waited for them to quiet down, we watched a cow and newborn calf grazing in the pasture across the street.

"That's not for me, is it?" I finally asked, gesturing toward the paper.

"Yes, ma'am," he said. "If that's your blue van right there, then this is for you. I'm here to repossess it."

In the hour or so that followed, the man waited while I called David, who somehow managed to come up with the money we owed. The bank was called. A payment was made. The man was sent home without my van. I was tremendously relieved. Our van had *almost* been repossessed but not *actually* repossessed. It had been an oversight on David's part, a slip of memory, and the incident was over, forgiven and forgotten.

The next month, however, the man was back, and this time, he took the van. It took us weeks to get it back, and in the meantime, I drove the old Ford Explorer David had bought used for two thousand dollars several years before. The handles for the driver's-side door and window were broken, and David had wedged a brick underneath the driver's seat to keep it upright. I could not move the seat forward or back, so I sat crooked on the edge of the seat, stretching my right leg to reach the pedals.

Up until now, all the things I should have seen as warning signs had simply seemed like minor inconveniences. Somehow, David always managed to fix things. The lights came back on. The phone worked.

The subpoenas to appear in court for unpaid bills were withdrawn. It never once occurred to me that the power might be out for good, that one day we might *actually* find ourselves in court. I was engrossed in the day-to-day aspects of my life, which were distinct in my mind from the day-to-day aspects of David's life.

I taught three college classes per semester—seventy-five students or more per semester. I prepped for classes and graded papers and attended my students' concerts and football games. I volunteered in my own kids' classrooms. I organized their birthday parties and Halloween bonfires and cookie decorating gatherings. I shuttled them from one activity to another—soccer, chorus, theater, swim team, school dances. I coaxed them through struggles in school, arguments with friends, breakups with love interests. I fed and walked our menagerie of dogs. I helped care for my aging grandparents. Money was the last thing on my mind. David was in charge of the money, and as naïve as it sounds, I always believed that whatever our financial problems were, he would eventually sort them out. In fact, that was what he told me over and over again: *I've got it.* He never suggested I take a more active role in managing our finances, and he continued to evade my questions. Every "discussion" about our finances quickly turned into a heated argument. Finally, for what I thought was in the best interest of our family—for peace between the two of us—I stopped asking.

Perhaps I should have asked longer or harder. Perhaps I should have insisted on being an equal partner in our finances *or else*. He was not willing to considering moving somewhere where I might have been able to find a job more easily, but perhaps things would have turned out differently for us all if I had been willing to move without him, if I had taken a job that offered more financial security, if I had worked four jobs, five jobs, whatever it took to make David's life less stressful and our kids' lives more secure. *If, if, if...* Of course, I see these choices now, but for whatever reason—perhaps because I was raised in a household where the husband was the sole provider, perhaps because I tended to have tunnel vision, perhaps because I was selfish and I wanted what I wanted—I did not see them then.

"This has to stop," I told David after our van was repossessed. "If the sheriff comes to our house one more time, I'm leaving."

"Okay," he said. "Okay. I'm doing the best I can."

Which he was. The truth—the truth he didn't want to tell me—was that he had no idea how much money he was going to make from one month to the next. Because his income varied wildly and because the terms of my employment varied from one semester to the next, we had no real way of planning for the next week, the next month, the next year. So we were trapped in a cycle of putting out fires, of throwing money at the most pressing problem at hand without any real long-term plan. It was an unsustainable lifestyle, one that was destined to come spiraling down around us.

Lying in bed that strange spring night after David told me about our taxes, I realized that this time, David had no idea how to fix things—no pending real estate deal that might yield a big commission, no credit card we could use. For what seemed like forever, we lay silently, not touching, barely breathing. Wind howled through the walls. It was yet another construction flaw—not enough insulation.

"I'm sorry," David said again. "I'm so sorry. I will get us out of this. You will not be held responsible."

Later, I would be angry. Later, I would say to him, "If I had taken care of our children like you took care of our finances, they would all be dead by now."

And he would look at me and say, "I know. You're right. I know."

But now my brain felt sluggish. It took all of my energy to simply keep up with what was happening. Slowly, very slowly, the reality of the situation began to sink in: David could go to jail for this. I could go to jail. At the time, I didn't know how bad it could be or even what exactly the charges would be, but later, I looked it up. If the offense was considered a misdemeanor, we could be fined up to twenty-five thousand dollars or sentenced to a year in prison for every year we had failed to file a return. And that was the better case scenario. If the offense was considered a felony, we could be fined up to one hundred thousand dollars and sentenced to five years in jail.

In the coming months, we would be subjected to tax liens. We could not sell our house or our cars, and though there was a cap on the percentage that could be taken in any one paycheck, my wages would be garnished, and the little money we had in our bank accounts would be routinely seized by the state. We had no savings. Our credit was too bad to borrow money from a bank. And when we were finally able to negotiate a monthly payment with the IRS, the payments were set at six thousand dollars a month, a hopelessly large amount, an amount we never once managed to pay.

Many Americans equate paying taxes with patriotism and not paying taxes with subversion, but it was not that we didn't *want* to pay our taxes. We had paid the bills that seemed most imperative at the time, the most immediate, and now we had no money left. In our small town, word got around about our situation, and at the oddest times, people would come up to me and tell me their stories. One night, a woman I had known for years came up to me at a party. She grabbed my sleeve, lowered her voice, and leaned into me.

"We owed back taxes too," she whispered.

And while I was struggling to figure out exactly how she had heard about my tax problems, she added, "A *lot*. It was a lot of money."

Later, I would get used to these sudden confessions. Every single time, they were stories, not of intentional deceit, of hiding money in foreign accounts or not reporting income, but of too much optimism and too little foresight, of believing that the current state of things was temporary, that things would surely soon get better. Estimates of the number of Americans who owe money to the IRS range from eight million to twenty million. Some of those people are rich and hiding their money in the ways that rich people have always hidden their money. Others are ordinary, middle-class Americans who somehow got swept up in the current of the bad economy.

For the next several years, David worked more and more, making less and less money each year, growing increasingly tired and despondent, and despite the fact that I had a master's degree and was constantly searching for a permanent teaching position, I was unable to find full-time work. The college where I taught part time relied almost exclusively on adjuncts to teach entry-level English courses. Every semester, they intimated that they might soon be looking to hire someone full time, and then the following semester, they would hire three adjuncts to fill one teaching position. I considered trying to get a job teaching high school, but I didn't have a degree in education or a teaching license, so teaching in the public school system was out of the question. I couldn't even work as a teacher's assistant because of the requisite credit check. Finally, I began to look at jobs in other fields, secretarial positions and receptionist positions, but every job description I found read like a description of areas in which I was particularly lacking: "Must be highly organized. Must be a self-starter. Must be detail oriented." They might as well have said, "Must not be, nor ever have been, nor ever aspire to be, an English teacher or a writer." I repeatedly applied for every opening that seemed even a remote possibility, but I never got an interview or even a phone call. At one particularly low point, a close friend suggested I apply for a job at the Belk department store in town.

"Have you seen how I dress?" I asked her, exasperated. "Do you really think they would hire someone like me?"

She looked at my short skirt and cowboy boots, my necklace made of recycled Coke bottles.

"Well, I guess not," she said.

Finally, in a last ditch effort to save our old house, David took a second job in addition to his more-than-full-time accounting business. He had some clients who owned a Chipotle-style Mexican restaurant that was quickly losing money. When they decided one day to simply walk away from the business, David offered to take over. While he was still in college, David had successfully managed a seafood restaurant, and he thought he could do it again—turn this business around, make it profitable—so despite the fact that his cooking expertise was limited to scrambled eggs and toast, he moved his accounting office into the same building as the restaurant and split his days between the two businesses.

He was excited to be doing something different, and he poured his energy into this new venture. He loved the challenge of trying to make the business profitable. He analyzed costs and prices, overhauled the menu, hired new employees, and developed rules and systems for all sorts of things that needed rules and systems—ordering food, storing food, cleaning, etc. The restaurant was across the street from my office at the college, so some days after my classes, I walked over and tasted new foods, made menu suggestions, and wrote promotional material for flyers and newspaper ads. I suggested craft beers to add to the beverage selection, convinced David to switch to antibiotic-free, hormone-free chicken, and, with a friend of mine, came up with new meat marinade recipes. Savory steak. Ground beef. Spicy chicken. Citrus chicken.

However, the newly revamped menu did nothing to increase our earnings. It turns out good quality juices and olive oils are expensive, and we were never able to raise the prices enough to compensate for our increased expenditures. At best, we were breaking even, and David was spending long hours at the restaurant. If we had been able to invest some money—buy a margarita machine, start a catering business—it might have eventually been profitable, but after over a year of trying to turn things around, David was exhausted and not at all hopeful that he could put the restaurant back in the green. He told the owners he was finished, and a former manager took over.

David and I were very busy those days, but when I did pause to think about our futures, I was able to convince myself that we were just on the verge of finding our way out of this deep financial hole. Other times, when the full reality of our circumstances hit me, my own desperation frightened me. Driving home alone late at night from book club or class, speeding along the curvy mountain road toward our house, I thought of just letting go, of taking my hands off the wheel and closing my eyes. What would it be like, I wondered, to feel the swift rush of cool water as the car careened into the river or hear the splintering of wood and metal as it crashed into a tall oak tree? In the end, would I be sorry or simply relieved? *At least this would be over then*, I thought. *Over*.

These were brief moments, half-formed impulses flitting in and out of my consciousness, not something I truly planned to do, but an idea I toyed with: *What would it be like?* I saw myself there in a heap against a tree, no longer someone anyone was counting on or someone counting on anyone else, just an odd amalgamation of singed clothes and tangled metal. And each time, after I eventually arrived home, healthy, whole, not slammed against a tree or overturned at the bottom of an embankment, I was immensely relieved. I had survived.

Finally, one afternoon after I had come home to find our power turned off for the third time in just a few months, I drove to David's office. Together, we sat down in the empty waiting room that should have been full of clients.

"We have to do something," I said.

David slumped against the chair, his head resting against the concrete wall behind him.

"What?" he asked. "What do you want to do?"

I hadn't planned to say it. I hadn't even known I was thinking it. But the answer was as clear to me as if someone else had spoken it.

"We have to stop this," I said. "We have to give up our house."

And very, very slowly, David nodded.

In the days that followed, we told Jeff and Denise, separately—me in a tearful, apologetic email to Denise, David in a private conversation with Jeff. *We can't keep up our house payments*, we said. *We want to, but we can't. We're really, really sorry.* It would be the last conversation we would have with our long-time friends. After that, we just stopped making our payments. The house was going to be foreclosed, and everything we read about foreclosure told us that you don't make payments on a house you know you are going to lose. Instead, you make a calculated play: You run out the clock. You pocket your mortgage payments to pay for your moving expenses, for attorney fees, for rent on another place. In reality, it was the only choice we had.

I didn't blame Denise or Jeff for pursuing foreclosure. It was what they had to do under the circumstances, and I knew we had left them in a hard place. Still, I was stung by what felt like their lack of empathy for our situation. Perhaps if Denise and I had had a different kind of friendship, if we had been old college friends or hiking buddies instead of friends through our children, we might have been able to navigate through this difficult time. As it was, she did not contact me again, and I did not contact her. Just the thought of a conversation with Denise exhausted me, drained my last bit of emotional energy. I had apologized. I didn't know what else to say. I did not even understand my role in all of this myself.

Thankfully, though, Denise made no effort to contact me. Eventually, I deleted all of our conversations from my email, and I avoided going places in town where I might run into her. In the coming months, I mourned our friendship. We had raised our children together. We had a history together. Something funny would happen, and I would want to tell Denise. Or I would have a question that I knew she could answer, like whether or not to hyphenate a certain word, and I would want to email her and ask her what to do, but I knew she felt I had betrayed her, that we had betrayed them, and I couldn't bring myself to contact her again.

By the time David and I started looking for another place to live, Alex and Aaron were in college, but Eli was a rising high school senior. He had one more year at home, and David and I wanted to find a place to live where Eli could have a space of his own. After much discussion, we also decided to let him finish his senior year at the same private school he had attended since sixth grade. His friends were there. His teachers were important mentors and role models, and besides, at this point, a few thousand dollars for tuition wasn't going to make any difference anyway. *He needs stability*, we said. It was the very thing we couldn't give him, yet we said it anyway.

David and I also had six animals to consider—five dogs and a cat. At this point, most rational people would simply have given their animals away. Then again, rational people would never have had six pets. We spent hours scanning Craigslist for farms and farmhouses that needed tenants but found nothing suitable. Plus, it seemed as if we were talking about something that was going to happen to someone else. *Someone else* had made a series of bad decisions. *Someone else* was going to lose her home. *Someone else* might go to jail.

One afternoon that spring or early summer, David came to me with a proposition.

"You're going to have to be open-minded," he said.

We were standing in the kitchen, next to the stove that flashed "F4" for "power failure imminent," as it had been doing for weeks. It needed to be fixed, but why fix a stove we were going to have to leave behind?

"How open-minded?" I asked.

There was a house out in the woods, he said. Well, not *exactly* a house. More like a cabin, really. It was over a hundred years old, and it belonged to people we knew, the family of one of David's distant cousins.

Here were the pros: One, the rent would be nominal, almost nonexistent. Two, we could make any changes we wanted. Three, the cabin was on fifty-three beautiful wooded acres, and we would have full use of all of that land. And, four—and this was a great selling point— just outside the front door was a towering waterfall covered in lush moss and flanked by oaks and hemlocks and flowering rhododendrons. Beneath the falls ran a cool and rocky stream.

However, there were just a couple of minor drawbacks: The cabin was heated primarily by a wood boiler, which also heated the water. And the spring water ran into the creek before being diverted to the house and was probably safe for drinking, but it was hard to be certain because…

"Just stop," I said, holding up one hand. "Stop." I leaned on the kitchen island, a mug of coffee in my hand.

"So what do you think?" David asked.

Light poured through the front door. Just outside, the crepe myrtles were starting to bloom. Their blossoms sagged and fell onto the front porch, creating a brilliant pink doormat. In the pasture across the street, alpacas huddled together, grazing. Listening to David describe this way-more-than-rustic cabin, I wanted to walk out the front door, past the crepe myrtles and the patches of mint and poison ivy in the front flower beds, past the basketball goal with the torn net and the cracked driveway and the pasture where a neighborhood kid liked to camp in his survival gear, past the time when we were *we*, and into my own, separate life.

Maybe I could go to my grandmother's house in Canton. Already, I was spending at least one night a week there, caring for her. I could settle into the bedroom where, as a child, I had fallen asleep to the sound of a distant train whistle and woken to the smell of bacon. Or I could go to my parents' house, to the three-story house in the upscale neighborhood where I was raised, where the beds were always made, where the floors were scrubbed clean with vinegar, and neat rows of vacuum prints streaked the carpet, like mower imprints on a lawn. Or perhaps I could go to my brother's house in Florida, sit by his kidney-shaped pool, soaking in the sun and buying myself some time until I could think of what to do next.

I knew, though, that none of these options were realistic. I had pets to care for, a son to finish raising. And I had a husband who looked like a man close to his limit, and though I wasn't even sure what that meant, I had some vague idea of what a man that desperate might do. *Maybe*, I told myself, *maybe I can leave him later, when he is stronger.* It was an ignoble thought, but it was the only way out of this mess I could see. In my mind, David was the problem. Or maybe David and I together were the problem, but in any case, if I could just get away, maybe things would be better. At least then I would always know exactly how much money I had. I would know which bills had been paid and which ones had not. I would formulate a plan that I alone would implement. Maybe then I would feel more in control of my life.

Maybe things would stop happening *to me*, and I could start making things happen.

Some days, I truly believed this was the solution to our problems. Other days, I was torn between wanting to leave and believing that there might still be hope for my marriage. David and I had been married for more than twenty years. We met at a high school football game when I was just sixteen and he was eighteen. Early one morning a few weeks after we first met, David parked his blue Fiesta just across the hill from the high school. I parked my car in the lower parking lot as usual and strolled down the hallway toward my homeroom. Then, just before the first bell, I ducked out the back door and darted over the bank to where David was waiting. We drove to his grandmother's house off Haywood Road in West Asheville. David's grandmother had moved to a nursing home, and he lived here with a roommate, a roommate who was not home that particular day. The floorboards in the house shifted and creaked, and the house was tilted over the bank. When you stood in the kitchen, you felt like you might slide off into the yard below.

David had worked all night the night before, and while he took a nap, I rummaged through his refrigerator. There was a twelve-pack of Budweiser, a package of hot dogs, and a loaf of Sunbeam bread. I popped open a beer and headed to the living room, where I took out a notebook and pen and began compiling notes for a story I was working on for the school newspaper.

All morning long, I sat on David's sofa, drinking beer, editing stories, writing. By midmorning, I had filled a spiral notebook, and I had made a large dent in David's beer supply. I was starting to feel queasy, light-headed. Maybe I needed something to eat. But when I went into the bedroom to tell David this, he stopped me before I could speak.

"Come here," he said, pulling back the covers.

And the quiet boy I had met at the football game was so confident and strong that I forgot all about how sick I felt. Later, driving me home, he would say how glad he was that I wasn't drunk the first time we had sex, and I would laugh, amused that he didn't know, surprised that it mattered.

David and I dated most of my senior year, then broke up when we both moved away to attend college. There were other guys after that, including Scott, a man I met in college and was married to for a year, but there was never anyone else who understood me, who got my quirky sense of humor, who knew all my flaws and insecurities, like David did.

Now, part of me wanted to be flexible and open-minded and easy to please—all those things David so clearly needed me to be—but the other part of me was too stunned to be generous, too weary to feign enthusiasm.

"What do you think?" David asked again. I downed my coffee.

"Do we have any other options?" I asked him.

We had been fighting constantly—one endless, circular argument—about who and what was to blame. For years, during tax season, David worked sometimes seventeen, eighteen hours a day. Lately, he had begun to take on a gaunt and haunted look. He was now a specter of the man I had married, the warm, funny boy I had met when we were both teenagers, and I could only assume I looked the same to him, a stranger, an interloper in our lives. Looking at my husband's bloodshot eyes, I felt very old, not in my early forties anymore but something far beyond forty. David stared intently at a barstool. Teeth marks from one of our puppies surrounded the leg like etchings.

"Not really," he said.

I sank onto another stool and rested my head in my hands. This was not real. This was not happening to us.

"Okay," I finally said. "Okay. I'll go look."

Later that morning, Hester and I headed out, following David's directions to the cabin. *Turn into the plant nursery and then keep going, past all the "Private Property" signs.* The gravel road was filled with potholes and mud. Sagging phone lines scraped my windshield. I passed a series of greenhouses, then piles of all the things needed to run a greenhouse—hundreds of empty plastic pots, bags of fertilizer and soil, immense plastic pipes, empty Sunkist bottles, cigarettes stubs, candy wrappers.

Finally, I came to a sign marking the property line. There was a lone rock chimney, a bridge of sorts, the remnants of an old barn. And then the road opened into a clearing where there was a rectangular indentation, the remains of an old garden plot. A creek ran the length of the cleared property, and rhododendrons, hemlocks, oaks, and pines covered the steep banks. At the end of the gravel road, just before the house, was an old outhouse, its sides split and rotting. Just beyond that, spanning the whole side of the mountain, was a towering waterfall. The falls were partially obscured by shrubs and brush, and the flow was moderate at best. Still, it was impressive. About 150 feet tall, it cascaded over smooth rocks and moss before emptying into the creek bed.

I pulled up and opened the door for Hester. She dove into the creek, then headed up the bank toward the waterfall, her pink nose down. Though it was still summer, it was chilly here in the hollow. I zipped my sweatshirt. David stood at the foot of the falls, his hands in his pockets, his back to me. For twenty years, David had worn the same basic outfit he was wearing right now. *His uniform*, the kids and I called it—khaki pants, a light blue oxford.

"We could clear all this brush around the waterfall," he said, "and at the top of the mountain, there are trails and an old road."

Just feet from the base of the waterfall, the house was set deep into the opposite bank. It was larger than I had expected—three stories tall. The porch and lower part were rock, and a row of wide windows covered the second story. One window had a long, diagonal slice through it. The tin roof was splotched with rust. *Shabby chic*, my friends would later call it.

"Are we going in?" I asked David.

He hesitated, then headed to the porch. Wasps and yellow jackets swarmed the front door and the eaves, but as we walked inside, David left the door wide open. Immediately, I understood why.

The house had stood vacant for many years, except for the

occasional brief stint by a relative of the family who owned it. It had the stale, musty stench of a house long forgotten, of mold and mildew and decay. In the coming weeks, while we were ripping out carpets and repairing walls, that thick, pungent odor would cling to my hair and permeate my clothes. I would smell it at the oddest times, when I woke in the middle of the night or when I was rounding a bend on my mountain bike. Even long after the house had been patched and scrubbed and Cloroxed, I still smelled it, and I would come to associate that scent with something akin to longing and regret.

Though the house had some unique and distinguishing features—a front door handmade from poplar planks, a rock fireplace, handcrafted wooden kitchen cabinets, beautiful wooden bookshelves—generally, the interior was, well, collapsing. The carpet downstairs was damp and soiled. Electrical wires covered in spiderwebs dangled from the ceiling. The second floor was covered in orange shag carpet and dark paneling. The third floor had the same orange shag carpet, but it also had green camouflage carpet *on the ceiling*. I noted all of these things from somewhere outside my body. I was a mouse peering down from the rafters, a tree frog gripping a wooden doorframe. The taxes, the foreclosure, this broken-down cabin—all of these things were part of an elaborate ruse, an extravagant hoax, an intricate and terrible joke. I had been snatched out of my comfortable life and propelled into a world where people put carpet on their ceilings.

"We can take that off," David said as I surveyed the camo carpet. "No problem."

He watched me carefully, held my gaze for what seemed like hours. He was waiting for me to spook and run, and though I wanted more than anything to bolt out that door and sprint down the gravel drive back to my old life, I knew I couldn't. My son would soon begin school, and though I didn't know much right now, I knew that he needed me, and I was determined to be there for him. I had no money, no available credit, not even a decent car. No matter how I felt about this place, I realized that David was right: we had no other options.

So we headed down to see the one dilapidated bathroom with its sagging light fixtures, rotting cabinets, a cracked sink, a cracked toilet. I was the kind of person who had three bathrooms. I had a vanity with matching his and her sinks, an adjacent walk-in closet, real ceramic tile. Or at least I had been that kind of person just moments before. The air pressed in on me, obstructing my breathing. My throat felt filled with mothballs. My eyes watered.

"Do you want to go on the roof?" David asked.

"No," I said. "I'm good."

"Come on," he said. "It's perfectly safe."

Upstairs, he opened a window at the top of the staircase, and I followed him outside. To the left, the waterfall spilled down the mountain. In our county, Transylvania, there were more than 250 waterfalls, and the water was often rough and tumultuous. Beauty and wildness, danger and majesty, the physical world and the hereafter lived in close harmony, and this paradox was something we locals grew up knowing. We knew how strong the undercurrent in the rivers could be, how the rocks on waterfalls were as slippery as ice, how if you tried to climb the falls, one misstep could send you plunging onto the jagged edges below. Every year, visitors to the area ignored the warning signs about the dangers of walking across the falls with often fatal consequences.

But the waterfall at the cabin wasn't like the other, more treacherous falls on public lands. It was narrow and slender and stretched as far as I could see, all the way to the ridge, a gentle series of mossy stair steps and cascading water flanked by rhododendrons, laurel, and ferns. Light shimmered through the pines and cast a glow on the rippling water. It was enchanting, otherworldly, a magical, mystical force. In the coming months, these falls would become the soundtrack of our lives, an ever-present, gentle crooning—a heartbeat—and whenever I was away, the sound of water—of rain spilling into creeks and rivers and oceans and dams—would act like a homing device, pulling me back to this cabin, this place that was not ours yet somehow was. Now, David and I stood side-by-side, gazing up the mountainside. Next to us, hummingbirds hung in midair.

"We can make a fire pit over there," David said, gesturing to the side yard. "We can raise our own eggs. We can clear a hiking trail and let the dogs run free. We can build a brick oven and make pizza outside…"

He was not looking at me, not even talking to me, really. He stared into the woods, seeing something I could not yet see, believing something I did not yet believe. In an instant, he had taken our old lives and shed them, like the black snake we would later find hanging from the eave of the house, its long, discarded skin draped from a wooden plank in our attic.

"How long?" I asked him. "How long do we have to live here?"

David shrugged.

"A year? Two years?"

"Maybe," he said.

"Which one? One or two years?"

"A couple," David said. "Maybe a few."

"Okay," I said finally. "Okay."

Looking back now, I feel immense compassion for the man standing on the roof, for his forced cheerfulness, his quiet yet palpable sorrow, but back then, I was too stunned to feel anything, too wrapped up in my own grief, in the shock that I could not rightly claim but that I felt nonetheless. I had idealized my life, *our* lives, until I could no longer see what was right in front of me, no longer distinguish what was real from what I simply wanted. And somehow in that moment, my mind took me back over two decades, to another time when I had taken a snapshot of reality and zoomed out until the picture was faint and hazy, a warped and toxic version of the truth.

Citrus Chicken Marinade

- 1 cup orange juice
- 1 cup lime juice
- ½ cup lemon juice
- ¼ cup ancho chili powder
- 2 tablespoons ground paprika
- 4 cloves garlic
- 1 cup olive oil
- 6 to 8 boneless, skinless chicken breasts

Combine all ingredients in a blender and puree. Pour the marinade over chicken breasts and refrigerate overnight.

Chapter Three

THOUGH DAVID AND I CONTINUED to see each other occasionally after I graduated from high school, we had been officially broken up for three years when one day during a poetry class at UNC Asheville, a guy wearing cowboy boots and tight jeans sat down next to me. He was hot, in a rough-and-tumble sort of way, and while I was staring out the window and gnawing on my pen cap, I realized my professor was talking to me, that he had, in fact, *been* talking to me.

"Pardon me?" I asked.

"I said, 'What does this passage mean to you?'" he repeated.

I looked down at my book. The cowboy's name was Scott. I knew this because the professor routinely called on him. Now, I could feel his stare. I could see the tips of his boots and the outline of his thighs through his faded jeans. I stammered something about imperialism, and my professor looked at me strangely and moved on. After class, Scott followed me out the door. I pretended to hurry ahead, but at the foot of the stairs, I paused at the Coke machine. When he touched my shoulder, I feigned surprise.

"Hey," he said, "there's a play here tonight. Would you like to go?"

When I met him later, I wore a short black skirt and black heels and my mother's snug, gray cashmere sweater, and my dyed red hair was cut blunt at my chin. I don't remember what play we saw or anything we said. I only recall that I loved Scott's awkwardness, his deep, furry voice, the way he pushed back on his glasses with his fingers when he spoke. His eyes were deep brown, and he had an intense way of looking at me, as if I were the only person he had ever really seen.

Scott was engaging, charming, affectionate, creative. He was majoring in marketing, but he also loved history. He could passionately expound on every significant military conflict in history, the lesser-known causes and aftermaths, the more obscure battles. He could give you the dates of uprisings and overthrows and impeachments and dethronements. He was similarly well-versed in the history of film. Name any film, and he could list the director, the entire cast, part of the crew, and the musical scores. He also loved to draw, and he kept a black notebook full of animal sketches.

A few weeks after we first met, Scott and I moved in together, in an old apartment near the school. That winter, we rarely went to class at all. We lay in bed, our legs wrapped tightly together, my ear resting against his hard chest as he read *The Godfather* aloud. Days passed that way, the snow pouring down outside, trapping us together in a white cocoon. One night, we had just fallen asleep when we heard a tremendous crash.

Without even opening my eyes, I said, "Scott, the ceiling just caved in."

He flicked on the lamp. A massive pile of debris and ice and snow lay at the foot of our bed. He turned off the light again, and together, we watched the snow falling past the stars.

Three months later, we got married with no more forethought than one might give to ordering a skinny latte with a double shot of espresso. We were twenty years old, and we told no one except our two witnesses, a broad, dark-haired Swede named Klas and his girlfriend, Beth, an earnest, pale girl from somewhere in the Midwest. That night at the courthouse, we were just four college students doing something crazy, like downing Jell-O shooters or whipping up Purple Jesus in the bathtub. Somehow, neither Scott nor I envisioned this impromptu wedding interfering with our future plans. We planned to simply carry on as we had been. But a couple of months after our wedding, I was pregnant. We had planned to wait until after we graduated from college to tell our parents about our marriage, but now we needed to do it sooner.

Soon after my first doctor's visit, Scott and I sat across from his father at a Pizza Hut in Fayetteville, North Carolina, where Scott was raised. Scott and his father shared a thin crust meat lover's pizza while I sipped a Sprite.

"Dad," Scott said. "We've got some good news to tell you."

"Oh?" his father said.

His father was in his midforties, balding but trim and fit. Scott's mother was prone to hysteria, but his father was generally calm and cheerful, which was why we had asked only him to lunch.

"It turns out," Scott said, "we got married."

His father put down his slice of pizza and breathed hard. I looked at Scott. *Tell him. Tell him the rest.*

"And we just found out that Jennifer is pregnant."

Scott's father swayed. He grabbed the edge of the table and began speaking quietly, seethingly under his breath. I remember nothing else from that lunch, not what he said or what we said in our defense. I only remember that afterward, Scott and I stopped outside the Fort Bragg apartment where Jeffrey MacDonald, a former Green Beret and medical doctor, murdered his pregnant wife and two young daughters in 1970. The crime was chronicled in Joe McGinniss's bestselling book, *Fatal Vision*. The book, which later became a made-for-television movie of the same name, described how in February of that year, MacDonald called authorities at Fort Bragg to report a stabbing in his home. When military police arrived, they found MacDonald's pregnant wife dead on the floor of the couple's bedroom. She had been clubbed and repeatedly stabbed with both a knife and an ice pick. The couple's daughters, five-year-old Kimberly and two-year-old Kristen, were each found stabbed to death in their beds. MacDonald, who had superficial stab wounds to his hand, blamed the killings on a Manson-like group of hippies, but he was subsequently convicted of all three murders.

When Scott and I visited the crime scene, the MacDonalds' apartment was still dark and empty, a bleak and tangible reminder of what had happened there, and as we headed back toward Asheville, I was dizzy, nauseated. Next to me, my new husband was young, handsome, doting, the ideal mate, and yet the grim and grisly details of the killings coursed through my pregnant body, filling me with nameless dread. As I struggled to regain my equilibrium, Scott chatted about the snow that was forecast, about a movie he had just seen. Though on the surface, we were a perfectly happy, young married couple, I would later look back on that day and see in it the very first warning signs, the first searing sensation in my gut that something was not right.

A few days later, Scott and I told my parents we were married, and they hastily arranged a proper reception at the Presbyterian church they attended. By then, my belly was already beginning to bulge against my dress, and my new husband and I floated around the fellowship hall greeting guests and sipping nonalcoholic punch. Waves of nausea rolled over me, subsided, then returned again, stronger, more insistent. In the pictures, Scott and I look like high school students after prom— my new husband lean and tall and slightly panicked looking, my face flushed and round, my fuchsia lips the exact shade of the flower blossoms dotting my white dress. There are photos of us feeding each other cake, photos of us each with our parents, their arms stiffly around us, their smiles pinched.

After the reception, we piled our gifts—china, silverware, a pewter bread tray, a set of stainless steel pots, a blender—into our car and headed to the little house we had just rented on Annie Street in West Asheville. The house sat on a hill overlooking a cluster of abandoned and soon-to-be-abandoned warehouses. Later, the area below would become the River District, an enclave for artists, potters, painters, and glassblowers along the French Broad River. But back then, it was a place to be avoided, especially at night.

During those first weeks of our marriage, we were simply playing house, and to that end, I did what I believed a married woman did: I cooked. I only had two cookbooks—Betty Crocker's 1978 cookbook and a copy of *The Joy of Cooking*, a gift from my mother-in-law. The latter seemed overwhelming. It had too many recipes, too many instructions, not enough photographs. But the Betty Crocker book transported me to the childhood I had so recently left behind, and every night, I made something new from that book—London broil, Hungarian goulash, economy beef stroganoff, tomato-pepper chicken, sloppy joes. In fact, the only recipes I ever tried that *weren't* in the Betty Crocker book were spaghetti with clam sauce and Cajun shrimp. The shrimp dish was spicy and garlicky and buttery and, to this day, is hands down my favorite shrimp ever.

I know people say that you have some sort of warning when your partner is capable of violence, an overpossessiveness, a quickness to jealousy, and later I would learn to see it coming—the darkness in his eyes, the tightening in his jaw, the rhythmic opening and closing of his palms—but at first, Scott just yelled a lot. I told myself that he was under a lot of pressure, that things would get better. But soon the yelling was followed by physical outbursts. He threw things across the room—books, silverware, plates. He punched a hole in the living room wall with his fist. And then one night, over a dinner of spaghetti with clam sauce, he leapt from the table and punched me in the jaw. I was three months pregnant.

Over the coming months, I watched as the sweet and doting man I had married transformed into a violent, raging stranger. One evening, I was sitting on the sofa, my socked feet stretched across the coffee table. Scott was across the room. One minute, we were talking about where his parents would stay when they came to visit, and the next minute, he was pulling a razor blade from his back pocket and walking steadily toward me. I pushed myself off the sofa and backed slowly toward the front door.

"You'll never get away," he said calmly. "There's a place where I can bury you, and no one will ever find you."

He crept toward me, the razor blade glinting in his outstretched fingertips.

"I am going to cut the baby from your stomach, and then I'm going to cut you into tiny pieces and bury you down in the basement, and no one will ever know."

He smiled, his movements steady and slow. A red line ran down the center of his forehead. His temples pulsed. I thought of the cool, dirt basement floor and then of the baby squirming beneath my breasts. I eased backward, feeling for the door handle. I knew I needed to do something, *anything*. I needed to throw open the door and run, make a dash for the neighbor's house. And yet I was frozen, transfixed. I was underwater in a murky lake, trying to make my way to the surface.

Everything was hazy, distorted, out of focus, and I was confused about which way was up, which way was out. Scott saw my hesitation, and he pounced. He grabbed my right arm with his left and pushed the razor blade against my throat. His breath was hot.

"I'm going to kill you," he whispered.

I closed my eyes and waited. He paused then, the cool tip of the blade pressed against the base of my throat, and I knew he was making a decision, to do it or not. He was on the very edge, and in that moment, I knew my best bet was to be quiet and still. We stood like that for what seemed like forever. And then I felt the blade pull back, and I heard his footsteps, walking away. When I eventually opened my eyes, Scott was gone—asleep or out, I didn't know which. I thought then of running out into the night, of going home, to my parents' house. But how could I tell my parents this? How could I possibly explain that the father of my unborn child wanted to slit my throat? It did not even feel possible to me.

In the days that followed, Scott was warm and loving. He was sorry, *really sorry*. He never really meant to hurt me. It would never happen again. So I forgave him. I know now that this is part of the pattern of abusers, a period of violence followed by a calm, loving period filled with apologies and promises to do better, but back then, I didn't know anything about domestic violence. I had never known anyone in an abusive relationship. I didn't even know that term.

Over time, though, I learned to be relieved after one of these episodes because it meant that Scott would be "normal" again for a while. It meant we would take long walks and cook dinner together. It meant that, at night, he would sleep with one hand on my belly, cradling our unborn child. It meant that he would be the gentle, sensitive man I had married. In those moments, I not only believed that Scott would never hit me again, I also almost believed that it had never happened at all.

And then one day when I was six months pregnant, I got a phone call at the substance abuse clinic where I worked part time.

"I have Aggie," Scott said. "I have Aggie, and I am going to break her neck."

Aggie was the dog we had found standing in the middle of a busy intersection a few months before. We had called to her, and she had followed us to our car.

"No, Scott," I whispered. "No, not Aggie."

"I will break her neck right now if you don't come home."

"Scott, not Aggie. Please," I said.

"Do you know what I'm doing now?" he asked. "I'm burning your poetry, all of it. Listen…"

Paper crinkled through the phone.

"Scott, listen, I'll be home as soon as I can. You know I can't just leave work…"

"She'll be dead when you get here."

And there was a click. I hesitated. Maybe it was a trick. Maybe he just wanted attention. Or maybe he really would do it.

"I have to leave," I told my boss, the head mental health counselor.

He had been standing behind me while I was on the phone, and now he looked at me hard.

"He is going to kill you," he said. "You know that, right? This man will kill you."

In a way, I believed that, and in another way, I didn't. Certainly the man on the phone seemed capable of almost anything, but he was not the man I had married. The man I married was sensitive and thoughtful. He had a father who was a veterinarian, a mother who was a preschool teacher. He loved art and music and literature and plays. He loved hiking and dogs and chopped celery with Beau Monde–seasoned dip. The man I had married was not a killer.

I left work and drove straight home. Scott's car was not in the driveway, and as I eased to a stop in front of the house, I noticed the curtains in the house across the street part just a little, then close. I hesitated for only a moment before jumping out of my car and throwing open the front door.

Inside, the house looked as if we had been robbed. Magazines and books covered the floor. Lamps and tables were overturned. The sofa stood on one end. It looked like a crazy person had been there. Scott had done that. My husband was a crazy person.

"Aggie!" I called. "Aggie!"

There was no sign of her, no sign of Scott, so I made my way into the bedroom. There, on the floor, was a pile of white—white feathers, white fabric. It took me a few seconds—five, ten, sixty—and then I realized what I was seeing—the down from our pillows. When I looked closer, I saw pieces of my favorite white jacket, shredded, maybe, or cut. And then I realized the pile was yellow in places, dark yellow. And that's when I smelled the sharp, pungent scent of urine.

Your brain has a way of slowing way down at moments like that, of thinking, *Okay. Something is very wrong. I have to get out of here.* And then somehow your brain allows you to keep your voice calm and steady, to see yourself from way off in the distance. You are able to call the dog easily and lightly, like you're out hiking on a trail and she has just run off to chase a squirrel, and when she appears, trembling, tail down, eyes wild, from behind a pile of tumbled furniture, you are able to coax her into your outstretched arms and stumble to your car.

I had no money of my own, nowhere else to go, so that day, I went to my parents' house and told them everything. I don't recall what I said to them or how I said it, nor do I recall what they said. I simply returned to my childhood bedroom with the canopy bed and the gingham curtains and the dollhouse my dad had made me for Christmas the year I turned eight, and I stayed there until late fall.

During that time, I still occasionally talked to Scott. I kept hoping that his violent behavior had been temporary lapses of judgment, that he would soon recover from whatever had taken hold of him, and that the old Scott—the one I had met back in poetry class—would reemerge. He was seeing a counselor. He had been diagnosed, and he was taking medication, a mood-stabilizer. I thought he was better. And I desperately wanted to have a home of my own, a home to share with my baby. So one afternoon early that fall, I stood once again in the doorway of the house on Annie Street.

The house was the very picture of domestic tranquility. The furniture had been righted, the debris cleared away. All indications that something terrible had happened there were gone. Scott reached for my suitcase, and I eased onto the tattered sofa. I wore navy stretch pants with an old-lady waistband and a blue-striped sweater I had gotten at the hand-me-down shop. I rested my hands across my massive belly.

"Would you like a glass of tea?" Scott asked as if I were a neighbor who had stopped in to say hello.

"Yes, thank you," I said.

Two months later, on a frigid November morning, Alex was born—an enchanting baby girl with dark-brown hair and deep-blue eyes. The following months are a blur—my beautiful daughter, the spot on her forehead that blushed red and crinkled when she cried; my crazed, out-of-control husband, no better at all, perhaps even more vicious now that he had a baby to care for; my own mental stability shaky at best. At night, I slept with a steak knife under my pillow. *Am I crazy?* I constantly wondered. *I must be crazy.*

One evening when Alex was nine weeks old, Klas and Beth, the witnesses from our wedding, came over for dinner. We had finished eating, and Alex was asleep in her room. After debating what to do next, Scott and our guests settled on watching an action film. I had always been sensitive to violent films, but now I was even more bothered by the slightest suggestion of violence—guns, knives, fighting, even yelling—so after the movie began, I picked up a book from the end table.

"Are you *reading?*" Scott asked.

"Uh-huh," I said.

"*Don't read.*"

Something about his tone made me look up.

"I don't like this movie," I said.

"You're being rude," he said.

I knew by his eyes I should put the book away, but it was late, and I was tired. And he had had counseling. He was supposed to be okay. I got up and walked to our bedroom. I was sitting on the bed reading, my back to the doorway, when he came behind me. He snatched the book from my hand and hurled it through the air. Then he grabbed my shoulder and spun me around. First, he punched me hard in the jaw. His eyes were dark and wild, moving rapidly around the room before settling on me.

"Cunt!" he screamed. "Why do you do this, you goddamn bitch? You goddamn, motherfuckin' whore, I'll kill you!"

He was on top of me then, his fingers curling around my throat. The room began to turn smoky and gray, and I gasped for air. Somewhere in the distance, I could hear Klas yelling at him to stop. Scott turned to yell back at him, to tell him to *mind his own fucking business*, and that was just enough time. I kicked Scott hard in the groin and broke free. And then I ran to the nursery.

Awake now, my daughter gazed quietly at the multicolored mobile above her crib. She was so very tiny, so incredibly vulnerable. Maybe I was too broken, too weak to protect her. Maybe she would be safer without me. For one brief instant, I considered leaving her. And then I grabbed her and ran.

Perhaps Scott considered letting me go, or perhaps this was just part of his fun, watching me run. In any case, I had time to get out the front door and to the car, to fasten my startled baby into her car seat. Her eyes, the eyes that had been so dark blue when she was born, were now a deep brown. She watched me silently.

Just as I was backing out of the driveway, the front door slammed, and as I started down the curvy mountainside, I heard the sound of squealing brakes behind me. Then, out of the blackness, a flash of headlights. His car jerked forward into the lane beside me. I turned to face him.

"*Pull over!*" he mouthed.

He smiled and edged nearer. I steered as close to the edge as I dared. He swerved to the far left, then back again, closer. There was no question in my mind that he would do it. He would run me over the side of that mountain, down onto the abandoned warehouses below.

I pressed the gas while Scott zigzagged behind me. Finally, the road spilled into the Westgate shopping center parking lot. I thought about trying to run for help, about screaming until someone heard me, but the parking lot was deserted. In the backseat, my daughter wore a pink onesie with a tie at the bottom, like a miniature cinch sack.

One of her feet had broken free, and she bounced it up and down, five tiny, perfect, pink toes. I slowed to a stop, turned off the engine, and unfastened my seatbelt. Scott met me outside the car. From somewhere above all this, somewhere just above the roof of the car, I watched a young woman being beaten. And the only coherent thought that I had was to wonder what that baby in the backseat was thinking.

Scott punched my jaw, then my arms, my stomach. He grabbed my hair and pulled my head backward, spitting obscenities in my ear. I sensed that I should not fight back, that saying anything might get my daughter and me killed. So I tried to go somewhere else in my mind, to believe that instead of being in a dark, empty parking lot being beaten by my husband, I was curled up in bed reading a book or strolling down a sunny street with my dog. Finally, Scott's anger subsided. He stopped punching me and simply stood there, his fists clenched at his sides, his chest heaving with each breath.

"I want you to get in that car and go home," he said. "Do you understand me?"

I nodded. And then I got in my car and drove home. I realize now how crazy that sounds, but that's what I did. I went home. As Klas and Beth were leaving, I put my daughter to bed. I filled the kitchen sink with Dawn and warm water, and I did the dishes. It was a normal thing to do, and I desperately needed to do something normal. I rubbed a warm dishcloth around the soft edges of two iced tea glasses, scraped the bits of dried lasagna from our dinner plates, wiped the breadcrumbs from the countertop. And then Scott appeared behind me.

"Why do you make me do this?" he said softly.

I stared at the wall beyond me, at the soft green lines of the wallpaper.

"Why?"

I turned. Tears streaked his face. He looked like a child. I wrung out the dishcloth, draped it over the faucet, and dried my hands on a towel by the drain. Then I reached for him and slipped my arm around his waist.

"I wish you wouldn't make me do that," he sobbed.

I patted his back. My jaw was stiff, my arms burning. I smelled like lemons. He collapsed in a heap on the floor, and I crouched beside him until he noticed. Then he pulled me down to him until my head rested in his lap. Rocking back and forth, he gently stroked my jaw.

"I'm so sorry," he said. "I'm so, so sorry."

I think now that if it had been just me, I would never have left. I would have stayed in that house and let him wear me down until I could no longer distinguish pain from love, fear from fondness, crazy from not crazy. As it was, crouched on that kitchen floor, my husband's bloody hands smoothing my hair, I closed my eyes and saw my infant daughter, her knowing brown eyes, her easy smile, the spot on her forehead that crinkled when she cried. I was a mess, a twenty-one-year-old wreck of a woman, but she was so beautiful, so perfect, so very brand-new. I did not yet know that I deserved better. I only knew that she did, and I had to get us out of there.

The next day, while Scott was at work, I pulled a suitcase from the hall closet, the same suitcase I had packed to take to the hospital just weeks before. While Alex and Aggie sat side-by-side, Alex in her baby seat, Aggie crouched next to her, I hurriedly emptied the contents of Alex's crib into the bag—stuffed animals, pacifiers, a cheery teal clown, the red-and-blue blanket she curled between her fingers while she slept. I opened her dresser drawers and dumped out a dozen brightly colored onesies, stretchy pants, tiny, embroidered tops, and lacy dresses. I threw in diapers, diaper ointment, baby nail clippers, pink hair bows. And then I moved to my bedroom.

There, I had a full view of the front lawn and the driveway. Our house was the last house on a dead-end road, and once, when I heard a car rumbling up the hill, I thought, *this is it. We are dead. All three of us*. But then the car pulled into the driveway next door, and I frantically threw in a couple pairs of jeans and slammed my suitcase shut. And then, cradling my daughter in one hand and dragging the bag behind me, I opened the front door, called to Aggie, and ran.

My car was maybe ten feet from the front door, twenty at most, but it may as well have been thousands. Terrified that Scott was somewhere nearby—waiting, watching—I imagined him in the hedge between the driveways, in the shadow of the single oak tree in the yard. It took every bit of strength and courage I had to look straight ahead and put one foot in front of the other. It was the longest journey of my life, but finally, I was there.

"Hurry!" I told Aggie, opening the back car door.

She jumped in the backseat, and I tossed my bag on the floor, then lowered Alex into her car seat. Fastening her buckle, I looked into her solemn eyes and said the one thing I had no right to promise her.

"It's okay," I told her. "Everything is going to be okay."

And then I jumped in the driver's seat and sped down the mountain, my sweaty palms gripping the wheel, my breaths coming so rapidly, my vision blurred. Every time I saw a red car, I thought it was Scott. Every time a car passed me, I could see his menacing sneer, feel him edging closer and closer and closer.

Do not faint, I told myself as I pulled onto I-26 and headed east toward my parents' home. *You cannot faint.*

For days and weeks and months and years to come, I would still see him there, the ghost of him, the ghosts of both of our pasts, intertwined. Even now, I see the remnants of snow on the grass, the fading sun low on the horizon, my baby's silent and solemn eyes in the rearview mirror as I raced down the interstate. They say the average battered woman goes back over and over before she finally leaves, but after that day, I only went back once, one dreary winter afternoon when Scott called and begged me to come over.

"Please," he said. "I just want to talk."

I should never have answered the phone. I should have hung up the minute I heard his voice. But even with all the evidence to the contrary, part of me still believed he might change. And the other part of me—the part that knew the truth—still grieved for the loss of the husband I had wanted.

So I left Alex with my parents and drove to the house on Annie

Street. Cautiously, I pushed open the door. It was dark in the house. Only a sliver of moon shone through the heavy shades in the living room.

"Can you see?" Scott asked, closing the door behind me.

I nodded. Soon after I had moved out, my father had come and collected the rest of my personal belongings and the few pieces of furniture I had had before Scott and I got married. Now, the house felt different with all my things gone. On the carpet were the outlines of our old coffee table. The musty smell of wooden walls blended with the smell of forsythia coming from the open windows, and I thought of Scott all those months ago, just after we had met, how we used to study together in the college library, his curly head of hair bent low while he scribbled in a thick, blue notebook. Standing there in the desolate living room, I could still smell his musky cologne. And then I was crying, loud, gasping cries. Scott wrapped his arms around me and guided me into the bedroom, onto the softly worn sheets, and for a few final moments, I allowed myself to remember the man I had wanted him to be.

Afterward, I lay beside my husband and gazed through the doorway to our daughter's old room. A freight train passed by outside and sounded its low, mournful whistle. I closed my eyes and watched the train cross under the Westgate Bridge, weaving past the warehouses and abandoned buildings before rolling along the French Broad River, until finally, even the rumbling faded into nothingness.

Moments later, I got up, dressed, and drove back to my parents' house. It was the last time I ever saw Scott alone. Going to see him had been stupid and reckless, but it had also given me closure. I knew then that we were over for good. A few weeks later, at my parents' house, I picked up the phone and called David. We hadn't spoken in over two years.

"David?" I said when he answered.

"Hey, Jennifer," he said.

It had been forever, yet it had been no time at all. A year later, we were living together in a rented duplex in the country. Two years later, we were married.

Now, it felt odd to think of David and Scott in the same breath, as if they were at all similar. David was the one who had loved and protected and restored me after I left Scott, the one who had told me how much I mattered until, gradually, I had come to believe it. And yet something about losing our home felt familiar, an old wound ripped open and oozing once again. Perhaps it was because, though the circumstances were different, I had remained stubbornly unchanged. Whatever it was that had allowed me to ignore the warning signs with Scott, to endure his abuse with futile optimism, had also allowed me to pretend that David and I had no real problems, that whatever financial difficulties we had were trite, trivial, inconsequential.

Cognitive dissonance, psychologists call it, this ability to hold two contradictory ideas or beliefs at one time. On the one hand, your husband beats you. On the other hand, you believe that is not who he *really* is and that, one day, your real husband—the kind and loving one you see in your mind—will emerge. On the one hand, you know you and your husband are having trouble paying your bills. On the other hand, you believe this is not actually a problem, that the money is there somewhere and your husband just needs to look harder to find it. And when the money doesn't materialize, you are astounded, your fantasy world obliterated.

Cajun Shrimp

- 1½ cups butter
- 8 ounces clam juice or seafood stock
- 5 cloves garlic
- 4 dried bay leaves
- 4 teaspoons dried rosemary
- 1 teaspoon dried basil
- 1 teaspoon dried oregano
- ¼ cup lemon juice
- 1 teaspoon ground red pepper
- 1 teaspoon salt
- 1 teaspoon ground nutmeg
- 1 tablespoon ground paprika
- ½ teaspoon ground black pepper
- 6 pounds shrimp

Melt the butter. Add all ingredients except shrimp. Cook uncovered for 20 minutes. Add shrimp. Cook 10 to 12 minutes or just until pink. Serve with thick, crusty bread, and plenty of napkins.

Chapter Four

THE MOMENT WE DECIDED TO move to the cabin, David seemed less burdened, more optimistic, and while I was still adjusting to the whole idea of rustic, back-to-the-land living, he jumped right into making the cabin more habitable. Using the money we had saved from not making our mortgage payments over the last few months, he worked on home improvements. Every evening after work, David cleaned the cabin floors and painted cabinets and walls. He tore out the ancient dishwasher and stove and replaced them with appliances he found on Craigslist. Every time we thought one project was finished, a new one presented itself. David patched a decaying spot by the kitchen counter, only to find another huge hole when he moved the refrigerator. He tore out the linoleum, only to find that the floor underneath was wet and mildewed.

And then we found the mice—or evidence of mice. A lot of mice. We found droppings on the kitchen counter and on the cabinet with the cooktop. They were all over the boxes we had brought over to the cabin, wedged in the lid of my food processor, in the base of my blender. And then we found a nest in the utensil drawer—on top of an unopened baggy of forks and spoons and knives. David removed the nest and bleached the drawer. Still, I couldn't bring myself to use the utensils.

We weren't eating at the cabin much anyway. The kitchen still reeked of mold and mildew, but occasionally, I cooked a meal at the old house and took it to the cabin. The kitchen counters at the old house were covered with boxes, some of them full, some of them not, but I left out some basic items—a can opener, a soup pot, a strainer—and using those bare necessities, I was able to create a few hearty meals that lasted for days. For example, my taco soup had all the qualities of a meal prepared *by* and *for* people in distress: It was simple. It was filling. It did not require overthinking. And it packed enough heat to jump-start our endorphins.

Once the soup was ready, I wrapped a dish towel around the pot and wedged it into an empty box along with all the toppings. Then I threw the box into my van and carted it over to the cabin where David and I ate outside on the patio by the waterfall. Hawks circled overhead while our dogs, running free for the first time in their lives, darted in and out of the water and up and down the mountain. Tails up, fur drenched, bellies caked with mud, they yipped and yapped with unencumbered delight. Their enthusiasm for their new home was breathtaking. Chasing and calling each other, they squatted or lifted their legs, sometimes both at the same time, peeing on absolutely everything in their vicinity—bushes, shrubs, trees, rock, grass. Thus clearing the mountain of deer, squirrels, rabbits, groundhogs, bears, bobcats, coyotes, and foxes, they swiftly and surely made this place their own, and I envied their passion, their adaptability, their certainty.

Sitting next to my husband, satiated with pepper-fueled endorphins, I watched as the sun dipped behind the waterfall and the moon took its place—one single motion, one solitary breath—and I imagined living a good life here. It would be one endless summer camp session. When the air was crisp and new, the fog lifting off the mountainsides like a curtain slowly raising, I would walk my dogs to the bridge and back. In the afternoons, I would meander along the mountain ridges, searching for the break in the trees that afforded a clear view of the Pisgah National Forest. In the evenings, David and I would build a bonfire and roast marshmallows under a starlit sky. Later, drifting off to sleep under a pile of quilts my great-grandmother made, as haunting screams of screech owls pierced the night, I would snuggle into David, pressing myself hard against his back, willing him here forever, believing in that moment that we were suspended in space and time, hidden from the outside world. Here, we would never get sick or frail. Here, we would never grow old.

In those moments, I could see how things *could* be, how they *might* be one day, sometime later, in the future. But after the sun had set, and David and I headed back into the house, the moment of serenity passed, and the sight of my new kitchen jolted me back to reality. Terrified that the mouse droppings were going to infect us with something deadly, I constantly, obsessively, washed my hands. Of course, this wasn't entirely rational, since I was washing with nonpotable water—creek water, essentially.

However, my thinking at the time was something along the lines of, *if I have to die alone in a secluded wooded holler, I would rather it be of giardia than hantavirus.* Though neither disease sounded exactly *pleasant,* violent, uncontrollable diarrhea somehow sounded more appealing than hemorrhagic fever or pulmonary distress. I would be hard-pressed to justify this position now, but at the time, everything seemed relative. Instead of thinking, *What color palette might be most suitable for the kitchen?* I thought, *Of all the various ways I might die out here, which one is slightly less terrifying, somewhat less excruciating than the others?*

Finally, David installed a UV water purifier, which somewhat but not entirely eased my fears about the water. He also wanted to poison the mice, but I read that mice that are poisoned die of thirst. To a former PETA member, this seemed exceedingly cruel.

"No way!" I said. "No!"

So David devised a humane mousetrap. He rigged the trap using an empty toilet paper tube balanced on the end of the kitchen counter, half on, half off. He put peanut butter in the end that hung off the counter, and on the floor beneath the tube, a large white bucket.

The plan, David enthusiastically explained, was that the mouse would step into the toilet paper tube to get the peanut butter and subsequently be gently, humanely catapulted into the bucket where he would then jump and jump and jump—which would be a great cardio workout for him but totally harmless. The next morning, we would find him still trapped in the bucket. He would be exhausted from all that jumping but otherwise perfectly fine.

David set traps all around the house, and then we left for the night. Early the next morning, I stopped by to drop off some boxes. I pushed the front door open with one hand and shielded my eyes with the other hand. The house was utterly silent—except for a high-pitched shrill coming from the wall. At first, I thought the phone was malfunctioning. It had taken the phone company days to find the telephone lines, presumably because the wires were so deeply buried underground, but perhaps the workers didn't know what they were doing after all.

I pressed my ear close to the wall but not on it, and the sound grew louder. It sounded like a nest of bees, only definitely *not* bees. I called David at work.

"Something is living in the wall at the cabin," I said.

"Where? What does it sound like?"

"It sounds like an entire family of mice," I said. "A *big* family. But it could also be the phone."

That night, David pressed his ear to the wall, then went outside to the gas tank.

"What are you doing?" I called from the porch.

"Do you really want to know?" he called back.

And, of course, I didn't. So I left.

A few days later, David and I stood in the tile aisle at Lowe's.

That afternoon, he had torn out the carpet in the great room downstairs and stripped the floor to the concrete. We were trying to decide what to put over that. We were also arguing about what to do about the mice that had evaded the humane traps and were still leaving droppings all over the counters. David wanted to use conventional traps, ones where the mice wouldn't end up romping in fields of daisies after we caught them. I didn't want them to suffer, but I didn't want mice droppings in my toaster either.

"Look, do you want me to kill the mice or not?" David asked.

I was a hard-core animal lover. For years, I had not eaten red meat, only farm-raised poultry and sustainably sourced seafood. It seemed like bad karma to kill the mice. They had been there before us. In a way, it was as much their house as it was ours. Still, I pictured my utensil drawer, the droppings that covered every single box in the house. Then, as I stood holding a mesa beige sample in one hand and a Sedona slate cedar in the other, something deep in my ethical core snapped. The mice weren't going to attack us. They weren't going to stampede out of the cabinets and slaughter the weakest among us for food. Still, on some fundamental level, it felt like it had come down to me or the mice, the mice or my sanity. So I chose me.

"Fine," I said. "Just kill them. Do whatever you have to do."

I put the cedar sample back on the shelf, handed the mesa beige tile to David, and headed to the laminate flooring display. I was looking for something to tack down in the extra bedroom, the one where I had moved Alex's things, carefully transposing her teenage bedroom into this one as if she might walk in, sixteen years old again and in need of all the childhood mementoes she had abandoned when she left for college—boxes of letters and cards and photos and ticket stubs mixed in with well-worn T-shirts and limp socks. What I really wanted was real hardwood flooring to cover the original wood that was warped and torn with jagged edges and large, gaping holes. But real wood was too expensive. So I perused the laminate shelves—oak, chestnut, hickory, walnut—before finally settling on a light shade of pine, on sale for eighty-seven cents per square foot.

I heaved a box over one shoulder and headed to the checkout to meet David. He carried three rolls of duct tape, a gallon of bleach, and a value pack of mousetraps. I met his gaze, then looked guiltily away. He might be a premeditating killer, but I was an accessory before the fact, a stone-cold accomplice, the Bonnie to his Clyde.

During those first weeks when we were moving, David and I were humbled by many offers of help from friends and family members. They loaned us their pickup trucks to haul furniture, brought us firewood and hot meals, helped us paint walls and tack down laminate over rotting floor boards. I knew we were incredibly lucky to have so many people to help us. I also knew that some families—in fact, some who lived very close to us, in the mountains surrounding Brevard—had always lived this way, had never known anything else. Still, I was stunned, incapable of doing much more than simply going through the motions of daily living.

At the cabin, we had no landline, no cell service, no internet, no cable, nothing to distract us. It was a strange, in-between time.

Our bed was at the other house, and I kept it there as a symbol of my lack of commitment to this place. David slept in a sleeping bag on the cabin floor. Meanwhile, I packed and organized our things at the old house, and sometimes I met David at the cabin. We changed into old, paint-stained clothes in the driveway, then opened all the doors and windows and blared bluegrass from a stereo David propped on the top of the refrigerator. We painted and sweated and drank Little Hump from Highland Brewing while our dogs raced up and down the falls and in and out the open doors.

Though Asheville had dozens of breweries, more per capita than any other U.S. city, Highland Brewing was the oldest and our favorite. Named for two grassy knobs on the Appalachian Trail along the North Carolina–Tennessee border, Little Hump was an American pale ale, and it was just one of the seasonal brews on which David and I counted to mark the passage of time. In and around Asheville, beer was more than just a beverage, and we loved it in that mad, fanatical, hormonally crazed way other cities like sports teams. It was an integral part of our culture, so we drank with both wild abandon and snobbish particularity, musing over notes of cardamom and orange, waxing poetically about hints of vanilla and currants, the essence of figs. And though it may seem that beer was a ridiculous indulgence at a time when David and I could not afford to indulge, the topic of beer and all the related topics—the various aspects of brewing, the appropriate beer-food pairings, the myriad festivals and concerts happening to celebrate new releases—constituted common ground, a safe place for the conversation to go, where we were pretty certain that neither one of us would end up crying or shouting or slamming doors.

Those nights at the cabin, we worked late, past midnight usually, and the feeling was something akin to how I felt after I ran a long distance. I was beyond tired. I was spent, empty. Empty, though, was better than desperate, stunned, shell-shocked. Empty, at this point, was a good thing.

First, I turned my attention to the enclosed front porch. I bleached and scrubbed, then organized the long row of cabinets. I placed medicines in plastic containers labeled according to ailment—*cold*, *upset stomach*, etc. I organized bags full of ink pens, Post-it Notes, colored pencils, and regular pencils. I lined stacks of graph paper beside calculators and rulers, organized bath towels according to size and color, arranged blankets according to thickness. *This is not me*, I thought. *I am not the kind of person who puts pens in plastic bags.* But I craved order, structure, some outward indication that the universe had not come undone, that my world was not spinning out of control.

And then one afternoon, when I was at the old house, a sheriff's deputy knocked on the front door. Of course, this was not the first time this had happened, but now the deputy had news that was shocking even to me: David had borrowed money—a few thousand dollars—without discussing it with me or even telling me. And since he had failed to repay the loan, he was now being subpoenaed to appear in court.

After the deputy left, I drove to the cabin, where David was working. The door to the house was open. David stood in the unfinished kitchen. He looked up at me, and instantly, he knew I knew. Neither of us said a word. Outside, a steady rain began, then quickly became a downpour. Above us, hail pummeled the tin roof like artillery fire. I did not ask why he had borrowed the money. In fact, I did not even think to ask.

Instead, I said, "I am only coming here for my son."

David's khakis and gray T-shirt were covered in dirt and paint. He had lost weight in the last weeks, and his pants hung off his waist.

"That's okay," he said. "That's all I ask. That you give this a try."

I hadn't slept well in days. Our other house had boxes everywhere. This house had boxes everywhere, boxes now sprinkled with mouse droppings. I took a beer from the refrigerator and popped it open with the opener on my key chain. David stared at the floor and shriveled into himself.

"I don't trust you," I said.

"I know," he said, shrinking, retracting.

I wanted him to tell me that this would get better, that one day this would all seem a little bit funny—sad, but funny too. I wanted him to tell me I wouldn't get *E. coli* from the drinking water or hantavirus from the mice, that the wood boiler wouldn't spontaneously combust, that he could humanely trap the completely benign yet somehow still terrifying wolf spider from the area just above his desk. Instead, he stared at the floor.

"Don't do that," I said. "You don't get to be the victim. *I* am the victim here."

"Okay," he said, looking up, his eyes the color of clay. "Okay."

Heavy rain pelted the stone porch and sprayed in the open doorway. Just beyond the porch, the waterfall surged. I grabbed my rain jacket from the counter where I had left it the night before, pulled the hood over my head, and ran for my car. Winding around the dark mountain roads, the car ensconced in thick fog, I shook so violently, I could barely drive. My husband had been hiding things from me. And while at the time that seemed like the overriding and most pressing truth, later I would realize another, simultaneous truth: my husband did not trust me either. If he had, he would have told me about the money. If he had, he would have told me how bad things were sooner. At least he would have tried.

I could *see* the problems. I just could not see a way to fix them, so I did the only thing I knew to do, the same thing I had done years before when I had left Scott: I simply kept going. I focused on the tasks at hand, on grading papers and teaching my classes at the college, on packing and dropping off boxes of old toys and games at Goodwill, on making sure Eli was fed and rested, on maintaining a cheery tone when I talked with my older two children on the phone. Only my two closest friends knew how devastated I was, how very close I came to walking away from David and never going back. This was not all his fault, of course. I shared some of the blame. Still, I could not see around this problem or through it, could not envision a way to repair the damage to our relationship, could not imagine an *us* after this.

Taco Soup

- 1 pound ground turkey
- 1 small onion, chopped
- 2 cloves garlic, minced
- 1½ cups water or chicken broth
- 3 (16-ounce) cans beans—a combination of black, pinto, kidney, navy, and/or great northern beans, drained and rinsed
- 3 (14½-ounce) cans canned tomatoes, diced, stewed, pureed, or fire-roasted
- 1 (15½-ounce) can hominy, drained, or 1 cup fresh or frozen corn
- 1 (4-ounce) can chopped green chilies
- 1 package taco seasoning
- Salt and pepper to taste
- Grated cheese (cheddar or Monterey Jack)
- Sour cream
- Tabasco or chipotle sauce

Sauté the turkey, chopped onion, and garlic in a large soup pot. Drain fat, if necessary. Add chicken broth, beans, tomatoes, corn, chilies, and taco seasoning. Simmer for at least an hour.

Season with salt and pepper to taste. Serve with grated cheese, sour cream, and plenty of hot sauce. Since hot foods increase your endorphin levels, the more distressed you are, the more hot sauce you will need.

Chapter Five

One evening in August, David and I sat on the front porch drinking Gaelic Ale from Highland Brewing and watching Eli clear the brush along the waterfall. Slender, dark-eyed, and introverted, Eli reminded me more of the men in my family than the men in David's family. Wearing long pants and boots and wielding a large swordlike tool, Eli whacked at the bushes obscuring our view of the waterfall. Every now and then, I called to him to be careful, but he couldn't hear me over the falls, so finally, I stopped shouting and just watched.

Since I had first told him about our move, explaining as best I could about the foreclosure, he had said very little about it other than to ask practical questions—*Should I take this or that? Which bedroom will be mine?* Ultimately, he claimed the top floor of the cabin—the space with two bedrooms, a beautiful view of the waterfall, and access to the roof. In his free time, when he wasn't at school or working his part-time job at the movie theater or hanging out with his girlfriend, he was into making movies—writing scripts, filming, editing, making props, and so on—and since I had told him about the move, he had been working to convert the spare bedroom upstairs into a makeshift studio. He painted the walls bright mauve, a cheery, optimistic shade, and he added a green screen and editing and sound equipment. He was doing what we all were doing, groping at what was familiar, trying to make this run-down cabin feel like home.

Watching him slash the brush, I thought of the boy he had been just moments before, all wide-eyed and creative and mischievous, and I wondered how he might remember this moment when he was grown. Would he think back and realize that David and I had done our best, that we had made mistakes but that we had loved our children as hard as we could? Or would he judge us more harshly and wonder how his parents had become so hopelessly lost, so utterly fucked up? I simply had no idea. David and I hadn't done a lot of talking lately, and we weren't really talking now. Still, we were here together, on the porch.

"Where is the top?" I asked David. "The very top?"

He pointed to the peak of the mountain, where, through the bushes, at the very top of the ridge, as far up as I could see, the water spilled down the mountainside.

"Let's climb it," I said.

"The waterfall?"

"Yes."

David looked at me hard for a minute. He knew this was a concession on my part, though what I was conceding would have been hard to say. His T-shirt and jeans were covered in paint and sweat.

I was dressed for my book club meeting later that evening—Chacos, corduroys, a better-than-usual shirt.

"Okay," he said.

Though "The Land of Waterfalls" is our county's official motto, locals have a twist on the saying: "The Land Where the Water Falls." It is our own inside joke, our way of acknowledging one of the few constants in our lives—water. It rains a lot here, especially in the summer months when thick thunderclouds roll over the mountains, bringing us almost daily deluges of hail and rain and strong winds. Transylvania County between seventy and ninety inches of rain per year, far above the national average.

One would hardly think that this sort of weather would attract tourists, but in fact, our waterfalls are frequent tourist destinations. People flock to the most popular spots to photograph the falls and to swim. Looking Glass Falls, Rainbow Falls, and Turtleback Falls in Pisgah National Forest and Triple Falls, High Falls, Hooker Falls, Bridal Veil Falls in DuPont State Forest are among the most popular spots. Parts of *The Last of the Mohicans* and *The Hunger Games* were filmed in DuPont, and tourists can now pay to ride into the forest on buses and see the site where Katniss, all ablaze, plunged into the icy water near Bridal Veil Falls. The more adventurous tourists strap cameras to their heads and tear down Ridgeline Trail on mountain bikes at breakneck speeds. Sometimes, they do it at night—with headlamps, GoPros, and a strong dose of courage or recklessness, depending on how you look at it.

Years ago, though, long before DuPont Corporation, before

white pines were planted and harvested to produce paper for Champion International, before water-powered sawmills at Corn Mill Shoals and Bridal Veil Falls in the 1900s, before Micajah, patriarch of the Thomas clan, was beaten and blinded by Union soldiers during the Civil War, Native Americans lived here. Today, centuries-old petroglyphs still speak to their presence.

David and I both knew that you should never, ever climb a waterfall. Nonetheless, we jumped over the creek that ran along the yard and headed straight up, over the moss-covered rocks. David went first, and I followed his lead, stepping wherever he stepped. The falls were staggered with ledges created by the rocks. One pool of water led to another drop-off and so on, and the moss overlying the rocks was surprisingly thick and firm, a brilliant emerald-green carpet. At one particularly steep ledge, David turned to take my hand to give me a lift.

"I've got it," I said.

He waited while I found a foothold, grabbed a nearby limb, and heaved myself up. When we were finally at the top, we stood on a rock next to the falls to catch our breaths. From there, we could see the tin roof, the smoke coming from the chimney, and Eli waving from the driveway. We hollered and waved back.

Instead of climbing back down the waterfall, David and I bushwhacked our way back down the mountainside, through the rhododendron thickets. Inside the thickets, it was cool and dark. Leaves whacked my face as I grabbed at branches to slow my progression down the hill. The air was sharp and pungent, filled with the scents of mud and moss and rotting leaves. Finally, I gave up trying to be graceful. I sat and scooted down the mountain. When I reached the bottom, my pants were covered in dirt and mud, my palms bleeding.

I took off my shoes and whacked them against the edge of the porch while David went inside. He returned with two towels and two beers and handed me one of each.

"Why don't you skip book club?" he said. "I'll heat the leftover soup. We can listen to some music and watch the sunset."

David's shirt was filthy. Bits of leaves clung to his hair. His hands were cracked and calloused. And as I took in all this evidence of...what? His love? His recklessness? His never-ending optimism? I almost said yes. *Almost.*

Part of me wanted to pretend none of this had happened—the foreclosure, the taxes, the borrowed money. The rest of me was deeply angry. I had been excluded from specific knowledge about our finances and from decisions about how our money was spent. Perhaps David had been trying to protect me, to save me from the stress and worry he experienced daily, but in the end, it had all come to this, and though I truly only had myself to blame—for walking around with my head in the sand, for expecting him to handle our finances on his own as if I were from another generation, another time in history—my self-pity got the best of me, kept me from moving forward or backward or around. I was both literally and figuratively trapped here in this hollow, and it would be a long time before I could see how much of this mess was of my own making, the result of my unwillingness to assert myself and make the hard choices that would have made our lives better. I wanted to move forward, but I couldn't.

"I can't." I said.

David held my gaze for a moment. I looked away. Then I put the unfinished beer down on the picnic table, climbed into my car, and drove away.

Finally, at the first of September, Eli walked into the kitchen at the Cape Cod house and announced he would be staying at the cabin from then on. The cabin was closer to school and would cut his driving time by twenty minutes. Perhaps he also dreaded the move and just wanted to get it over with, to put it behind him. So my final step toward moving in was not so much a decision as it was the result of indecision. I needed someone to tell me what to do, even if that someone was my eighteen-year-old son, so I left with him, my toothbrush and pillow wedged in the front seat between us.

For the next few months, the three of us—David, Eli, and I—walked gingerly through our new lives. When the shower leaked through the ceiling and into the toaster downstairs, we simply dried out the toaster. When a fuse blew whenever we tried to microwave a cup of coffee, David quietly replaced it. When the spring clogged due to heavy rains, he hiked to the top of the mountain and cleared the obstruction from the pipe that siphoned water from the creek. And on hot, muggy days when we still had to have a fire in the boiler to heat our water, we sweated profusely, as if it were a cleansing ritual. Thanksgiving passed, then Christmas, and we did not yet have all of our things from the old house. We were still two months away from the official foreclosure date, and we figured we had plenty of time. The longer we were at the cabin, the less we liked to think of the lives we had left behind. So we kept putting off the final move. And then one day in January, as I was driving home from visiting my brother in Florida, I got a call from David.

"You're never going to believe this," he said.

But of course, I would have believed anything at this point.

"I stopped by the old house to get some things, and the locks have all been changed."

I was near the Green River Bridge at the foot of Saluda Mountain, almost home. *Home,* I thought. *What a strange and complicated word.*

"Are you there?" David asked. "Are you still there?"

"Yes," I finally said.

"All the outside lights are on too, so they've had the power turned back on."

We hadn't actually meant to turn off the power. We had just forgotten to pay the bill—one of the many things we lost track of during those months when we lived in a daze, going through the motions of our lives like we were actors in someone else's sad drama.

"I looked in the windows, and the house looks empty," David said. "But the garage is full. I think they've moved all our stuff out there."

"Call Tom," I said.

Tom was our lawyer. According to Tom, the house still legally belonged to us, and no one had the right to enter without our permission. We could get in however we wanted, he said. We could call the sheriff's department and ask for access. We could hire a locksmith to break the new locks. Or we could just smash a window and break in.

David and I discussed all of those options. A locksmith would cost money, which we clearly did not have. And any interaction with the sheriff's department was to be avoided, just as a general rule. That left option three. So the night after I got home, a frigid January night, I rode shotgun with a sledgehammer wedged between my knees while David drove the getaway car, the van that now had 250,000 miles on it.

"Are you sure we won't get arrested?" I asked David.

"No, I'm not sure," he said.

"What if one of the neighbors calls the police?"

"We'll just have to be fast."

We passed cow pastures and empty cornfields, then wound along the French Broad River. The sky was vast and clear, the moon a tiny sliver. When we had lived here, I used to stand outside at night, searching for the Big Dipper and listening to the coyotes calling in the distance. Now, as we neared the house, it looked like a runway. Every exterior light was on, the driveway brilliantly lit.

"Oh, shit," I said.

David pulled into the drive, then turned off the ignition and reached for the sledgehammer. He got out of the van, and in a couple of moments, I heard several vigorous *thwaps*, followed by the sound of metal hitting concrete. In a moment, the garage doors slid open.

"We're in," David called to me. "Come on!"

I put on a knit cap and gloves and got out of the van. In the garage doorway, I paused. Here was every single thing we had left in the house—televisions, a sofa, a chair, tables, books, and ten or twelve giant trash bags. I opened one of the bags and recognized the contents of a kitchen drawer. I moved on to the next bag, then the next, opening each and sifting through our possessions—cards, letters, drafts of stories I had written, medicines, cosmetics, photographs.

"Look," David said, holding up a toilet wand. "They've bagged up everything in the house that wasn't nailed down. I think they had a firm do this."

Just then, a car drove past. It slowed, then turned and came back, pausing at the end of the drive before finally moving on.

"Let's just get this loaded up," David said.

I began filling the van seats with boxes while David heaved trash bags into the hatch. Finally, we had loaded everything we wanted except for one bag. I opened it, and there on top, wadded into a ball, was the watermelon-colored dress I had worn to both my daughter's and my son's high school graduations. I lifted the dress, smoothed the wrinkled fabric, and held it to my face, inhaling the scent of my old life. Outside the open door, katydids chirped, and somewhere in the distance, coyotes howled.

In the backyard, three of our animals were buried—a half-lame corgi mix named Julie, a beautiful, sleek border collie named Luke, and an orange cat my daughter had named Simba, after the hero from *The Lion King*. Also in the yard were countless Airsoft pellets, the rosebush my parents gave us on our twentieth wedding anniversary, a bullfrog we had dubbed Ernest, a row of towering Leyland cypress trees we had planted when they were saplings, a white lily a dark-eyed girl had given my older son on prom night.

"Are you ready?" David asked me.

He stood in the doorway. His blue jeans were covered in dust and dirt, and from a hole in his down vest, tiny feathers spilled onto the garage floor. He was perfectly still, a snapshot of a husband. It was something he did a lot now, silently watching me, weighing how close I was to hysteria, to running into the night and never turning back. He was sorry, I knew—sorry for me, sorry for our kids, sorry for the things he could have done differently and for the things he couldn't have done differently, sorry for all of it. And I was sorry too—sorry that I had not been better, sorry that I could not be better now.

Of course, I knew there were many worse things than foreclosure. There were deaths and accidents and illnesses, people who, by no fault of their own, had horrific things happen to them, people who would have loved for their biggest problem to be that their house was being taken away. There were also men who would have given up and walked away long ago, who would not be standing in the doorway right now, waiting. No, I wasn't ready, but clearly it was time to get ready. So I nodded.

"Good," my husband said. "Let's go."

We headed out to the car with the last of our belongings, and as we wound along the river on our way back to the cabin, I checked and rechecked the rearview mirror to see if we were being followed. Maybe the neighbors had called Jeff and Denise. Maybe they had called the police. When we finally turned down the gravel road that led to the cabin, I rolled down my window and took huge, gasping gulps of air.

It was over, this part. Done. In a few months, our former home would be sold at auction to the highest bidder, everything we could have done and should have done a matter of court record. Then we could begin our new lives in earnest. And gradually, very gradually, I would begin to see that this was not so much an ending as a beginning, that my life was not so much a line as one intricate loop, winding back, back, back through time and then spiraling rapidly forward, the past, the present, and the future, the person I was and the person I had yet to become, all tangled into one.

Chapter Six

DAVID AND I WERE JUST beginning to settle into our new lives at the cabin when my grandfather's youngest brother, Bill, died. Three months later, my grandmother's closest sister, Beatrice, died. Ten days after that, on the first day of summer, the longest day of the year, my grandmother died. A few months later, my grandmother's only living sister died—an entire generation of my family gone.

I had been very close to both Bill and my grandmother, and the close proximity of their deaths left me reeling, unmoored. To make matters even harder, in a frenzy of grief, my parents and aunt and uncle had begun cleaning out my grandmother's home immediately after her death—as if death could be swept away, piled neatly into clean trash bags and dropped off at Goodwill or bargained away in a yard sale. This was the house my mother had grown up in, the place I had always considered my second home. Still, the day after my grandmother's funeral, I helped my mother dismantle the kitchen, a task we could have completed blindfolded if someone had asked us to.

Sweat poured from my neck and onto my shirt while my mother and I sorted through over sixty years of plates and glasses and pots and pans. We drank tall glasses of iced tea sweetened with thyme syrup, and every now and then, my mother paused, a coffee mug or cast iron skillet poised above a box. Then she set the object on the table and walked away.

That afternoon, I found her standing at the kitchen sink by the window to the backyard. The bird feeder was empty, but it was a habit bred from years of watching cardinals and robins and gold finches vying with squirrels for seeds. I followed her gaze to the back field where a fat bunny languidly nibbled a patch of clover. When she spoke, her voice was a trembling whisper.

"I am really going to miss watching the bunnies," she said.

That day, I loaded almost everything my grandparents had owned into my van. I brought home my grandmother's soft, white hairbrush, her cantaloupe-colored bathrobe, her Tupperware and cast iron skillets, her china cabinet, a dressing table filled with bobby pins and curlers and packs of zinnia seeds. I brought my grandfather's saddle, his soft, flannel shirts, a half-drunk bottle of Jacquin's Rock and Rye.

Within days, my grandmother's cast iron cornbread mold hung on my kitchen wall. Her old washboard was propped on the porch window ledge. The quilts my great-grandmother had made by hand were on our beds. Sometimes, I felt comforted by the presence of those remnants of my grandparents' lives. Other times, I felt them pressing in on me—one thick, heavy weight. I couldn't go back. I couldn't go forward. And in the midst of all this, Eli graduated from high school. In a few short weeks, he would leave for art school a few hours away, and though I was thrilled for him, here was yet another change, my last child leaving home.

Then one morning late in the summer, I was sitting at my desk on the second floor of the cabin when I heard Reba barking furiously. Sleek and stealthy, Reba was as close as a dog could get to being a coyote without actually being one. We had rescued her eight years before, when she was just a couple of months old, from a smokehouse in rural Madison County, and she never had become quite as tame as our other dogs. David and I were in Reba's pack, and with us, she was a gentle and loving companion. She carried box turtles down the hill in her mouth and set them, softly, gingerly, at our feet. She rode shotgun in David's truck when he went to the bank or grocery store.

However, despite our attempts to socialize her, she did not like other dogs. Once, she so viciously attacked our beagle mix, Kate, that years later, Kate still had a memento of that afternoon, a V-shaped cut in her left ear. And on more than one occasion, she and Hester had scuffled over access to the front door. So to keep the confrontations to a minimum, the five dogs rotated times outdoors. Reba was now downstairs, in our great room, because our dachshund, Pretzel, was outside.

At first, I wasn't overly concerned. Reba was David's constant companion, and she often barked to go out when he was outside working. But she was going to have to wait. When the commotion escalated, however, a series of frantic, high-pitched yelps, I headed downstairs. Even then, I still didn't perceive what I should have perceived, that this was an unusual bark. A warning bark.

"Reba!" I yelled, running down the stairs. "Shut up!"

At the foot of the stairs, I stopped. Instead of barking at the door to go out, Reba faced my grandmother's china cabinet in the corner of the great room. Her hair stood on end, and she repeatedly lunged at the base. *A mouse*, I thought. *Another fucking mouse*. And that was when I saw it. Long and lithe and unmistakably copper-colored, it weaved in and out of the china cabinet legs. For a moment, I could not move. I could not breathe. And then I threw open the front door and ran down the driveway, mud splattering the backs of my calves. Pretzel sprinted beside me, his long, taut body propelled on flailing legs.

"David!" I screamed. "David! There's a fucking snake in the house!"

David was hoeing weeds in the far field. He wore a large straw hat, and he stopped and smiled a little—as if to say, *how strange and yet absolutely believable is that?* Then he headed up the drive, hoe in hand. I stood outside in the driveway and covered my ears with my hands while David ran inside. Moments later, he came outside carrying a bucket, which he set on a far corner of the patio.

"You can come back in now," he said.

The dogs were quiet. I was quiet.

"It's a copperhead," I said finally.

"Are you sure?" David asked.

I was sure. I had seen the flat, pointed head, the telltale diamond pattern on its thick, copper back. Copperheads were one of two kinds of venomous snakes in our area. They were not as deadly as rattlesnakes, but a single bite would certainly send you to the hospital. Copperheads, I learned later, were attracted to rocks and water, two things we had in great supply. Our dogs could have been bitten. We could have been bitten. And worst of all, there could be more.

In the days that followed, I compulsively inspected every surface of the house—kitchen drawers, bathroom cabinets, sofa cushions, the boxes of my grandmother's china, stacks of towels, under my bed, and under the covers. At night, I slept with a light on, our cat stretched across my chest. I was anxious and skittish, constantly on a state of high alert—code red.

On those nights, everything piled into one heap in my mind: Our tax problems. The foreclosure of our home. Bill's death. My grandmother's death. My grandmother's empty house. My kids leaving home. The copperhead. Each event had jolted my center, severed my sense of stability and security. Each thing collapsed into the other, mingling, overlapping, entwining, until I was unable to discern the greater trauma. Too much had happened at once. I was not safe.

Since we had moved here, I had been grieving, unsettled, unsure of who I was anymore, but after my grandmother's death, I had become fragile in a way I had never been before. I had a hard time concentrating. I couldn't remember my phone number or the kids' phone numbers or my ATM password. I cried a lot at odd, unpredictable times. I needed to do something. I knew that. And the only thing I could think of was to go somewhere new, start a new job, a new life. So with only a casual mention about it to David, I began applying for teaching jobs out of state.

For years, I had been using an online database, HigherEdJobs, to search for positions in our area, but now I expanded my search. I would take a job anywhere in the country, anywhere that would hire me full-time. I could start immediately. I would load up my mountain bike and my dog and my Chacos and be gone, far away from here, from all this sadness. Somewhere else, I might be able to sleep without a night-light. Somewhere else, I might be able to remember things. Somewhere else, I might feel sane.

The place that would hire me, it turned out, was a university in Macomb, Illinois, a school that heavily recruited students from both Midwestern farms and inner-city Chicago. The day after I posted my resume, the composition program coordinator contacted me to set up a Skype interview. The next day, I did the interview, and the following morning, I had an offer. The job was temporary, just for the semester, but it could be extended, perhaps even become permanent. The program director seemed nice, her teaching philosophies in line with my own. The pay was good, way better than what I was getting as an adjunct at the college here, and it would be a change of scenery. Classes were set to begin in less than a week. I had twenty-four hours to make a decision.

When I told David, he was leaning with his back against the kitchen counter, waiting for a pot of coffee to brew. Already, living at the cabin had been good for him. He was still doing accounting, but when he was home, he was spending more and more time outside. He was now trim and muscular and tan, and he had a certain lightness about him. He talked more. He joked more. And he waited more often to hear what I had to say. Now, he looked at me as he had been looking at me a lot lately—perplexed, alarmed.

"Huh," he said. "That sounds interesting. Is that something you want to do?"

We were just a few feet from where the copperhead had been. Both our sons were home. Eli had not yet left for college, and Aaron had a few weeks off from work before heading back to school. Their belongings were scattered all over the kitchen—computers, backpacks, guitars, rain coats. Eli was sitting at the kitchen table, eating chips and finishing off a container of guacamole while watching a movie on his computer. Aaron was upstairs doing the same thing with a container of hummus. I wandered around the kitchen, wiping things down, hanging things up, putting things in the dishwasher, tossing cans and bottles in the recycling while I considered what to say.

David loved living here. He loved the quiet, the privacy, the fact that it was always ten degrees cooler at the cabin than it was in town. He loved chopping wood and building fires. He loved the fact that our rent was so cheap.

"Two hundred and fifty dollars!" he would say each month when he wrote the check. "I just can't believe it!"

David's enthusiasm for the cabin, however, was not contagious.

I was still struggling to adjust. One night, when I was eating dinner at Rocky's Hot Chicken Shack in Asheville with my book club, one of my friends had asked me what I missed most about our old house. My friends had all been kind and supportive. No one had said, *You're a total idiot. What did you think would happen, walking around all those years with your eyes closed?* Instead, they had listened to me cry, helped us move, prepared us meals. And they had been full of suggestions about what to do: *Leave David. Stay with David. Move in with my grandmother. Move to Costa Rica. Live alone in a yurt in the woods.* But this was the very first time anyone had simply acknowledged my grief: *What hurts most?*

Seven women watched me. We were eating spicy fried chicken on Texas toast. My eyes burned. I took a swig of my beer. *Don't cry,* I told myself. *Do. Not. Cry.*

"The light," I finally said. "I really miss the light."

At the old house, my desk had faced a large window overlooking the alpaca and cow pasture. I had a view of the mountains. I had watched the school bus pull in every afternoon, the neighborhood kids skateboarding up and down the hill outside. But at the cabin, my desk was in a dimly lit room full of dark wood.

We had torn out the low, white, industrial ceiling, hoping to replace it, but for now, the ceiling was basically a black tarp covering the insulation. On rainy days, water leaked onto my desk and into my coffee mug, and the only lights were long, bare, fluorescent tubes— business lighting. When we first moved in, David had talked about putting in skylights, but like so many other improvements on our list, that had never happened. There just wasn't enough money. And even if there had been, it would have seemed silly to spend a lot of money renovating a rental home.

Throughout the day, I alternated between states of despair and rage. I was furious when David forgot to check the gauge on the hot water tank, and I had to take a cold shower. I was embarrassed by the fact that my clothes, my hair, my jackets, my blankets and towels all constantly smelled like a campfire because of the wood boiler. I was depressed by the unfinished ceilings and floors, frightened by the gunfire we occasionally heard in the woods outside our house.

David and I had known each other since we were kids, and he was a loving father to all three of my children. And yet, I didn't want to live in an old, ramshackle cabin with snakes and spiders and mice, in a house full of painful reminders of my grandmother. I didn't really want to move to the Midwest, but I didn't want to stay here either.

While I considered how to respond to David's question, I opened the kitchen door and threw a handful of empty beer bottles into the recycling bucket outside. They made a deafening crash.

"I think so," I finally said to David. "Yes. I want to go."

If David had said don't go, I might have reconsidered. If he had promised me that I would feel better soon, that we would be better soon, I might have said, *Okay. Let's try it a while longer.* But he didn't. He said, "Go then. If you want to go, you should go." Later, he would say that he did not know what to say then, that he was afraid if he told me not to go, I would be even angrier than I was already, that I would blame him even more. So he told me to go, and I went.

Three days later, I grabbed a few essential items—my mountain bike, my computer, Hester—and loaded my Mountaineer. Aaron and Eli and David stood in the driveway together and waved goodbye as I drove away.

Hester rode shotgun as we drove through torrential rain all the way from North Carolina, through Tennessee, and over the rolling hills of Kentucky. Then, just as we hit Indiana, the rain eased, the sky grew wide and clear, and Hall & Oates came on the radio. I rolled down the windows and cranked it up, and Hester and I jammed all the way through the Hoosier National Forest. Finally, we were passing mile after mile of corn and soybean fields. I did not yet know whether the decision I had made was the right one. I only knew that it had not felt like a decision at all. It had felt a little like freeing myself from an intricate web. Every few miles, I felt a little less trapped, less ensnared. The blue sky deepened. The air smelled greener. My lungs expanded. I could breathe.

Admittedly, the Midwest is an unlikely place for a pilgrimage. In the vast and wide-open landscape, one doesn't have the sense so much of going inward but rather of being exposed, flayed open like a trout. I had lived my entire life in the Appalachian Mountains, and the only things I knew about living on a grassy plain I had gotten from *Little House on the Prairie*.

As I looked across the varying hues of green that grew deeper and darker before finally dipping into the horizon, that information seemed a bit dated. Eventually, I passed some signs of civilization—gas stations, signs announcing village populations (four hundred, eight hundred, twelve hundred), a hotel, a billboard promoting the university, and then a row of high-rise dorms. Looking at those stark dorms with their bleak, concrete façades, I considered for the first time that I might have been too hasty in choosing this place.

"We have made a mistake," I told Hester. "A really big mistake."

But there was no time to reconsider. Moments earlier, the writing director had called to make sure I was on the way to sign my contract. My first class was at 8:00 the next morning. I turned left at the campus, eased up the hill past the cemetery, and followed the directions to the renovated boxcar where I would live for the next five months.

Before I left home, I had looked at the structure on Google Earth. Flat and oblong, it was a Lego project in progress. When I had zoomed out, the Legos—and the tiny town around it—became an island in an immense sea of fields. Now, I could see that the building was low-lying and red. On one side, a fenced yard was full of lovely, untamed things—a sagging fence bordering a bed of wild, overgrown asparagus, an unruly thatch of mint that brought to mind a really strong mojito. On the other side of the house, hundreds of thick, ripe tomatoes hung from a vine wound through the fence.

The boxcar was actually what remained of three railway boxcars that, years ago, a homeless man had hauled over from the nearby railroad station. He had sawed and hammered and nailed until he connected the cars in such a way that they made a house. Sort of. *The Hobo Arms*, the neighbors dubbed it. Eventually, the "hobo" decided to build a church onto one end, so he sawed off part and added on, creating a "sanctuary" where he proselytized to his family and anyone else who would listen.

Years later, the structure was divided into a duplex, and in the 1970s, a rock band called the Rainbow Riders lived in the back apartment. They had large, rowdy rehearsals in the front yard and a pet goat that occasionally wandered over to the neighbor's pool. Everyone I met here had a story about this place. People had smoked weed there, dropped acid there, made love there. The boxcar was not just a makeshift house. It was a character in a richly complex story, a fascinating piece of local lore.

I pulled up to the entrance and opened the door for Hester. Inside the boxcar, the bathroom was separated from the kitchen by only a curtain, but there were wood floors and plenty of large windows and a nice kitchen with pine countertops. There was also a gas stove that had to be lit with a match, and while I quickly got the knack of lighting the burners, I never did learn to light the oven, so I bought a Crock-Pot on sale at Aldi and resigned myself to living off food that could be prepared in a slow cooker—soups and stews and whole roasted chickens. I set up my computer on a desk overlooking the neighbor's tomato-laden fence, my mountain bike in the entranceway. Most mornings, I rode over the railroad tracks and past the rows of frat houses to campus. I rode home at lunchtime but then drove back to campus as it was too hot by then to ride back for my afternoon classes.

Of course, had I researched the climate before leaving, I would have known that summers on the prairie were sweltering. I would have known that north didn't necessarily mean cooler, and I would have packed shorts and sundresses instead of sweaters and wool pants. As it was, I sweated constantly. I showered two or three times a day, and my sheets dried on the clothesline in the time it took me to run inside and eat a tomato sandwich. One day in late August, when the temperature peaked at 112 degrees, I found myself standing in front of the Redbox at Walmart. My shirt was drenched in sweat, my breathing heavy, and for a moment, I considered getting into my car, picking up Hester, and heading back to North Carolina. Maybe this had been a bad idea. Maybe it had been, as my grandmother used to say, a *bad miscue*. But the heat made me sluggish, unable to think straight, and leaving then would have taken more energy and initiative than I had. So I chose three movies and spent that afternoon watching them, back-to-back, inside the air-conditioned boxcar with all the blinds closed.

In the evenings, when the temperature dipped to the upper nineties, Hester and I, downright giddy, headed to Lake Argyle in nearby Colchester. The lake was surrounded by the steepest hills I had seen since Kentucky. Prairie grass stirred in the hot, thick wind, old ladies fished for walleye from the bank, and teenagers stretched on blankets by the water, cans of beer and bottles of sunscreen scattered among their prone bodies. Hester and I walked along the paved road and across the dam, retracing the steps of the coal miners who had lived and worked here in the 1800s. At dusk, we made our way to a dirt road where we stood in the fading light and watched the sun sink over the prairie, a hot, red orb that turned pink, then orange before dipping below the horizon.

During the day, I was so busy, I thought of little else except for my job. But on those evenings by the lake, after those long walks, I no longer thought of how many papers I had to grade or how I was going to manage an unruly student. Instead, I thought of my grand-mother. I could not yet think of her in the earlier years, when she was healthy and happy and whole. I was stuck in the memories of her last weeks and days, of everything I didn't do and should have done on the last night she was alive. In recent years, as she had become increas-ingly frail, my mother had devised a complex schedule that provided my grandmother round-the-clock home care. I had been the person staying with her the night before she died, and that night, she was extremely agitated. The instant I walked in the door, she began a line of questioning that involved a missing suitcase—*Was it mine? Where had it gone? Did someone take it?* And on and on and on. I tried distract-ing her, but to no avail.

It's the Case of the Missing Suitcase, I texted Alex.

A geriatric Nancy Drew, she texted back.

If she doesn't stop this soon, I'm going to have to unplug her oxygen machine.

It wasn't funny, really, certainly not in retrospect. But it was an ongoing joke, albeit a very dark one, something we said sometimes to get us through the evenings when our efforts to pull back the witty, compassionate woman we had known failed. When I tucked my grandmother into bed that night, I took the hearing aid from her outstretched hand, pulled the covers over her, and patted her legs.

"Good night, Mamaw," I said. "Sleep well."

"Good night, Jenn," she said. "I'll see you in the morning, the good Lord willin'."

It was how she always said good night, how my grandfather had always said good night—not a prayer exactly, but something like one. I pulled her door halfway closed, then went into the kitchen and poured a big glass of merlot. The suitcase line of questioning had left me drained, and I was worried, not in a specific way, but in the general way you worry about someone who has been sick for a long time. And then I heard sounds coming from my grandmother's room. Wine glass in hand, I stood in the hallway and listened. She didn't seem to be saying actual words, so I moved to the recliner in the living room and waited.

"Oh!" she said. "Oohhh."

It was not a loud cry but more a soft moaning, as if she had a cramp in her leg or a catch in her side. Maybe it would pass. And it did. In a moment, she was quiet.

The next morning, I woke at daybreak. Though she was usually up by six or seven, that morning she was still sleeping, her oxygen tank humming. I made myself coffee and turned on the local news. From my grandfather's old recliner, I could see the outline of her body. She was curled on her side, her head resting in the crook of one arm.

When she wasn't awake by eight o'clock, I made her breakfast—oatmeal, French toast, coffee. I set out sugar and syrup and prunes. When she wasn't awake by nine, I went in the bedroom and stood beside her. Her breaths were long and heavy, her mouth slack, her chestnut hair dipping like waves onto her cheeks. She seemed deeply asleep. Increasingly uneasy, I checked her oxygen tube. When I determined the air was still flowing, I went back to the living room.

Finally, at 10:30 a.m., I called my mother. Something was wrong. In a way, I understood that. Still, although my grandmother had been in hospice care for almost a year, although she was ninety-two years old and weighed less than seventy pounds, although in the preceding weeks she had become increasingly weak and short of breath, I thought maybe she was just exhausted. Or perhaps coming down with something—a stomach bug or a cold.

"Should I try to wake her?" I asked my mother over the phone.

"I think maybe you should," she said.

And that's when I knew.

Later that morning, when the hospice nurse stopped by to officially pronounce her dead, I stood outside under the maple tree in the front yard. The tree had been pruned so thoroughly, it looked naked. When I was a kid, my grandfather used to lift me up to reach the lowest branch so I could climb up and up until finally I dangled over all of Canton, over the white, clapboard houses and the stone garages and the Pintos and Novas lining Trammel Avenue. I was a robin. A shape-shifting cloud. An angel.

"Are you Jennifer?" the nurse asked. She stood next to me, her hand pressed gently on my forearm. Her eyes were soft blue. "You must be Jennifer."

She waited for me to say something, but my body was no longer my own. My hands looked odd, wrong, someone else's hands. My feet were someone else's feet, my lungs, someone else's lungs, breathing in and out against my will. The nurse watched me for a moment, then continued.

"I wanted to tell you that your grandmother chose to die when you were there, and that is very special."

Cardinals circled and dove around us, brilliant red flecks against the harsh June sun. The air swished between their wings.

"Well, that was not very nice," I finally said.

She laughed, a gentle trickle of a laugh. She was a kind person. In the few, brief moments I had known her, I could tell that. Still, I didn't believe her. I had been one of my grandmother's caregivers as long as she had needed help. She had almost always preferred my company to anyone else's, but in the weeks before she died, she had repeatedly asked for someone to be with me when I stayed with her. And now I believed this was the reason: she didn't want me to be alone with her when she died.

She didn't want me to feel this way, and yet, I did, and nothing the nurse said or that David said or that my children or my parents or my aunt and uncle said could take that away. For weeks and months and years to come, I would wish I had done things differently that night. I would wish I had gone to my grandmother when I heard her cry out. I would wish I had sat with her and held her hand, that I had brushed her damp hair from her forehead and smoothed her wrinkled gown and whispered how much I loved her. I would wish I had not let her die alone.

"Listen to me," the nurse said. "I know something about loss. I lost a sister-in-law I was very close to. And I want you to know that there was nothing you could have done that would have changed the outcome here. Nothing, okay? And whenever you remember how you found your grandmother today, you just need to think of the best memory you have of her. Okay?"

Staring into the empty field that used to be my grandfather's garden, I nodded and tried to think of what that might be, of how one could possibly choose one best memory out of forty-five years of memories. And then I tried to imagine what remembering this might feel like a week from now, two weeks from now, two years from now, when my grandmother's death wasn't something that was happening but something that had happened in the past.

The friendly, down-to-earth people in Macomb, the intimate cafes, the strong pro-union sentiment, the elaborate Labor Day festivities that essentially shut down the town, the incessant, mournful sound of trains passing through were all reminiscent of my childhood in rural

Appalachia. Gradually, I began to make new friends and immersed myself in my work, and by mid-September, I was starting to feel a little bit settled. One afternoon, I was sitting in my office catching up on some grading when my officemate cleared her throat. I finished the sentence I was reading, then gave her my full attention.

"So," she said, "what *exactly* are you doing here?"

It was a question people repeatedly asked me in different ways, but the question was always essentially the same: *What is wrong with you? What was so wrong with your old life that you ended up here alone?* When most people asked, I told them part of the truth, that I needed the money. But for some reason, maybe the fact that I was particularly tired that day, that I had pulled out a shirt to wear and it had smelled so strongly of wood smoke, of home, a home I no longer recognized as my own, I told her more. I told her about our house, about Bill and my grandmother, about my strained relationship with David. And I told her something I was only just beginning to understand: I felt responsible for my grandmother's death.

My officemate was in her early thirties. She wore a short red dress and high heels. Her long hair was tinted blond, her freshly manicured nails crimson. While I talked, she nodded and groaned sympathetically.

"Oh," she said when I was finished. "So you're resetting."

"Yeah," I said, tapping my pen on my desk. "Yeah, I guess that's what I'm doing."

Instantly, instead of being a dropout from my old life, this thing

I was doing had a name and a purpose. *I'm resetting*, I told myself over and over in the days to come. For the first time in my adult life, my time was truly my own. I could have wine and cheese for dinner, and no one would care. I could drive all the way to Iowa for spicy apple pie, and no one would notice. I could spend my weekend bike riding and playing with my dog, and no one expected me to do anything else. If my doorbell rang, I would not feel sick to my stomach because I would know that it wasn't a sheriff's deputy coming to deliver a subpoena or someone from the power company coming to turn off our power or someone from the loan company coming to repossess my car because that sort of thing did not happen here. It only happened back in North Carolina.

One evening in late September, a colleague, Karen, invited me to a potluck picnic, sponsored by a local food advocacy group. The guests were an odd amalgamation of professors and farmers and hunters. We sat at cloth-covered tables surrounded by vases of flowers and decanters of water and wine and ate curried sweet potato soup prepared by a former member of the Rainbow Riders and pound cake made by a biology professor who was also a jazz singer.

Then, as the sun began to set, we gathered our jackets and made our way to the fire pit outside. A circle formed—men with harmonicas and fiddles, women with guitars and voices like lazy rivers. The sky was wide and full of stars, and in that moment, I was one of them, a tiny yet still significant spark in the universe. I was so immersed in my reverie that I didn't notice at first that the man next to me was speaking.

"They're pretty good, huh?" he repeated.

He was older than I was, in his sixties. He wore jeans and a ball cap and held a Heineken in one hand. He gestured toward the circle of musicians.

"They're great," I said.

The harmonica was somber and woeful, a long coal train bound for the Mississippi.

"Do you teach at the university?" he asked.

It wasn't a hard call. Pretty much everyone in Macomb taught at the university or had taught there at one point.

"English," I said. "I'm just here for the semester."

I took a sip of my Blue Moon and moved to a log by the fire. The man eased down beside me.

"Tell me, where did they find an English teacher just for the semester?"

"Online," I said. "I found the job online."

"Like on a rent-an-English-teacher website?"

He had bright-blue eyes and a certain thing about him, a spark, a glow, an easy smile. Together, we chuckled about the low prestige of my position, the crazy randomness of it all.

"I'm Chris," he said.

"Jennifer."

While the band launched into a rendition of "Wagon Wheel," Chris leaned in and asked, "How old are you? About forty?"

I frowned and downed the rest of my beer.

"Don't even," I said.

He laughed, and though I never sang back in North Carolina, I begin to sing along. I sang to Chris and to the fire and to the stars, which seemed to be stretching further and further across the sky. When the song was over, Chris was ready to leave. He got his coat, then came back over and crouched beside me.

"Are you homesick?" he asked, leaning into me, putting his hand on my back.

Had he asked me this earlier, I might have said yes. Never before had I spent so much time alone, and at first, the large spaces of silence in the Midwest had seemed infinite. Anxious for the sound of someone else's voice, I lay in bed at night, mentally clicking off how many days I had left before the end of the semester. Hester sprawled beside me, her head on the pillow, her hazel eyes peering into mine, as if she too were pondering the strangeness of our circumstances. But then at some point, not at a particular time or during a particular event but at some vague, indefinite moment, I had begun to ease into this new life, and the silence, instead of being a void, began to have its own weight and texture.

Now, the Big Dipper hung just over my head, so low, I felt I could reach up and take a gulp of cool, clear sky.

"No," I told Chris. "I'm not homesick."

The band was playing a Gillian Welch tune—"Elvis." Karen sang, her voice a low, longing croon.

"That's good," Chris said and patted my back. "That's good. Sometimes we need to do new things."

Long after he had left, I sat there, the fire warming my back, the harmonica strains drifting through the trees.

In the weeks that followed, Chris and I kept in touch. He and his wife were separated, and he was dating someone in a neighboring city. Still, we talked on the phone, emailed, occasionally met for lunch. He was cheerful and easygoing, and being with him reminded me of the early days with David, of the time when our relationship was unfettered and uncomplicated. I told myself that Chris and I were friends, friendly, nothing that crossed the line into romance, but the line itself was becoming blurry for me.

That fall, I repeatedly asked David to come see me in Macomb, but he never did, so that October, Hester and I drove back to North Carolina. I met David at Bouchon, a French bistro in downtown Asheville. He had on a new shirt and pants, and we ordered wine and mussels and made polite small talk about our children and our pets. I told him about my students and about the new friends I had made. Everything about our relationship felt strange and new. He felt different. I felt different.

When we got home late that night, I could see that David had done the dishes, that the bathroom had just been cleaned, that he had put fresh sheets on the bed. We fell into bed, exhausted, content, for the moment, just to be together again. The next morning, we woke to the sound of rain and to the churning, pulsating, gushing of the waterfall. The air coming through the cracked window smelled sharp and green, like pine saplings. Pulling the quilt over my shoulders and snuggling in close to David, I let the sounds of the water wash over me. I soaked in his deep, steady breathing until finally, the torrent outside began to ease, and I threw off the quilt and climbed from bed.

That afternoon, we planned to go to the Lake Eden Arts Festival in Black Mountain, about an hour away. It took me forever to decide what to wear. I wanted to look cool but not too young, not trying too hard. Finally, I chose a thick, hooded cotton dress and my favorite cowboy boots, and I pulled my long, gray hair back in a clasp. David too spent longer than usual picking out his clothes.

"Is this okay?" he asked, holding up the brown L.L.Bean shirt that I had gotten him for Christmas years ago.

"Very okay," I said.

It was officially a date—more officially, I suppose, than any date we had ever had before we were married. So I felt sixteen again or perhaps the way sixteen is supposed to feel, giddy and nervous and a little uncertain, but in a good way. At the festival, we listened to music and drank craft beer and ate organic, farm-raised chicken on sweet potato biscuits. Then we wandered past the music tents to a picnic table near the lake. It was a beautiful fall night with a full moon. We could hear the reggae band from the lakeside stage. Barefoot kids with glow sticks chased each other in the nearby field. A steady stream of people passed by on the gravel walkway—young women in short skirts and boots, young men with dreadlocks and combat boots, gray-headed couples perfumed with patchouli.

And in that moment, it occurred to me that this was who we were now. Perhaps it was who we had been all along. All those years of dressing for success, of attending one function after another in homes so large, we occasionally got lost, of hanging out with people who summered in Europe and owned their own planes and thought nothing of giving their kids a thousand dollars for a trip to the mall—this was infinitely more true to who we were. It was both oddly comforting and unsettling, and I struggled to think of what our futures might look like, of who we would become now that all the extraneous things had been stripped away.

"Do you sort of feel like we're separated?" I suddenly asked David.

We had never called this time apart a separation, never called it anything really, but while I had been away, I had begun to think of myself in the singular. *My house. My dog. My life.*

"No," David said. "Not at all."

He almost stopped there. I could feel him watching me as I stared into the lights reflecting on the water. And then he said, "Do you?"

I took a sip of my beer. Maybe he would forget he had asked. Maybe my silence would imply the answer. But he wanted to hear me say it.

"Do you?" he asked again.

"Yes," I whispered. "Sometimes."

"Well, then," he said. "It's time for you to come home. When you finish in December, I want you to come home. Okay?"

I loved my newfound freedom in Macomb, my break from the stress of our lives. I loved all the new people I had met, all the things

I was learning, the way I was reinventing myself. In Macomb, I was teaching kids who desperately wanted and needed an education. In Macomb, I was not just someone's wife or someone's mother. I was interesting and fun, someone who got invited to parties and picnics and bike races. In Macomb, I was not a total fuckup.

I wanted David to say he would come with me if I got a more permanent offer. We could start our new lives together in the Midwest. He could work remotely, and I could teach. We could go to the grocery store without worrying about running into Jeff and Denise. We could make new friends, friends who didn't know all about our fuckedupness. He could be married to a woman who had a future. But even as I wished these things, I knew David would never leave the mountains. He would never consider living anywhere else. He just didn't have it in him.

"Okay," I said.

The next day, I loaded Hester back into my car and, once again, made the fourteen-hour drive to Macomb. For some reason, leaving home was harder this time, but I was also eager to see my friends and glad for the distraction of work.

A few nights after I got back, Chris and I went to dinner at a Mexican restaurant just down the street. It was a place we had been many times with other people, but this time, we were alone. Chris was thin, and his face was starting to show signs of age, crow's feet at the corners of his eyes, lines framing his cheeks, but his eyes were a dazzling blue. We talked about our jobs, our past relationships, and, finally, our current relationships.

"You know what your problem is?" Chris said.

We were splitting an order of chicken fajitas. I was eating all the vegetables. He was eating all the chicken.

"What?"

"Your problem is you don't tell your husband what you want. You need to just speak up and say what you want."

I wiped fajita juice off my chin while I considered this. Was it true? Was I unwilling to communicate what I wanted? Maybe. Or maybe the real truth was that I didn't know what I wanted or, perhaps, that what I wanted was constantly changing.

"You know," Chris said before I could speak, "I wish we had met a long time ago."

For once, Chris wasn't smiling, and when he looked at me, all serious and wistful, I could see him now, sixtysomething years old with a soon-to-be ex-wife and a girlfriend and two just-grown sons, but I could also see him back then, twentysomething years old—long hair, wiry frame, a wild and charismatic hippy full of quiet dreams.

"We would have had a lot of fun together," I said.

"We sure would have."

It was as close as we ever came to naming what there was between us; though perhaps under different circumstances it would have been more, as it was, we were destined to remain friends. We looked at each other for one long moment, until a birthday celebration began at a nearby table. *Cumpleaños feliz*, the waiters sang. So we sang along.

Chipotle Chicken Burritos for a Crowd

- 10 pounds boneless, skinless chicken breasts
- 30 chipotle peppers in adobo sauce (about 5 small cans)
- 20 cloves garlic
- 2½ teaspoons ground cayenne pepper
- 2½ teaspoons ground paprika
- 1¼ teaspoons ground black pepper
- 1¼ teaspoons ground cumin
- 1¼ cups lime juice (not diluted)
- 1¼ cups Worcestershire sauce
- 1¼ cups honey
- 2½ cups balsamic vinegar
- 2½ cups olive oil
- 3 tablespoons salt

Puree all ingredients except chicken in food processor or blender. Place chicken in pan. Pour marinade over, and turn to make sure it is thoroughly coated. Cover and refrigerate for several hours. Grill. Chop into cubes.

Serve buffet style with warm tortillas, rice, beans (a choice

of refried or black beans is nice), shredded cheese, lettuce and/
or spinach, chopped red onions, chopped tomatoes, salsa,
sour cream, guacamole, etc. Accompany with margaritas or a
smooth, nutty amber ale such as Green Man ESB from Green
Man Brewery in Asheville.

Chapter Seven

ONE DAY IN LATE OCTOBER, just after the harvest, when the Asian beetles swarmed from the fields and clung to car windows and doors, to light fixtures and porch railings—a modern-day plague—a tornado skirted Macomb and devastated a small community just outside of Peoria. Hester and I were walking at the lake when the storm hit. The sky turned gray, then an odd, purplish black. Tree limbs hurled through the air. We jumped in our car, and as we drove home, streetlights and power lines shook so violently, Hester huddled on the floor and refused to move. We arrived home just as the storm was easing. I parked the car under the breezeway in the driveway and called David.

"You wouldn't believe the storm we just had," I told him. "The wind—the wind was incredible."

I described the eerie, lonesome howling, the way the lake water had turned dark and fierce, the cracking of the tethered boats as they slammed against the dock. And then, as if the storm had pried something loose in me, I was filled with panic at the thought of leaving this place, of leaving friends who had loaned me spare bikes and baked me homemade bread, who had invited me to Sunday dinner at their farms, who had helped me trap mice and shared their homegrown tomatoes.

"They've asked me to stay here another semester," I said.

David cleared his throat. "But you won't, right?"

I paused. "I don't know."

"We talked about this, remember? You're coming home in December."

Lightning streaked the sky. Branches and leaves littered the yard. The scent of mint filled the air.

"I mean, it's just that I can imagine this whole other life," I finally said.

The pause on the other end was so long and deep, I took the phone away from my ear and looked at the seconds ticking away to make sure we were still connected. Finally, David spoke.

"You have a life here," he said.

"But I have a life here too," I said. "I have friends. A job. People I have formed attachments to."

They were disjointed thoughts, disparate pieces trying to come together to say something about how I was not the same person who had left home months before. Somehow, in the midst of teaching eighty-five eighteen-year-olds, of learning what YOLO and turnt up meant, of scuttling down canyons in Starved Rock State Park and bike riding along the Mississippi and chatting with my next-door neighbor while our dogs chased an errant rabbit back and forth in an endlessly entertaining game of bunny volleyball, I had come to understand important things about myself and who I was. For a few moments, there were people whose lives had lined up next to mine and eased my grief, made me feel less broken.

Still, as much as I loved my new life in the Midwest, I knew that part of what I loved was the break from all the pressures of home, pressures that would soon follow me here.

And in the heavy silence that lingered between David and me, I thought of a story my grandfather told me just before he died—his very first memory. In July 1917, when he was six months old, my grandfather had sat in a cornfield, propped against a thick stalk. His five older siblings were at school, and his mother had brought him there where she could watch him while she worked. The baby could see his mother through the stalks, a shifting shadow in the changing light. The ground beneath him was dark brown, almost black. Above him, the green sky swayed in the wind. The baby dug his tiny fingers in the dirt and then sucked them, drinking in the rich, loamy soil, swallowing the earth that belonged to his grandfather and to his father and his father before him.

And then the baby noticed something—a tiny, twitching animal with large, floppy ears and shiny, sable eyes. At first, there was only one, but then there were more, ten or twenty smaller ones, darting in and out among the cornstalks. The baby was amazed, enchanted. He rocked back and forth, held out grubby baby hands. He called out in his own, special way—a cooing, gurgling chortling that rippled through the leaves and found his mother, bent over, twisting an ear of corn from the stalk. A moment later, she knelt before him, her damp hair matted to her forehead, her balled-up apron overflowing with corn.

"Bunnies!" she said. "Do you see the baby bunnies?"

My grandfather was well into his ninetieth year when he told me this story, and when he was finished, I was quiet, trying to find the right words. I wanted to tell him that I too saw it all so vividly—the hem of his mother's homemade dress, the brilliant sunshine, the frolicking, magical bunnies, the way the cornstalks moved together like waves. I wanted to tell him that I too would remember that image for all of my days, through all of my growing old. I wanted to say I understood what he was telling me, that this place, these mountains, were my legacy, my birthright. But I couldn't find the words.

Instead, I said, "That sure must've been something, Papaw."

And he said, "It sure was."

Though my grandfather had been dead for five years now, his story glided across the years, found me parked next to a boxcar in the Midwest. It reminded me of my rootedness, of the deep and abiding knowledge that *who* I was was inextricably tied to *where* I was. If I stayed in Macomb, I would have a good job, good friends, a nice place to live. If I went home, I was going back to snakes and mice and spiders, to lukewarm showers and the occasional clogged water pipe.

But I was Appalachian in a bone-deep sort of way. I missed the mountains. I missed running by the Davidson River with my dogs. I missed mountain biking and hiking. I missed hearing those voices I grew up with—the thick, unhurried speech of my people. And I missed David's smoky, familiar smell, the way his beard scratched my neck when he hugged me, the easy way he held me. For me, David and the mountains, my kids and home, my ancestors and my identity were all hopelessly tangled into one. In order to know who I was and what I believed, I needed to go home. Now, David's silence was filled with raw, shrill aching.

"I'm coming home," I told him. "I am. It's just going to be hard."

The holidays were just around the corner, and all of my kids would be home, all of us together in one house, under one rather suspect roof. That is what I pictured: the house smelling of cinnamon and cloves and nutmeg, the five of us gathered around the breakfast table eating cream cheese braids and sipping Russian tea and somehow getting through Christmas without my grandmother. It was what she would have wanted.

"It don't matter if we have any gifts or not," she used to say, "just so long as we're all together."

That winter would be one of the coldest, snowiest winters on record for the Midwest, and the December day I left Macomb for good, it was six degrees below zero. My front porch was covered with a thin layer of ice. I had packed all of my belongings the day before, and the entranceway was cluttered with bags and boxes. Before dawn, bundled in two coats, a pair of gloves, a hat, and boots, I gripped the handrail on the porch and staggered outside, carrying box after box to my car. Hester stood shivering on the porch, her eyes roaming from the boxes to the car.

"Come on, girl," I said to her when I was finished.

She bolted down the steps, out the front gate, directly onto the box of student papers in my back seat.

"Jesus Christ," I said. And then, "We're going home, girl."

Hester flicked her tail. On the way out, I checked the mailbox one last time. Inside was a book Chris had recently mentioned to me, Nora Ephron's *Wallflower at the Orgy*, with a sticky note on the front that said, "Take good care. C." I put the book on top of one of the boxes and made a final run to campus to return my students' papers, and then Hester and I headed south. For hours, we rode past snow-covered fields until, finally, the ground became wavy again, then rocky and jagged. Twelve hours later, we hit the Smokies.

It was dark outside and misting rain as we zigzagged through the gorge outside of Knoxville. Fog hovered over the highway. I turned on the defroster, and as we crossed into North Carolina, I could hear my grandmother naming each community along the way. *Fines Creek. Jonathan Creek. Crabtree. Newfound Gap.*

They were places she had known her entire life, places she understood in relation to her own life and the people she had known. She had cousins who lived in Crabtree, in-laws on Newfound. She could tell you the weather in any of those other areas simply by looking out her living room window.

"We've got about five inches of snow out here," she would say, "so they've got upward of eight inches out at Fines Creek."

In another two months, my grandparents' home would be sold. The garden, the walkway lined with peonies, the grapevine where, as children, my brother and I flicked Japanese beetles into mason jars— all of those things would belong to someone else. I had promised myself I wouldn't cry when I passed the Canton exit on I-40. It had been six months. I should be doing better now. But as soon as I saw the plumes of smoke from the paper plant, the tears came, not soft, quiet tears but a terrific rush. Hester whined and pawed at my shirt sleeve, and for a moment, I thought I would not be able to breathe, that I would never be able to breathe again.

When my grandmother and my uncle Bill were still alive, it felt a little like my grandfather was still here too. Through their storytelling, their humor, their humble ways of being in the world, they had kept him alive, and I had been part of something larger, something I understood. After my grandmother died, my extended family were all really gone—not just my grandparents and their siblings but everyone who came before them. These mountains were rapidly changing. Factories and tobacco fields had given way to craft breweries and mountain bike trails, and as this generation passed, an entire way of living and speaking and being had passed with it. For me, the loss was unfathomably deep.

I knew that eventually I would be able to sort through my grandmother's dresser drawers. I would be able to throw on my grandfather's flannel shirt without stopping to see if it still smelled like him. I would be able to wear my grandmother's watch and her scarves, to dump out the canister of self-rising flour and the jar of honey peanut butter I would never use. I would be able to tell funny stories about my grandparents, listen to their favorite songs on the radio, summon their voices at the times when I most needed them. But feeling better would not mean the loss was less real, only less raw and exposed. Instead of being on my skin, my grief would seep through my pores and adhere to my heart and lungs, to my blood and guts. And now I had to figure out how to live like that, how to behave like a normal, sane person, a person who was not haunted.

As I passed the exit to my grandmother's home, I thought of a worn black-and-white photograph she had kept in an old shirt box along with all the family photographs. In the photo, two young men wore cowboy getups—jeans, boots, hats, flannel shirts. Each man had a guitar slung over his shoulder.

"Who's that?" I asked her once.

"Just an old boyfriend," she said. "They were musicians. I liked that one," she said, placing her forefinger on the shorter guy, the one with the shy, crooked smile, "and Beatrice liked the other one."

My grandmother had been married to my grandfather for almost seventy years. Their relationship had been so close, their roots so deeply intertwined, that I rarely thought of them as individuals. Together, they had been one powerful spiritual force, a two-tiered anchor, a double-sided talisman. Now, for the first time, I wondered if my grandmother had ever longed for another life, if she had had any regrets, if on that last morning, while I was cooking oatmeal and spooning Folgers into her mug, she was dreaming of all the places she had been and the people she had loved, or if, in the end, she had simply taken one giant leap and become a part of it all.

Mamaw's Cornbread

- 1½ cups self-rising cornmeal
- 3 tablespoons self-rising flour
- 1 egg, beaten
- About ½ cup milk (whole, evaporated, or buttermilk)
- 1 to 2 tablespoons oil or shortening for pan

Preheat a cast-iron skillet coated with oil or shortening in oven at 425 degrees. Mix dry ingredients. Stir in egg, and add milk until the batter is the consistency of thick pancake batter. Pour into hot pan. Bake about 18 minutes or until brown on top.

Chapter Eight

THE FEBRUARY AFTER I CAME home from Macomb, our region saw our first real snowstorm in many years. Over a foot of snow fell, followed by ice, resulting in treacherous roads for days afterward. Our driveway was impassable. David chopped wood and tended the boiler while I cooked soup and cornbread, creamed chicken and biscuits, lentil stew. Finally, one afternoon, bored from being stuck indoors, we donned our boots and down coats and set out walking. Reba and Hester ran ahead, skating gracefully on the ice, while David and I trudged through snow up to our knees.

The four of us followed the creek until we came to a second waterfall just beyond our house. Sheathed in ice, the falls were white and hard and eerily quiet—a magnificent ice sculpture. We watched, listening to the silence, and then we angled up the mountain to the ridge above the house, then down to the property line, across the driveway, and up the other side of the mountain. We lumbered over fallen limbs, searching for the pink markers Aaron had used to mark the trail the previous spring.

The Earlobe Trail, Aaron had dubbed it, an allusion to the Art Loeb Trail, a 30.1-mile trail that began near the entrance to the Pisgah National Forest, just down the road. Aaron had trimmed overhanging branches, added footholds, marked the path. Like sorting markers into baggies or converting a spare bedroom into a film studio, it had been a way of putting his imprint on this place, of making it home. Ultimately, however, the markers proved unnecessary. Reba had been Aaron's constant companion during the long afternoons on the trail, and she remembered every twist and turn. Navigating downed hemlocks and rhododendron thickets, she perched high on a bank and waited. *Like a gargoyle*, we said. At the top of the trail, near the spring basin, we paused.

Beneath us, the world was white—the trees, the tin roof, the smoke furling from the chimney. Rhododendrons sagged with snow, and all around us, tree limbs popped and cracked. Bundled in layers of clothing, only our eyes and noses and mouths exposed, David and I stood with our sleeves touching, our breaths phantoms in the frigid air. And then I remembered another gray day like this one, over a quarter of a century ago.

In the spring of 1984, when David was nineteen and I was sixteen, we sat on a rock at the base of Looking Glass Falls, a cooler of beer and a pen and notebook wedged between us. Because I was editor of the high school newspaper, I was in charge of writing senior superlatives for our final issue, and since David also knew almost all the seniors, he was helping. Shouting over the roar of the falls, the water spraying our clothes and our hair, we made our way through the list.

The superlatives needed to be humorous in a tasteful, not offensive way so that my advisor would approve them. Or they had to be seemingly innocuous but not actually so. For example, two of our friends—Sam and Catherine—had recently been in a minor car accident, the result of Catherine giving Sam a blow job while he was navigating a curvy mountain road. Sam had lost control of the car and crashed into a bank, and though they were otherwise fine, the impact knocked out Catherine's front teeth. For Catherine's superlative, David suggested *most likely to need dentures*. I wrote that down. It was silly, perhaps even unkind, but I was not thinking of those things then.

More than thirty years had passed since that day, but looking over the glassy falls above the cabin, I could still feel the cool rock beneath me. I could see the dark, swirling pool beneath the falls, and I could still see David there—blue jeans and a light blue T-shirt, thick, tinted glasses, a bottle of Budweiser in one hand, the other hand resting on my bare thigh.

David and I had been married for almost twenty-three years, and yet our transformation from two carefree kids to a middle-aged couple seemed so abrupt, my mind struggled to keep up. I knew other people who had experienced a dramatic life change, a move from, say, a townhouse in the city to a home in the woods. But those people had chosen that path, sought it out, and then created a life that was still relatively comfortable. They had hot water heaters, cable television, regular phone service, hardwood floors, ceramic chicken sculptures, and quaint flower gardens.

Our situation felt different, not a Thoreauvian quest so much as an exile of sorts, a banishment from mainstream society. In the year and a half since we had moved to the cabin, our financial situation had only gotten worse. Because we had yet not settled with the IRS or the Department of Revenue, we were accruing exorbitant penalties on our overdue taxes, and because the payment plan the IRS had originally given us was way beyond our means, we were in a holding pattern— "wait and see" mode. The IRS had moved our status to "not collectable," which meant that though we still technically owed taxes, the IRS was not actively pursuing us. It was obvious that we didn't have the money to pay what we owed. Still, we kept hoping that our situation would improve enough for us to make the IRS an offer in compromise, an offer to settle for a portion of the full amount due. Just as often, we hoped that the money to pay off everything in full would simply fall out of the sky—that we would win the lottery or find a golden ticket in a chocolate bar. We hoped for something—anything—that would allow us to put this behind us and move forward, and the fervent hoping, the incessant pressure of thinking through every *what if*, cast a constant shadow over our lives.

Though I knew we were lucky to live in such beautiful surroundings, calling this place home meant embracing something I had not chosen. Even now, whenever I was away, I instantly pictured myself back at our old house, in my old kitchen, cooking a pot of corn chowder or baking a tomato pie. The self I knew and understood was back there, in that old life, not a perfect life certainly, but a life where I had an intact home and a house full of kids and a grandmother who was still very much alive.

In addition to our financial worries, I was still often stressed by the day-to-day challenges of living in this dusty, dark cabin. We had not replaced the fluorescent lighting. We had not renovated the bathroom. We had not finished replacing the floors. I constantly coughed and sneezed and wheezed due to the boiler smoke. I worried about the drinking water. Still, looking down at the cabin from the top of the ridge, the whole hollow illuminated in white light, the dogs running in circles, kicking up snow behind them, I felt something else too, something faint but sure—the very first tug of belonging, a low and steady rumbling. And with that came a steady surge of other realizations: *Maybe I could learn to love this place. Maybe I could forgive David. Maybe I could forgive myself.*

The wind, which had been blowing evenly all afternoon, picked up speed. A great howl began over the far ridge, swept across the hollow and up the mountainside. I cinched my hood tighter and leaned into David.

"Ready?" he asked.

I nodded. Our feet and faces tingly and numb, we walked sideways down the mountain—or perhaps more accurately, David walked, and I slid. He took a few steps, then waited until I crashed into him. Then he steadied me and took another step. Eventually, using the slide-and-crash method, we made our way down the mountain. Our hiking adventure complete, it was time to make snow cream.

I had left a mixing bowl and a long spoon on the picnic table, and now we scoured the snow for a spot free of dog pee. When we had located a good place, David chipped through the outer layer of ice, then filled the bowl with snow. We headed inside, stripped off our wet clothes, and hung them on chairs to dry. While David threw another log on the fire, I added vanilla and sugar and cream to the bowl of snow. Then, wearing only our long johns, we sat kitty-corner at the kitchen counter, listening to jazz on the radio, slurping snow cream and sipping Fireball whiskey, and in that moment, I felt a little like a kid again, content and giddy and hopeful, all at the same time.

Snow Cream

- Snow
- Milk or cream
- Sugar
- Vanilla

Go outside. Scout out a patch of snow that is free from dog pee, cat pee, rabbit droppings, pine needles, and other contaminants. Scrape off the top layer of snow. Being careful not to touch the ground below, fill a chilled mixing bowl with loosely packed snow. Once you are back inside, add just enough milk or cream to create a slushy mixture. Add more sugar and vanilla than you deem reasonable. Then add some more. Serve with straight whiskey or, for children, hot chocolate.

Chapter Nine

THAT WINTER, THANKS TO THE unusually cold weather, I found myself with time on my hands—lots of time. I had always wanted to try making my own cheese, and now seemed like the perfect time. While David chopped wood, I stocked up on rennet and cheesecloth, then perused the internet for instructions on how to make simple cheeses like ricotta and mozzarella. For now, I would use cow's milk from a local creamery.

Mozzarella was somewhat complicated to make, and to me, it didn't taste much different from standard, store-bought mozzarella, but making ricotta was easy—easier, in fact, than driving to the store to buy ricotta. It was also a great way to use milk that was approaching or even slightly past its due date. You simply brought a gallon of milk to two hundred degrees in a large pot, stirred in a quarter cup of lemon juice or three tablespoons of vinegar, brought the milk mixture back to two hundred degrees, then let it sit, covered, for about fifteen minutes. Then you drained the whey from the curds and hung the cheese. In just over an hour, you had heavenly homemade ricotta that was delicious in pasta dishes or smeared on toasted bread with plenty of garlic and oregano and a drizzle of olive oil.

I was also thrilled to discover that I could use the leftover whey in place of vegetable or chicken broth. I used it in soups, in rice, in puddings and pies. Then, encouraged by my success, I decided to try making yogurt, and though I knew a yogurt machine would greatly simplify this task, I wanted to make it the way my favorite homesteading blog recommended, the old-school way—on the stove top in quart-size mason jars.

None of my regular pots was large enough to hold four jars, but then I had an idea—my grandmother's Burpee canner, circa 1940. If I removed the enamel liner, the outer pot would be perfect. I dragged the canner from the bottom kitchen shelf, shook out the spiders and dog hair, rinsed it, and placed it on the stove. The directions said that if you placed a cloth in the bottom of the pot, the jars wouldn't rattle, so I folded up a dishcloth and set four quart-size mason jars filled with milk on top.

The next part was tricky. You had to add water until the jars were three-quarters covered, but you couldn't get any water in the jars. I was a big-picture person, and my method of approaching most things was hit or miss, but this required my utmost concentration. It had to be done slowly and gently. If water got in the milk, the yogurt would not set properly, and all this effort would be for nothing. Finally, the water successfully added, I turned on the stove. According to the directions, the milk should reach 180 to 185 degrees. You could measure that with a thermometer, or you could look for a layer of skin to form on top. Uncomfortable with ambiguity, I clipped a digital thermometer onto the side of one jar and waited.

Every few minutes, the screen on the thermometer automatically shut off, so with one of my grandmother's dishcloths thrown over my shoulder, I stood next to the stove, tending the thermometer, listening to Lake Street Dive on the radio. Eventually, the milk seemed to be doing something, shifting almost imperceptibly. The thermometer read 170 degrees. *Close*. From the kitchen, I could see patches of snow in the shady areas along the creek and underneath the low-lying shrubs. Icicles clung to the rocks in the waterfall and reflected the morning sun—tiny stained-glass windows.

I could also see the waterfall and the massive stacks of wood in the side yard. David had read on a homesteading blog that in pioneer times, a woman used to judge a man's potential as a husband by how he stacked his wood. Poor stacking technique did not bode well for the couple's future. Neat, careful stacks that allowed air to circulate and dry the wood meant a man was a keeper. His family would stay warm, and they would have plenty of fuel to cook their food.

Since we had been here, David had developed his own stacking process, a crisscrossing technique. He also knew which types of wood burned longest and hottest. He could eyeball a truck bed full of wood and say whether it was a full cord, a half cord, or something in between. Once, he ordered a cord from someone off Craigslist. The man drove all the way from Asheville, but when he tried to charge the price for a cord of wood when the truck bed was a quarter full, David refused to even negotiate with him.

"Get the hell on out of here," David had told him.

By then, David had given up his office in town. He put his office equipment and boxes of files in storage and worked from home. At first, it was odd having so much time together, but now, it seemed strange when one of us ran into town for coffee or milk and left the other alone at the cabin. *Our new normal*, we called it. Each morning, we tended to our dogs and cats. Then we drank coffee and talked about the day's agenda before departing to our separate work areas—my desk upstairs, his desk downstairs.

The thermometer screen went blank, and I pushed it on again. 177 degrees. Three more degrees. I loved this part of making yogurt. I loved that Hester sat on the cushion by the door and that Pretzel stretched at my feet, his nose pressed to the heat vent beneath the cabinets. I loved that in this space, my mind could wander, circling time and space, lingering where it needed to before spinning away again.

For the past fifteen years, I had taught composition to college freshmen, primarily underprepared athletes none of the full-time faculty wanted to teach. It was a job that required constant focus. Any lapse in my attention resulted in my students answering phone calls from their coaches or spilling spit cups on the floor or engaging in loud arguments about whether or not one of them did or did not look *exactly like Jesus*. Once, I zoned out for one second, and a student, a member of the golf team, raised his hand. He wore a pink knit shirt, plaid shorts, loafers without socks.

"Mrs. McGaha," he asked, "who would you rather sleep with, Brett Favre or Obama?"

I had missed the chuckles on that side of the room, the elbowing and the whispered dares, so this caught me unaware. For a few tense seconds, the students, all of them, had the upper hand. I stared at them. They stared at me.

"Get the hell out of my classroom," I said.

"But just tell me," the student pleaded as I shut the door behind him.

I had no idea who Brett Favre was, and I had spent those quiet seconds trying to figure that out. Later, Alex would tell me.

"He's a football player, Mom. How can you not know that?"

"Oh well," I said. "Then the answer is clearly Obama. You know how I feel about football."

Yogurt making was not emotionally taxing like teaching had been. Yogurt making was contemplative, meditative, forgiving. There was room for error, time for you to zone completely out without getting hoodwinked, usurped, outwitted. From my perch by the stove, I watched David whack a large chunk of wood. His arms were firm and muscular, his shoulders taut as he raised the ax above his head and dropped it, one clean sweep, followed by another, then another. There was the ping of the ax hitting the splitter, followed by a great *thwap*— the sound of breaking wood.

With both the stove and wood boiler running, the kitchen was at least ninety degrees. I stared at the milk, looking for the telltale wrinkles on top. The windows did not open, and the air was close and sticky, my shirt damp. Still, I sat close to the stove, pressing the thermometer over and over again until, eventually, it read 180. Then, I turned off the stove and, using my grandmother's dishcloth as a potholder, I moved the jars, one by one, to the counter to cool.

According to my directions, when the milk reached 110 to 120 degrees, it would be warm enough to stimulate the starter but not hot enough to kill it. At that point, I was to stir a couple of tablespoons of starter yogurt into each jar. While I waited, I went upstairs and answered a few emails. Then I came back and looked at the thermometer. 176 degrees. I showered, then checked again. 166 degrees. I threw on my farm coat and walked the dogs down to the bridge and back. I made a phone call. 150 degrees. I went upstairs and tweeted a photo of the mason jars in the pot. I posted the same photo to Instagram. *Making yogurt the old-school way,* I said. 145 degrees. I heated a bowl of leftover taco soup, doused it with Tabasco sauce, and sat down at the counter to eat. 140 degrees. Sweat poured down the side of my face. Wood boiler heat, I was learning, was fierce. The kitchen felt like a sweat lodge, or what I imagined a sweat lodge might feel like since I had never been to one.

"That wood heat is the best heat I've ever had," I had told my uncle Bill shortly after we moved in.

"You're gonna think that's good heat until that damn thing blows up on you," Bill had said.

Bill had been full of big, crazy talk like that. At his funeral, the preacher had asked if anyone wanted to say a few words, and one woman after another stood up and told about Bill flirting with them or propositioning them or proposing marriage. Finally, the red-faced preacher returned to the pulpit and said, "All right. All right. Let's just go ahead and have a show of hands. How many of you in here did Bill Boyd propose to?" More than half the women in the funeral home chapel raised their hands. If my grandmother had been there, she would have raised her hand too, but the day of Bill's funeral, she was at home, just weeks away from death herself. Shortly after my grandfather died, Bill, by then an eighty-nine-year-old widower, had heard a preacher say that if your brother dies, you should marry his wife. It was in the Bible somewhere, though Bill was vague on where, and although he had never been much for conventional religion, that passage particularly struck him. Immediately, he had called my grandmother and proposed.

"Ah, shut up, Bill," my grandmother had said.

It was still so hard to believe they were all gone—my grandfather, Bill, my grandmother.

The milk had reached 130 degrees. *Almost*. I put my empty soup bowl in the sink, ran some water in it, and got out the yogurt starter and a tablespoon. And then I resumed waiting. In my past life, I was impatient, high-strung, constantly flitting from one task to the next, but here, if I wanted hot water, I had to wait for a fire. If I wanted enough water pressure to take a shower, I had to wait for the dishwasher to finish running. If I needed to use the bathroom, I had to wait my turn. In fact, things were so serene here compared to the rest of the world that whenever I drove into town to the grocery store, I felt overwhelmed by the people and traffic.

"Where did these people come from?" I would ask David.

"I have no idea," he would say. "I was wondering the same thing."

When I visited larger cities, my sense of detachment was even more pronounced. Before, I had enjoyed the occasional weekend trip to a major city, but now, any metropolitan area larger than Asheville felt overwhelming. Subways made me panic. As did elevators. And traffic. And people blowing their horns. In fact, some days, even Asheville was too much. *Where was everyone going? Why were they all so loud?*

Finally, the milk reached 120 degrees. Still, I waited a few more minutes, just to be sure. At 117 degrees, I stirred a couple of spoonfuls of yogurt into each jar and capped the lids. Then I moved them all to a cooler and filled it with hot tap water until the jars were almost covered. For the next ten hours, every few hours, I scooped out some of the cooled water and replaced it with fresh, warm water.

When I came downstairs to check the milk one last time, it was dark outside. The dogs had been fed, and they were sprawled about the house sleeping. Moths pinged against the windows outside, and "Fare Thee Well" by the Dead played on the radio. Above the waterfall, a full moon loomed. I opened the cooler and shook the jars, one by one, testing for firmness. The yogurt jiggled but didn't slosh—a good sign. Satisfied, I moved the jars to the refrigerator. And then I went back upstairs and climbed into bed. David was still downstairs working. Kate, our beagle mix, was asleep in the clothes basket by my bed. I pulled my grandmother's quilts tightly around me, turned off the light, and dreamed.

In my dream, it was evening, and I was walking down a wooded path when I saw three wolves curled together in a bend. The wolves were thick and gray, their muzzles silver. Flicking their tails, they watched me through icy-blue eyes. I stood in the path, hesitant to go back up the trail because it was getting dark but wary of walking past. Very slowly, I took my cell phone from my pocket and called my mother. *There are wolves*, I whispered. *And I'm afraid.*

Shadowy figures emerged through the trees ahead, one set of ears, then another, a pair of tall, fluffy tails. Two wolves tore down the mountain, their legs taut and lean, their muscles powerful. Scarlet tongues dangled from their mouths. They were bold, majestic, intensely joyful, and I was no longer frightened. I wanted to catch them, lean into them, and run my hands through their coarse fur, feel their hot, wild breath on my face.

Never mind, I told my mother. *I'm okay. The wolves are friendly.*

I hung up the phone and sprinted down the path, my feet pounding the earth, the wind stroking my hair like fingers. I woke disoriented, thrilled by the image of the running wolves. And then before my mind was fully awake, I knew: I had dreamed of my mother and all the other mothers before her. I had dreamed of crossing over.

Homemade Yogurt

- 1 gallon milk
- 8 tablespoons plain yogurt with active cultures

Divide milk into 4 jars, leaving 2 inches of space at top. Place a folded dishrag in bottom of pot. Add filled jars. Fill pot with water ¾ of the way up the sides of jars. Bring water to a boil, and simmer until milk in jars has reached 180 to 185 degrees. Remove jars from pot, and allow to cool to 110 to 120 degrees. Once cooled, stir 2 tablespoons yogurt into each jar, and cap jars. Place jars in a small cooler. Fill cooler with warm water, exchanging the water as necessary to keep the temperature consistent. Let sit for 10 hours. Remove the jars from the cooler and refrigerate.

Chapter Ten

My grandmother grew up on a farm in the mountains of western North Carolina, and in her recollections, farm life was never idyllic. The work was backbreaking and constant, food hard to come by. On frigid winter mornings, she woke covered with snow that had drifted through the slats in the bedroom walls. Still, her stories made me dream of the three-room log cabin in which she was raised, of her nine brothers and sisters, of the mother who cooked dinner for twelve on a woodstove, of the father who spent his days plowing fields and hoeing potatoes, tending cows and hogs and chickens.

Perhaps, to a more reasonable person, my grandmother's stories might have seemed more like cautionary tales than inspirational ones. I'm sure that's how she intended them. But there was also a richness to her stories, a certain knowingness that drew me in and held me there. I could see my young grandmother hauling water from the well with her sisters, crawling into the hayloft to search for chicken eggs, fashioning hollowed-out acorns into makeshift cups for tea parties in the woods. Those images were as real to me as my own recollections of growing up in an upper-middle-class neighborhood just outside of Brevard. Farming defined my grandmother, made her who she was, instilled in her a rare combination of toughness and gentleness, and somehow, after she died, I had a vague yet definite sense that living closer to the land, raising our own vegetables and farm animals, would bring me healing—not just spotty, episodic moments of happiness but something deeper and more lasting.

For years, David and I had talked about the possibility of getting a few goats or chickens. However, though our across-the-street neighbors raised cows, alpacas, and chickens, our old neighborhood was part of a development that had a restrictive covenant forbidding farm animals. But once we moved to the cabin, all of that changed. There were no rules. We could do anything we wanted. And what I wanted was to raise chickens. All I had to do was convince David this was a good idea, which was easier than I had thought. I only had to promise him one thing: under no circumstances would I ask him to kill a chicken. The chickens would be for eggs and eggs only.

"Okay," I said. "Fair enough."

So I bought a copy of *Storey's Guide to Raising Chickens*. I read everything I could find online. I accosted farmers at the tailgate market and perfect strangers I found wandering around the homesteading sections of book stores: *Do you have chickens? What kind do you have? How many? What type of feed do you use? How many eggs per day do you get?* Finally, I asked a farmer at our local market where I should get chickens. McMurray Hatchery, he told me, a mail-order company based in Iowa. It seemed like an awfully long way for a baby chick to travel. Plus, it seemed odd to begin our foray into local food by buying chickens from halfway across the country.

"Iowa?" I asked. "Are you sure?"

He was sure. McMurray's offered a wide variety of chicks and would replace any that died during shipping. Though the thought of a chick smothering to death on its way from Iowa to North Carolina was disturbing, I knew that if I wanted to be a farmer, I was going to need to toughen up. These were not puppies. They were chickens, and if one died every now and then, well, so be it. I just wouldn't make the mistake of getting too attached to them. I would remember they were poultry, not pets. I would not name them or hold them. That afternoon, I called McMurray and ordered a rainbow variety pack of laying hens, to be delivered in March.

A few weeks later, David and I woke to the call we had been expecting. It was not even daylight, and while David told the postmaster we were on our way, I began throwing on my clothes.

"They're here!" David said when he hung up.

"I know!" I said. "I told you they would be! Get dressed!"

The night before, David had been skeptical. Do they really mail chicks halfway across the country the day they are born? Yes, I had told him. That's how it works.

"We should have just slept in our clothes," David said.

"You don't have to come," I said. "I can go by myself."

But he was up, pulling on jeans and the same T-shirt he had worn the day before. We made coffee, and David stoked the fire in the wood boiler. Then we hopped in the car with an inexplicable sense of urgency. The chicks had been in the package for a day already. What difference could a few more minutes make?

When we got to the post office, the sky was just beginning to lighten, a flush of yellow, then pink, then violet. Per the postmaster's instructions, we pulled around back. I jumped out of the car before David had even stopped. Another woman—an employee from Tractor Supply—was already there. I waited while the postmaster brought out her package, and when she walked past me, a dozen tiny beaks peeked through the box holes.

It had never occurred to me that someone else might be getting chicks at the same time I was. The whole idea of chickens seemed to belong just to David and me, and the fact that you could order them online from Iowa and they would show up at the post office in downtown Brevard was simply magical, as if they had flown in on a carpet versus an airplane. Or a truck. I wasn't sure how they had arrived, now that I thought about it. But the chicks were actually here, which meant that in just a few minutes, it would be official: we would be farmers. *Sort of.* I was more excited than I had been in years.

"Ma'am?" the postmaster was saying.

"I'm here to pick up my chicks," I said.

Moments later, I was holding the box from the hatchery. Very carefully, I made my way down the handicapped ramp and back to the car where David stood waiting to open the back door.

"I'm just going to hold them," I said, climbing onto the front seat.

On my lap, the warm box shifted and rocked and gyrated as the chirping chicks clamored over each other. I stroked their downy feathers through the air holes.

"It's okay, girls," I said. "You're okay."

Once we were home, David took the box from my lap and carried it to the boiler room where he had constructed a brooder from scrap wood. He set the box in the brooder and carefully cut the tape with his pocketknife. I watched, not moving, not even breathing, while he lifted the lid. And there they were—twenty-seven peeping, popping, bouncing babies in an array of soft colors, just like the catalogue had promised.

One by one, we lifted the chicks from the box and dipped their beaks into their water dish before releasing them into the brooder, where they promptly fell sound asleep on the wood chips. We turned on their heat lamps—one on either end of the brooder—and then stood admiring them like proud parents. There were white chicks, red ones, a downy yellow one, blue ones, black ones, black-and-white speckled ones, and two huge girls that looked more like swans than any chickens I had ever seen. They were positively fascinating.

That night, I hardly slept at all. I was up before dawn, and the girls were still asleep when I walked into the boiler room. As soon as I began stoking the fire, however, they woke in a frenzy, chirping and running around. All of them, that is, except for one. That chick, a Rhode Island Red, stood motionless, her head limp and hanging. I went upstairs to tell David, but what was he to do? We watched helplessly that day as she got more and more still, her body sagging closer and closer to the boiler floor.

Later that afternoon, David found her facedown in a corner. He got her body out, wrapped it in newspaper, and set it on the woodpile where we kept the stash of bones the dogs were constantly bringing home from the woods. Later that day, he would bury her. The next day, when a second chick started doing the same thing, standing languidly, head down, David attempted to feed it electrolytes through an eyedropper, but she too was dead within hours.

Though we knew it was not unusual to lose a couple of chicks in the first forty-eight hours, we still felt like failures. We had read articles online about people who had lost all of their chicks within days of each other, and we worried our chicks had something contagious. The fact that the hatchery would replace our chicks was little consolation. I wanted *these* chicks, and I wanted them to be healthy. I watched the remaining chicks obsessively, repeatedly checking the two thermometers in their brooder and adjusting their heat lamps. David even rigged a system so that I could monitor the brooder temperature from our bedroom at night.

It was March, and in our area, that meant one thing: uncertain weather. It might be seventy degrees outside one day and snowing the next. You never knew. But for the next week, the brooder needed to consistently be ninety to ninety-five degrees. After that, we would turn the temperature down five degrees per week until we got to seventy degrees, at which point the chicks would have all their feathers and would no longer need heat. The problem with this was that the room temperature was hard to regulate. The wood boiler seemed to have two settings—off and scorching. David would stoke the fire. Within minutes, the brooder would be ten degrees hotter. Other times, such as on windy days when air pulsed through the drafty room, the brooder temperature kept dropping, and I worried the chicks were too cold.

Eventually, David figured out how to keep the temperature more consistent—with a small fire regularly tended. During those weeks, we rarely left home. The house stayed dry and warm, our own little desert in the woods. It was cozy and close, and David and I spent many hours watching the tiny, fluffy balls waddling around, peeping, then falling asleep sprawled on the floors or tucked into corners or in tiny chicken heaps—twenty-five bodies illuminated by two warming lights and the orange glow of the boiler. Overhead, the pipes hissed and steamed, and something about the closeness of the room, of all the innocent lives depending on us, reminded me of another spring, the spring I was expecting Aaron.

David, Alex, and I were living in a rented duplex next to a cow pasture between Brevard and Asheville. Because we only had two bedrooms, David and I converted the walk-in closet in our bedroom into a nursery. We took out our clothes (though I have no memory of where we put them—Did we fold them and put them in drawers? Did we drape them over the furniture?) and pasted in a wallpaper border with bright blue trains. Our final touches were a black-and-white mobile over the crib and a changing table with a bright, cheerful bumper pad. After Aaron was born, I used to stand by his crib, watching my beautiful, towheaded baby sleep. I remembered his sweaty-sweet smell, his gentle baby laughter and his hiccupping cries, the way he used to run his fingers over the tiny mole on my neck when I held him.

Watching chickens sleep was not exactly the same as watching a human baby sleep. Still, there was a peacefulness about the dozing chicks, a quiet vulnerability that reminded me of mothering, of the frightening and awesome responsibility of having someone depend on me. One morning as I watched the slumbering chicks, I noticed a wood chip in their water. As I leaned in to remove it, I knocked the edge of the brooder, jostling the sleeping babies. One yellow ball hopped up and darted about, peeping frantically. In her alarm, she stumbled into a pile of sleeping chicks, and a cacophony of peeping ensued until there were twenty-five wide-awake, frantic chicks.

"It's okay," I cooed. "It's just me. Go back to sleep."

Again, they went through their bedtime rituals—food, water, peeing—and again, they settled in. One of the two Brahmas was sleeping bottom-up in the wood chips. Later, she would grow into a friendly, gorgeous white chicken with black plumage and feathered feet, but now she was fluffy and gray with a creamy yellow head. She looked more like a ball of dryer lint than a chicken, and upon closer inspection, I could see that her vent was blocked with dried poop. It needed to be cleaned, a process that would disturb all the chicks again, but according to *Storey's Guide*, it was imperative that a blocked vent be cleared immediately.

I headed into the kitchen to get a warm rag. Then, picking her up and holding her firmly with one hand, I wiped her vent with the warm cloth in the other hand. She squealed and squirmed, a beautiful, melodious peeping that woke all the other chicks. Once again, twenty-five chicks ran screaming and tumbling over one another until they finally settled down again.

At first, I was faithful to my promise not to name the chicks. But as the girls began to develop individual *tendencies*, if not personalities, it seemed necessary. David and I needed to be able to refer to them in conversation. We needed to be more specific than just, "The black chicken with green markings is acting peaked." We needed to be able to say, "Emmy Lou is acting peaked." For practical reasons, the birds needed names.

I had considered naming them after female writers I admired, my own little band of literary sisters—Charlotte, Edith, George, Louisa May, Eudora, Toni, Flannery, Zora Neale, Joyce Carol. But then a friend suggested naming them after country and bluegrass singers, so we named the blond, large-breasted one Dolly, the golden-laced Wyandotte June, the pearl Leghorn Crystal, the Brahma Wynonna, and so on. But every now and then, we broke the ladies of bluegrass pattern, such as in the case of the exuberant yellow chick that flew at David's chest every time he came near the brooder.

"Watch it, lady," I said each time. "He's mine."

It was our own little joke, just the three of us. Whenever I put my hand in the brooder, that chick would curl up next to my fingers like a puppy. Eventually, I began carrying her around the house with me, making rounds, showing her the layout. *Here is the kitchen. Here is the front porch. Here is the cat you should avoid.* She rode on the palm of my hand, making contented peeping sounds, hence earning the name Mella Yella, which was neither a literary name nor a musical one but at least an apt description. She even learned to like Hester and vice versa. Whenever I held her out for Hester to inspect, Hester whined and sniffed and tilted her head from side to side. She wasn't sure what she was, but she liked her anyway.

There was another New Hampshire Red hen too, exactly like Mella Yella. At first, we could tell them apart by their personalities, or at least, we thought we could, so we referred to them as "Mella Yella and her sister." Later, as they grew into hens, we often couldn't tell one from another, so we just referred to them both as "the Mella Yellas," a practice that carried over to the other duplicate breeds. Crystal became *the Crystals*, Wynonna, *the Wynonnas*, and so on.

A few weeks later, just after we turned the brooder to eighty degrees, I walked into the boiler room one morning and discovered a brooder full of miniature dinosaurs, little flying T. rexes with feathers protruding at peculiar angles. For some reason, we had not anticipated this. We thought the chicks would go from being baby chicks to reasonably mature adolescents who could go into their coop. It was now clear they needed more room. We needed a grow-out pen, so David began trying to figure out how to make one from discarded items he found in the field below our house—pallets, a camper rooftop, a black plastic dome.

"What on earth is that?" I asked, pointing to the dome.

"It's a casket holder," he said. "Someone was using it for a dog house, but I think I can use it for the pen."

"You've got to be kidding."

"It's not that bad. It just needs to be cleaned. I can pressure wash it."

"Absolutely not," I said. "It's too depressing. A bad omen."

The next morning, David began construction on what was basically an addition to our house—a wooden structure with a tin roof that abutted the right side of the house. The floor was made of salvaged pallets, and there was a real, functioning door and a large window from the Habitat for Humanity resale store. The chicks had a skylight too, a large slab of glass. From anywhere in their pen, they had a lovely view of the mountainside, of the daffodils and rhubarb and lilies growing on the bank. When it was finished, the new pen was almost as nice as our house. David moved the chicks to their new home Noah's-ark style— two by two.

And then he started on the coop. Because he was still working six days a week doing accounting work, David could only work on the coop on Sundays, and every single Sunday, it rained, violent deluges lasting hours at a time. Normally, our waterfall had a slight, steady flow, but now it was our private Niagara, slender but fierce, gushing off the mountain and dragging with it rocks and crayfish, whole branches of trees.

Our gravel driveway was full of ruts and gullies, our car windows sprayed with sludge. Inside the house, paper shrank and curled like palm fronds. Mold crept up the windowsills. Outside the grow-out pen, the chickens tossed clumps of mud onto their feathers. Donning boots and a raincoat, I took them tubs of Stonyfield yogurt.

"Are you buying organic yogurt for the chickens?" David asked.

"Of course not," I said, though, of course, he knew I was.

David threw up tarps, and wearing a poncho, he hammered and sawed until finally, we had a coop that was, hands down, *way* nicer than our house. On moving day, we ran around the yard grabbing handfuls of chickens in order of temperament—the Mella Yellas and the Wynonnas first, the two feisty blue chicks last—until, finally, all the girls were settled in their new space.

Within twenty-four hours, every blade of grass, every weed, every living thing in their area was gone—wiped clean. We threw out scratch and kitchen scraps, lettuce and carrots and the tops of fennel bulbs. We brought them tortillas that they flipped into the air with their beaks like pancakes.

"You haven't lived until you've seen a chicken eat a water-melon," a friend told me.

So we brought them watermelons, cut in two. The chickens squealed and dove in, face-first, twenty-five chickens at once. On warm, sunny days, they dug holes in the yard, then tossed dirt onto their feathers. The practical function of this was to clean their feathers and rid them of pests, but it always struck me as a playful, joyful act: chicken recess. I stood by the fence and watched as they bickered over the choice holes. *Box seats*, we called them. At night, the girls arranged themselves on the perch according to kind: Brahmas. Brown Leghorns. White Leghorns. New Hampshire Reds. Only Dolly, our sole buff Orpington, sat alone at the end of the perch.

Gradually, our lives began to wrap around the rituals of farm life. All those things that at first seemed so complicated—regulating the chick's water flow and food supply, mixing the right amount of oyster shells with the feed, and so on—became part of our routines. In the mornings, I walked down the gravel road to the coop with the "little dogs," Pretzel, Kate, and Piper. Piper was the oldest of our dogs. He was almost twelve, and he had cataracts and a bad hip. Still, he looked forward to our morning jaunts to the barn, and he walked right at my heels, ears up, nose down, as he sniffed for mice and bunnies and squirrels. Our cat, Chip, was an honorary member of the "little dog team," so he joined us on those mornings. The four of them waited outside the fence while I opened the coop and threw out scratch for the chickens.

The hens flew from their perches in rapid succession, colorful, winged parachuters. *Swoosh. Plop. Swoosh. Plop.* Twenty-five extreme adventurers. I refilled their feeders, then checked their outside water supply. David had run a line from the creek to automatically fill their buckets, but on cold mornings, I hacked apart the top layer of ice with a stick. Then the dogs and Chip and I walked back up to the house together to make coffee and let the "big dogs," Reba and Hester, out. In the evenings, David took the big dogs with him to shut the chickens into the coop for the night.

One afternoon, David and I were down by the coop. He was working on the fence, and I was planting a salsa garden—tomatoes, peppers, herbs—when all the chickens began screaming. A small, speckled hen twisted and flopped across the dirt, a speckled hot potato. Twenty-four frantic, panicked, yelling chickens ran inside the coop. Unsure of what if any action to take, David and I stopped what we were doing and watched.

"Look at that!" he finally said.

"Should we do something?"

"Like what?"

While I was trying to think of what might be best, the hen stopped thrashing and lay motionless in the dirt. I looked away.

"Is she dead?" I asked.

"Maybe," David said.

It looked a lot like a seizure, or rather, it looked how I remembered a seizure *felt*. I had had three seizures when I was a kid, the first when I was seven years old. I had been standing in line at McDonald's on Patton Avenue in Asheville with my mother when I felt strange. My head was heavy and light at the same time. My vision blurred. The people at the counter, the people in line, the tables and chairs and drink machines all went fuzzy. And then I saw only a blank television screen, black and white lines running together. I fell backward. My mother screamed.

"Call an ambulance!" someone yelled.

When I came to, I was lying on the floor. Shadowy figures hovered over me. Somewhere far away, my mother was still screaming. A man hollered for everyone to back away, then knelt beside me. At first, he was a gray man with gray clothes, but gradually, color returned. In a far corner, Ronald McDonald was a yellow, orange, and red giant. The man wore a light blue shirt with a red striped tie.

"Can you hear me?" he asked.

I nodded.

"Do you know where you are?"

I nodded.

There was more shouting, and two uniformed men rushed in. They unfolded a stretcher. Then one of them replaced the man kneeling next to me. He took my blood pressure. He put two fingers around my wrist and silently counted. Then he wrote in a notebook.

"Do you think you can sit up?" he asked.

Again, I nodded, and he put one hand behind my back and pushed me to a sitting position. The room was wobbly, the tables off-kilter. People sounded as if they were underwater. Or maybe I was the one underwater. Then gradually, everything slowly settled back into place. The napkin holders righted themselves. The walls straightened. I began to regain my senses. Which is exactly what must have happened to our chicken.

The hen was still for what seemed like a long time. One of our three spangled Hamburgs, she was smaller than the other chickens, and her feathers were white with black flecks, like someone had flicked a black paintbrush across her body. We still hadn't thought of a fitting name for her, so we had been referring to her and her sisters simply as "the speckled chickens." Now, very slowly, she raised her head, and one by one, the other chickens crept out of the coop. Some of the hens nudged her. Others walked around her. A few minutes later, she got up and began pecking in the dirt, like she had simply been taking a nap. The cackling and trilling of the other hens died down. The girls were relieved. David and I were relieved.

"I know what we can call her," David said. "Chicken Seizure Salad."

So that was her name for the rest of her days, which were, unfortunately, limited. Later that week, we came home after dark one night. David parked in the road next to the coop and left the car headlights on, but the lights pointed up the road, not toward the coop. Since chickens instinctively go into their coops at night, David assumed all the hens were already inside, but as he ran into the lot to close the door, he felt something soft beneath his shoe. And then he heard a loud snap. Chicken Seizure Salad gasped, then emitted one soft, faint cry before dying. Something had been wrong with her. That was evident. Still, David was despondent. He felt responsible for not looking before he went in the coop yard, and he could not get the sound of her dying out of his head.

"I felt her bones snap," he said over and over.

That night, he buried the hen in the barnyard by moonlight, then placed a cement block on her grave to discourage the other chickens from digging near the burial site. Other than the two chickens that had died within the first twenty-four hours after arriving, it was our first hard lesson in farming. If I had been a religious person, I might have thought of this lesson in terms of "The Lord giveth, and the Lord taketh away," but since I was not, I thought of it instead as a sort of bargain we had made with the universe: we got to start over, but we didn't get any guarantees.

All the information we had read said that hens began laying when they were around sixteen weeks old, so soon after Chicken Seizure Salad died, David prepared the nesting boxes—two rows of three boxes next to the perches. We filled the boxes with straw, then put a golf ball in each box, a strategy to trick the girls into thinking there was already an egg there, thus encouraging them to lay. It was the equivalent of erecting a sign: *Please lay here.*

At first, the hens completely ignored the boxes. They walked around them, flew past them, sat on the perch outside the boxes with their backs to them. Then one afternoon, four months to the day after we had gotten the chicks in the mail, I was walking Hester in the forest when David texted me: **A Leghorn is sitting on a nest.**

Until that moment, self-sufficiency had been a strange and abstract concept, something my forebears had *had* to do, but nothing I would have chosen. Now, the enormity of what I had been missing all along struck me—this, the simplest of joys, the pleasure of nurturing living things that would then give back to me in return. Hester and I began to jog. And then we ran—across the wooden footbridges, past English Chapel and the big grassy field, along the Davidson River until we reached the parking lot.

At home, I pulled to a stop in the driveway next to the girls' lot. The rain of the previous weeks had left the ground soggy, the girls' feet perpetually caked in mud. Inside the coop, the air was stale and sour. It took a moment for my eyes to adjust, but when they did, I saw on the nest one of the lovely brown hens that had only weeks before more closely resembled a chipmunk. I tiptoed over, and she greeted me with a soft coo. And there, right next to a golf ball, it was: a perfectly oval, perfectly pristine white egg.

Startled by my presence, the hen flew out of the nest. I lifted the egg from the straw. Warm and smooth and flecked with red, it was unlike any egg I had ever seen or held, unlike any other egg that had ever been laid. And I was the mother of all mothers. I was Eve.

Smoky Poached Eggs with Chickpeas and Feta

- 2 tablespoons olive oil
- 1 medium onion, chopped
- 4 cloves garlic, chopped
- 1 to 2 jalapeños, seeded, finely chopped
- 1 (15-ounce) can chickpeas, drained
- 2 teaspoons Hungarian smoked paprika
- 1 teaspoon ground cumin
- 1 (28-ounce) can crushed tomatoes
- Salt and freshly ground black pepper
- 1 cup coarsely crumbled feta
- 8 large farm-fresh eggs
- Chopped fresh cilantro for garnish (optional)
- Smoking J's Fiery Foods chipotle hot sauce or other good quality sauce

Preheat oven to 425°. Sauté the onion, garlic, and jalapeño in a large ovenproof skillet over medium-high heat until onion is soft, about 8 minutes. Add chickpeas, paprika, and cumin, and cook for 2 minutes longer. Add crushed tomatoes. Bring to a boil, reduce heat to medium-low, and simmer about 15 minutes.

Take off heat. Season to taste with salt and pepper. Sprinkle feta evenly over sauce. Crack eggs one at a time and place over sauce, spacing evenly apart. Transfer skillet to oven, and bake until whites are just set but yolks are still runny, 5 to 8 minutes. Garnish with cilantro. Serve with hearty brown bread and, of course, hot sauce.

Chapter Eleven

As MUCH AS I LOVED raising chickens, my adjustment to life at the cabin was still slow and fraught with setbacks. My emotions wildly vacillated. Some days, I loved the adventure—the wood fires and cozy jackets and wild creatures, the constant fine mist the waterfall sprayed over the grass and our cars, the way it grew foggy at the top when it rained, the falls spewing forth from the clouds. Other days, such as when heavy rains dragged debris down the mountainside and clogged our water pipes or when David forgot to build a fire and we had no hot water, I seemed to be back on page one, the mailman pulling into the drive, the foreclosure notice fresh in my hands. My new life was a constant exercise in patience and fortitude, and sometimes I just wanted everything to be easy again. I wanted my old life back. On those days, my anger at David felt fresh again, my sense of despair raw and new.

One day, I came home after mountain biking for hours. I was sweaty and muddy, my leg bruised and bloody from where I had grazed a tree. There was nothing I wanted more than a hot shower. When I stripped off all my clothes and hopped in the shower only to find there was no hot water, I was furious. I pulled a towel around me and went downstairs to find David.

"I didn't choose to live here," I said. "*You* did. And if you want me to stay, you will make sure we have hot, running water in this house."

It wasn't fair, but I was angry, and I needed someone other than myself to blame for my unhappiness. David looked stunned. He loved living here, could not imagine ever living in a real house or neighborhood again.

"It's like Disneyland here," he told me once. "There is so much fun stuff to do!"

Sometimes, after we argued, we went days without speaking to each other in any meaningful way. During times like that, I thought a lot about Macomb—about my cozy little boxcar, the long walks Hester and I took around the lake, the way we curled up at night, just the two of us. Macomb was more than just a memory for me. It was a safe place, a place where I had, for the first time in my life, felt competent and whole. It wasn't that I wanted to go back there, but I wanted to feel that way again, as if I had some power over the direction my life was headed, as if my future weren't so uncertain.

Maybe David and I argued because we wanted different things. Or maybe we had different ideas of what the same things looked like. David could live in this house forever and never want anything more. But I still thought of this as a temporary stop on our path to somewhere else, somewhere brighter, somewhere with better insulation, a paved carport, and good city drinking water. Homesteading, to me, seemed too hard, too unpredictable, and some days, I longed for things to be uncomplicated again. Even growing a basic garden seemed impossible here.

The garden we planted the first year—in the grassy field down the road—produced nothing. The space we plowed was a large rectangular indentation, an indication, we thought, that someone had once had a productive garden there, so we planted rows of tomatoes, peppers, beans, cabbage, lettuce, kale, squash, potatoes, corn. But the sun didn't rise over the ridge until midmorning, and it disappeared behind the ridge by three in the afternoon. And when it rained, which was very, *very* often, the water gushed down the mountainsides and gathered in pools, soaking green peppers on the vine, unearthing potatoes, rotting squash blossoms before they could produce. Eventually, we gave up, and instead, next to the chicken coop, David began building a barn out of pallets and tin and salvaged wood. If we couldn't grow vegetables there, maybe it would be a good spot to raise goats.

Though I knew nothing about raising goats, I had wanted dairy goats for over thirty years, ever since I had read *Heidi*. It seemed to me they were a lot like dogs—quiet, vegetarian dogs who slept in a barn. And while I enjoyed visiting goats during various farm tours in the area, I knew it would be different to have my own herd. I had watched other goat farmers with their animals, had seen how their animals ran to them when they were called, how the farmers could pick one specific goat out of a whole herd that all looked the same. *He calls his own sheep by name.* I had learned that in Sunday school when I was a kid, the message driven home by colorful illustrations of sheep and kindly shepherds and lovely green hillsides.

Now, though, the idea of knowing one animal out of an entire herd took on a new, more literal significance. What did it mean to know your animals that intimately, to know the source of your food, to be able to say, "This cheese was made with milk from that particular goat"? How did that change a person? Did it make you kinder, more grateful, less greedy? I wanted to know. I wanted to be able to look across a pasture and pick out a doe by the particular tilt of her head, the throatiness of her calls, by those traits that made her *her* and not just any other doe. I wanted goats of my own.

Of course, it wasn't reasonable to believe that getting goats would make our lives better. First, under the terms of our lease, our landlords could decide to no longer lease the cabin to us with six months' notice. If that happened, we would have to either find a similar situation— which would be next to impossible—or try to rehome all the goats. Second, we would be investing in animals that we hoped would eventually be able to produce food, but given our lack of farming experience, there was no guarantee we would be successful. And finally, there was the scary fact that we would be learning animal husbandry as we went along. If we got it wrong, there was so very much at stake.

And then there was the cost. David still had accounting clients, not as many as he had had years before but enough to cover the basics—our rent, utilities, food, gas, and so on—and I had returned to teaching as an adjunct at the local college. In addition, I made a couple thousand dollars per year teaching part time in a writing program through the state university in Asheville. Though the Department of Revenue still garnished my wages, I had enough money leftover to pay for essentials like gas. However, the state still occasionally wiped out both of our bank accounts, and they seized all the money I made from leading occasional workshops—a couple hundred dollars at a time—as there was no maximum on the amount they could take for work done on a contract basis.

The tax situation was an endless quagmire, a complex labyrinth we traveled around and around without finding any new insights. It was frustrating and demoralizing, a constant source of stress and strain. So since there was nothing we *could* do, we did nothing. Until we could reach settlement agreements for both the federal and state taxes, we were going to have to either go on with our lives or not. Those were our choices as I saw them. We could spend the rest of our lives being miserable—and still not free of the tax burden—or we could try to create the best lives we could under the circumstances while still hoping to settle our debts. In order to do that, I needed to do something new, something real, something that would soothe and strengthen my spirit. I needed to be ankle-deep in mud and goat poop, to sneeze incessantly from the scents of hay and straw, to have every shirt I own nibbled off at the hems. I needed to raise dairy goats.

So after much reading and research and discussion about what kind of goats to get, and where and when to get them, we found a listing on Craigslist for LaMancha does "in milk" in nearby Hendersonville. *In milk* was one of the many new terms I was learning. It meant that the does were currently producing milk, and in this case, it meant the does had recently kidded, or given birth. I didn't know anything about LaManchas. Still, they sounded perfect. We could have milk right away plus possibly two does in milk by the following fall.

In what would later become a familiar scene when we were buying goats, we followed a winding, mountain road until it dead-ended. And then we kept going, down a lonesome, treacherous dirt road until, finally, we came to a house perched precariously on a rocky precipice. There was no grass, no yard, no fence, just red clay and rocks. A buck was staked to a fence post just below the house, and several goats grazed on the brush on the hillside. The whole atmosphere was vaguely menacing.

"I don't know about this," I said.

In my old life, I had visited homes with hanging baskets, decorative doormats, seasonal wreaths. Here, there was no indication that anyone had attempted to make the place look cheerful or homey or even *not scary*. As we stopped the car, a woman stepped onto the porch. She was about my age and wore jeans, an oversized flannel shirt, and work boots. A teenaged boy dressed head-to-toe in black stood a few feet behind her, not speaking, not moving, his arms crossed, like a bodyguard. After we had all been rather formally introduced—a ritual that seemed odd under the circumstances—David and I followed the woman to the large, sturdy barn, just a few hundred feet from the house. Just outside the barn, two chained pit bulls snarled and lunged.

"Watch out," Sheila said. "They're not very friendly."

Giving the dogs a wide berth, we entered the barn through a series of locks and gates and large oak doors. Inside, we waited for our eyes to adjust to the dim light while Sheila's son lurked just behind us. He was not tall, but he was sturdy and muscular, his eyes watchful, and I thought of all the horror movies I had seen where bad things happened in barns—torture, murders, dismemberings. If we needed to, we could make a run for it out the back gate, which would give us a clear path. Well, except for the bull. We would have to go around one massive, angry-looking bull. I tried to convey all of this to David in furtive glances at the boy, then the door, but David was oblivious. He was already mesmerized by a white doe and her doeling.

"Look!" he said.

He leaned over the stall and rubbed her head. She reared back and butted the stall door. He tried again. She butted the stall again. Though she didn't look like any goat I had ever seen before, she was beautiful. Grumpy, but beautiful. Her eyes were watchful, her ears so tiny, so ungoatlike that she appeared earless.

"They're supposed to look like that," Sheila said, following my gaze.

Making our rounds through the barn, we looked at one lovely animal after another—tan does with hazel eyes, dark brown ones with chocolate eyes. Their coats were smooth and sleek, their eyes mesmerizing, and soon I too was able to forget the boy, to remember all the questions I had read I should ask: Have they had their shots? Have they been wormed? Will the babies be disbudded? All of Sheila's answers seemed right, but there was one problem: whenever we got too close to the does, they aggressively butted us.

"They don't like it when you touch them there," Sheila said after David touched a doe on the bridge of her nose and she almost rammed him to the ground. "That's a sign of aggression."

At the time, we accepted this as normal goat behavior, but later, we would realize this was not typical, and after things went wrong, we would begin to wonder how much human interaction the goats had had, how much time they had actually spent outside their stalls. Sheila seemed to be doing her best to care for them. Still, there were so many of them, and dairy goats needed to be handled from an early age so that they weren't afraid of people. That day, though, we were too enamored with the goats, or perhaps with the *idea* of goats, to realize any of this. We were simply overcome by their beauty. So after much debate, we chose a sable-colored doe named Maple and her doeling, Cinnamon.

David still had work to do to complete the barn and fence, so it would be a few days before we would be ready to take the goats, but Sheila agreed to hold them for us if we paid in full—$450. Those were her terms. We all signed an informal agreement, scribbled on a notepad, and David and I headed home. A few days later, when we returned, I was uneasy. We bumped and thumped down the worn-out road until we reached the house. Sheila's car was not in the drive. Instead, a tall, broad-shouldered, solemn man met us in the driveway.

"Oh no," I said to David.

Sheila, it seemed, was delayed getting home, but she was coming. We would have to wait. The man, who smelled vaguely of whiskey and motor oil, relayed this information to us, then asked if we wanted to see something. I was not at all sure I did, but David was game.

"Sure," he said.

We followed the man up the bank where, nestled in a pile of leaves and pine needles, were two tiny clumps, each the color and size of a batch of biscuit dough.

"They were just born," the man said.

The goats were silent and wide-eyed, their fur still wet. As the three of us knelt in the leaves, I was both thrilled to see these newborns and horrified that their mother appeared to be nowhere around, that they were out here in the open where dogs or wild animals could snatch them, where one of the many goats wandering loose could accidentally step on them. Finally, after what seemed like hours but was likely only fifteen or twenty minutes, Sheila arrived.

"Sorry I'm late!" she said, breezing by to check on the babies before leading us to the barn.

Relieved and ready to go home and get our goats settled, we headed to Maple's stall. As we walked in, another doeling slipped around us and into the stall. The doeling was very young, maybe a month old, and light brown—a miniature camel. As soon as she was in the stall, she headed for Maple and tried to latch on to her teats. Maple vigorously kicked and head-butted her. I watched, aghast, as the doeling backed up, then tried again. Maple growled and head-butted her into the corner. Finally, Sheila dragged the doeling out of the stall.

"Where's her mother?" I asked.

"Up the hill somewhere," Sheila said. "She just keeps running off and leaving her, and the baby keeps coming in here to try to get milk."

Finally, someone—I'm not sure which one of us—suggested that we take her too. Sheila would give us a special deal if we did. The doeling was so thin, we didn't know if she would survive. I felt certain, however, that she wouldn't survive here, so as Sheila led Maple and Cinnamon out to our car, I followed carrying the new doeling. David and Sheila lifted Maple and her doeling into a dog crate in the back of our car, and while David paid Sheila the amount due, I settled into the front seat with the errant doeling on my lap. Before we were even out of the driveway, she fell asleep with her head in the crook of my arm. We had to be prepared to lose this doeling. I knew that. She was so malnourished, I could see each notch on her spine. Maybe I shouldn't be holding her. Maybe we shouldn't name her. But we did. By the time we pulled into the driveway at home, it was settled. Her name was Willow.

Willow had not nursed all day, but Sheila had assured us that we could simply milk Maple when we got her home, then give Willow the milk in a bottle. Maple would make plenty of milk for both doelings. *No problem*. We weren't concerned that we had never milked a goat before or that Maple had never been milked. People had been doing this forever. Plus, we had read *Storey's Guide to Raising Dairy Goats* so many times, we knew it almost by heart. How hard could this possibly be? The answer was, pretty hard. At least until you learned how to do it. And then, once you knew how to do it, it seems simple, like riding a bike, and you couldn't remember ever *not* knowing how to do it.

When we first got Maple and the doelings, though, we knew nothing about how to milk or how to handle a frightened doe. We figured that out later, much later. That evening, once we had the goats in the barn, David knelt on the straw, squeezing Maple's teats at the top, then rolling his fingers down gently, just like *Storey's Guide* instructed. Terrified, Maple kicked and head-butted and threw her body sideways into the barn wall. Finally, David gave up. He stood and rubbed her neck, ran his hands through her soft fur.

"I just can't," he said. "She's not going to let me. We have to go to Plan B."

The problem was, we had no Plan B. I stood outside the barn door cradling Willow in an old towel like a human infant. She was sound asleep. Already, I loved her, and now, we had no way to feed her. It was almost 10:30 p.m., and all the farm supply stores in town were closed. However, a grocery store in Mills River, a twenty-minute drive away, was open until eleven. If I hurried, I had time to get there.

While David took care of Willow and settled Maple and Cinnamon into their stall for the night, I drove to Mills River, raced through the massive store until I located a quart of goat's milk, then hurried home. In my kitchen, I heated the milk and poured it into a bottle. Once again, I swaddled Willow in a towel and sat at the kitchen table. I had envisioned this as a special bonding moment, something like feeding my own babies. Willow would stare lovingly into my eyes, gulping the warm milk before drifting back to sleep in my arms. Instead, whenever I put the bottle near her lips, she squirmed and writhed and thrashed.

"Yum, yum," I told her, squirting milk on her lips. "Milk!"

She tightly shut her lips and turned her head. Finally, holding her with one arm and wedging her between my thigh and the table, I pried her lips open and squeezed the bottle. She gagged, then sputtered and coughed as milk ran out and down the side of her mouth. Hester sat beside me, nervously wagging her tail and licking up the milk that dripped onto the floor.

"Well, shit," I said.

David was back from the barn, and he offered support in the form of a Google search.

"It says to squeeze some milk on her lips," he called from his desk.

"I already tried that," I said.

Finally, using a squeeze and release and hold-the-goat-upright-so-she-doesn't-choke technique, I got her to drink a few ounces. The entire process had taken close to an hour, and we were both exhausted. We couldn't leave Willow in the barn with Maple, so after she fell asleep in my arms, I carried her into the boiler room, put her on a pile of newspapers, and pulled a baby gate across the doorway. Hester stretched next to the gate in what I hoped was a protective pose. Then I went upstairs and fell soundly asleep.

Early the next morning, I got up and repeated the entire feeding routine with Willow, and this time, she did ever-so-slightly better. After I was satisfied that she had drunk enough milk, I put her back in the boiler room, and David and I headed down to the barn to let Maple and Cinnamon outside. They bolted from the barn and huddled together in one corner—two sleek, graceful figures on the dewy field. Cinnamon occasionally dipped under Maple's belly to nurse, then quickly resumed her post by her mother's right front leg. Whenever I tried to pet her, Maple butted me away. Soon, I gave up trying and went back to the house to get Willow. All afternoon, Willow and I sat in the field while David worked in the barn. Once or twice, Cinnamon sidled over to me, nibbled my pants leg, and eyed Willow, but soon Maple scurried over and shooed her away. Maple did not trust me. It was going to take some time.

That evening, when David and I went inside to eat dinner, Maple and Cinnamon were still in the same spot in the corner of the field. Afraid to leave Willow alone with Maple, I put her back in the boiler room. She curled up on the newspapers and closed her eyes. Equally exhausted, David and I sank onto bar stools in the kitchen and silently shoveled down heaping bowls of pintos and rice and cornbread.

We had had the does exactly twenty-four hours, and it all still seemed surreal—this house, the chickens, the goats. Ten years ago, my life had been radically different. I had chaired a silent auction at the local playhouse. I had volunteered at my kids' private school. I lectured at the local college. I had taken nice vacations—to the Grand Canyon, the Florida Keys, Paris, Barcelona. I had attended tea parties and Longaberger basket parties and ice cream socials. It was, on the surface, a good life, a life I had thought that I wanted, and if someone had told me then that one day I would be sitting in a three-story cabin full of snakes and mice and wolf spiders eating pinto beans while a goat slept on a pile of a newspapers by a wood boiler that was my primary source of heat, I would have thought that someone was on hallucinogens. And yet, here I was. Here we were. Our transformation amazed me.

David and I had been inside for fifteen or twenty minutes, maximum, before he headed back down to the barn. Within moments, I heard him hollering. I had no idea what he was saying, but I could tell he was frantic. I grabbed Willow from the boiler room and ran outside and down the drive, and even after I got to the empty field, it took a moment for the words to sink in.

"They're gone!" David said. "They're gone!"

I looked from him to the fence, across the hollow, up the hillsides covered with rhododendron thickets so dense, you couldn't see more than a foot in front of you in places. There was no sign of the goats. No rustling leaves or stamping hooves. Nothing. Too astonished to move, I waited for David to say something else, to figure out what we should do.

"Take her back inside, and meet me on the hill," he said.

I ran Willow back to the boiler room and secured her gate. Then

David and I began scouring the woods, hiking up and down the ridge on both sides of the driveway. When that search produced nothing, we took Hester and Reba outside on leashes to see if they could pick up on the goats' scents. After they sniffed for a while at the bank across from the barn, on the side that eventually led to the highway, we drove around and searched the other side of the mountain. Again, nothing. At midnight, physically exhausted and emotionally spent, I fell asleep, but David continued to search. He paced the driveway, drove up and down the roads near our house, hiked once again to the ridgeline in the dark. Not a trace. It was as if, as David said, the goats had been beamed into space.

The next morning, we posted "Lost Goats" signs on all the major roads. We called our neighbors and animal control and sent our dogs on search missions through the woods, but we never found any evidence that they were close by or, in fact, that they had ever been here at all. As time went on, we even considered the possibility that someone had stolen them. It just seemed so unlikely that they had disappeared so quickly and so thoroughly. Perhaps that was easier than picturing what had likely happened, that they had run up the mountain and eaten rhododendron leaves, which would have quickly killed them. Or worse, they had made it until dark and been attacked by coyotes. Or worst of all, that they managed to survive for a few days before finally succumbing to hunger and cold.

We were devastated. Though we had thought their fence was adequate, it obviously had not been. We had read that goats could escape from fences easily. We just didn't know *how* easily. Somehow, the goats had managed to slip between the gate and fence or to climb over. Here was even more glaring evidence of our incompetence, our fuckedupness. And while I blamed us, I also blamed Sheila for selling people brand-new to goat rearing two animals that were so skittish, they were almost wild. Our friends who had farm animals said their goats often got out of their fences and just stood in the yard outside the fence or walked up to the house. But Maple did not yet recognize this as home or us as family, and with her doeling in tow, she must have bolted so hard and so fast, we would not have been able to catch them even if we had seen them.

In the days that followed, we continued to search. We kept hoping the goats would "show back up," a phrase so nebulous as to encompass all possibilities without dwelling on their probable fate. While David fortified gates and fences, I was Willow's constant companion. If I couldn't bring Maple and Cinnamon back, I could do my best to keep her safe, so I took her outside and followed her around with a copy of *Storey's Guide* opened to the "Bad Weeds for Goats" section, complete with illustrations. Every time she showed interest in a plant, I held up the book to determine whether it was one of the forbidden weeds. I offered her warm goat's milk infused with molasses every few hours, but she never really learned to take the bottle, so I began feeding her in the kitchen from a saucer propped on an upside-down soup kettle. At night, I wrapped her in a towel and held her while we watched *Columbo* reruns on my computer.

Still, I worried about her. Goats are herd animals. They should never be raised by themselves, so despite the fact that Willow was rarely technically *alone*, I worried she was lonely, that she needed another goat companion. Getting a new goat seemed to close forever the albeit remote possibility that Maple and Cinnamon had somehow survived. However, we finally accepted that they weren't coming back and began to search for another goat.

After calling everyone we knew and sort of knew, everyone who had ever raised goats or made goat cheese, after consulting Craigslist and Iwanna, and after a tense phone call with Sheila where she berated us for calling her on Easter Sunday before we could even explain why we were calling, I emailed the owners of Three Graces Dairy in Marshall, just outside of Asheville. Yes, they said. They had a doeling that just might work—a two-month-old Saanen. A few minutes after I got the email, David and I threw the dog crate in the back of the car and headed out to get her.

The doeling was in a stall in a large, open-air barn with at least a dozen other babies, and before I saw the goats, I heard them. They were raucous and boisterous—kindergartners on a field trip or frat boys at a party—but when the farmer brought our girl out of the stall, I was so enthralled, I no longer heard the other goats. Pure white with pink bunny ears and a pink nose, she baaed and cried. I dropped to my knees, whispering to her, telling her how beautiful she was, how we had a lovely girl at home she would love, but she was distressed to be away from her bunkmates and unimpressed with me. As we pulled out of the road leading to the farm, she screamed out the back window until we had wound around a curve and her old home was no longer in sight. Moving, it seemed, was not easy, even for a goat.

The new doeling had no name, just a red plastic chain around her neck holding a number: *11*. That night, Number 11 and Willow both slept in the boiler room. The barn was ready, but we were afraid to trust it, afraid predators could burst through the pallet walls or climb over, afraid the girls would get cold.

"Let me get this straight," Alex said when I told her. "You and Dad are keeping two goats *in the house?*"

"Not in the *house*," I said. "Don't be ridiculous. The boiler room. They're in the boiler room."

Finally, a few days later, we moved both Willow and Number 11, known now as Holly, out to the barn, which was protected by a complex system of gates and bungee cords and more bungee cords and more gates and metal locks and latches and more bungee cords. We wanted to do it *right* this time.

In the daytime, the girls were inseparable, moving together through the field like one being—nibbling leaves and dandelions, lying on their sides in the sun, stretching their necks to try to reach the brush just outside their fence. At night, they cuddled in their stall, one girl's head on the other girl's back. In addition to eating grain, Holly still took a bottle once a day, and whenever I brought the old Coke bottle filled with milk, she grabbed it and tugged so hard, I had to brace myself to keep from falling. The milk was gone within seconds.

Willow, on the other hand, still ate out of a saucer, and she still insisted on having molasses with her meal. If I forgot the molasses, she would not drink her milk. So four times a day, I carried out to the field a large pot, a saucer, a measuring cup full of warm milk, and a jar of molasses. And then David or I held Holly so Willow could eat.

After a very bad start, things were starting to look up. Our doelings were healthy and happy, and Willow was getting bigger and stronger. She slept less. She ate more grain and hay. She was playful. Still, even if we did everything right, we wouldn't have milk for at least another year, maybe two years if we waited a season to breed the girls, and now we had all this space, a nice barn and a secure field. So we began to talk again about buying a pregnant doe. That way, we would be able to enjoy the babies, and we would soon have milk. It would be a win-win situation. As before, we kept an eye on Craigslist, and soon we found a goat that sounded perfect—a pregnant Nigerian dwarf, due that summer.

Molasses Cocktail for Finicky Goats

Mix ¼ cup blackstrap molasses with 2 cups warm goat's milk. Pour into an empty, clean soda bottle fitted with a nipple, or if your goat is extra finicky, onto a plate propped on an overturned soup pot. Gently massage baby goat's ears while she drinks.

Chapter Twelve

THE MILK OF NIGERIAN DWARFS has a high percentage of fat, which means their milk makes rich cheese, and because they are small, they need less space than standard breeds. David and I had watched hundreds of Nigerian dwarf videos online. The babies were playful, precocious, adorable. They ran through and over and under obstacles, chasing each other, jumping on the backs of dogs and donkeys and other goats. Every goat owner I talked to loved Nigerian dwarfs. However, they were all quick to tell me that Nigerians could be stubborn, and they didn't give a lot of milk. And so, duly noting both the charms and drawbacks, one Saturday in May, David and I set out with Alex, who was home for the weekend, to get the pregnant doe.

The farm was in rural South Carolina, somewhere vaguely near Spartanburg, past megachurches and dairy farms and the occasional McDonald's. After several wrong turns and some backtracking, we were finally there, at a place that more closely resembled a petting zoo than any farm I had ever seen. There were turkeys, chickens, and a sow with a new litter of piglets, all in immaculate pens, and there were handmade wooden rabbit hutches with stoops where young visitors stood to feed the bunnies.

The farmers, Harry and Jill, were chatty. Harry told us about his children, his first wife and the farmhand she ran off with, the beef cattle he used to raise back in Pennsylvania, the heart attack he had the previous year. Buying a milk goat, I was learning, involved more than just cash exchanged for an animal. It was a delicate dance in which each party sized the other up, gauged the other's character. *Has this farmer taken good care of this animal? Can I trust what he is telling me? Will this buyer take good care of this goat, or does she intend to turn her and all of her babies into goat curry?*

I had taken a fair share of social work classes in college, so I knew a little about active listening, which came in handy now as I told Harry I could imagine how hard it had been when his wife cheated on him, how I bet the heart attack must have been really scary, but all the while, I could feel David getting impatient. He was not a chitchatter. He paced around, clearing his throat repeatedly, while I threw him furtive looks. *Stop. Stop being impatient.* Finally, he could no longer contain himself.

"Where's the goat?" he asked.

"Oh!" Harry said, as if this had just occurred to him. "This way."

He led us through a grove of oaks and pines to a broad gate that he unlatched. Inside the fence, we were instantly surrounded by massive cows, a rare, very large breed with thick heads and lovely, dappled coats—show cows. They edged closer and closer, bumping into us, pressing us closer to the gate. Jill carried a box of Nilla Wafers.

"Here," she said, passing Alex and me handfuls of wafers. "Feed them these. They love 'em."

We offered the cows the treats, and one particularly friendly bull sidled up to Alex, sniffed her hair, then rearing on his hind legs, placed his right front foot firmly on her back.

Alex crouched down and said quietly but urgently, "Dad. *Dad.*"

"Oh, he's just trying to say hi," Harry said.

David ran over and shoved the bull away, and just when I was thinking there were no goats, that this had all been an elaborate ruse designed to get us trampled to death by cows, a herd of Nigerian dwarfs darted through the trees—a dozen goats of varying sizes and hues, blacks and tans and pure white.

"There she is!" Harry said.

The goat he pointed to was white with long, lower lashes and brown and black markings around her legs and eyes—a short Sophia Loren with sides like heavy buoys.

"She's beautiful!" I said. "What's her name?"

"Katherine," Harry said. "After my mother."

While Harry launched into a long story about his mother, about her extended illness and subsequent decline and eventual death, David and Alex offered the goats cookies.

"Do you spell Katherine with a *c* or a *k?*" I asked Harry.

"I don't know," he said. "You can change it if you want."

Katherine/Catherine seemed perfect with one notable exception: she had horns. Everything we had read said not to get a goat with horns, but she was so lovely, so well cared for, so very pregnant, that David and I instantly decided the horns were not a big deal. She was tiny. How much harm could she possibly do?

David squatted down, wrapped his arms around the doe, and lifted her as if he were lifting a heavy box, with his thighs and calves. Holding her out so that her horns were at a safe distance, he made his way to the car. The rest of us trailed behind, and while Harry helped David settle Katherine/Catherine into the dog crate in the back of the car, we said our goodbyes. And then Katherine/Catherine began to scream, not a restrained, anxious babbling, but a frantic, maniacal bellowing that did not let up the entire drive home. Whenever David took a curve at over five miles per hour, I worried that she was being jostled too hard. I didn't know how careful one had to be with a pregnant goat, but I was pretty sure she shouldn't be slammed around in a dog crate just weeks before her delivery date.

"Slow down!" I said over and over, screaming to be heard over the goat.

The smell of goat poop and urine mingled with her distressed bellowing, a disturbing, nauseating combination. In the backseat, Alex covered her ears and stuck her head out her open window. At red lights, people pointed into our car, and we read their lips: *Is that a goat? There's a goat in that car!* Later, I would read Louise Dickinson Rich's 1942 memoir, *We Took to the Woods*, about the years she spent living in the backwoods of Maine, and feel a special kinship to the people Rich described as "woods queer." It was a term applied to people who had lived in the isolation of the woods for so long, they had gone a little nuts. Maybe we weren't completely crazy—yet—but the moment we decided to throw a pregnant goat in the back of our car and haul it across state lines, we had definitely lost touch with what most people considered normal behavior.

Finally, two hours after we left the farm, we were home. Alex and I bolted from the car and watched while David moved Katherine/Catherine into the pasture with Holly and Willow. This, it turned out, was a grave error, a rookie mistake. Katherine/Catherine chased and butted the other goats, knocking their underbellies with her sharp horns. As we watched her try to gore Holly and Willow, we decided that, although she had seemed perfectly fine at the farm, there was something terribly wrong with this goat—maybe a genetic defect, some mental problem that was the result of inbreeding or injury.

Finally, we put her in a stall with grain and hay and called it a day. That night, we did what we always did when we had a goat question. We Googled it. And lo and behold, it turns out that you should never, ever, *ever* just throw a new goat in with your existing herd. You were supposed to introduce them slowly, over time. At first, they should be kept in separate areas, where they gradually become accustomed to each other's scents and sounds. Then, after a week or two, they can be together for short periods under supervision. And then, if they were doing well, they can be left together unsupervised.

So over the next few days, we backed up and did what we should have done to begin with, which seemed to be our modus operandi: *Proceed at breakneck pace until a problem occurs, then furiously backpedal.*

Those first few days, while Katherine/Catherine screamed and Holly and Willow stared horrified through the fence, David and Alex and I debated about her name. I worried that it was disrespectful to change it since, after all, she was named after Harry's dead mother, but we often referred to our dog Kate by her formal name, Katherine. It would be too confusing to have a *goat* named Katherine/Catherine and a *dog* named Katherine. Finally, Alex, who had spent some time in Ghana when she was in college, suggested we rename the doe Ama, the Fante name for a girl born on a Saturday, the day we had gotten her—a Saturday birth, or in this case, a reinvention. It seemed fitting.

For days, Ama continued to scream. More than once, I thought something terrible had happened, that her head was stuck in the fence or one of her horns had been ripped from her head. I ran down the driveway only to find her standing by the gate, perfectly fine, bellowing at a truly shocking level. Eventually, I figured out that she was crying for David. Whenever he was working down at the barn, within her sight, she was fine. Whenever he came up to the house, she panicked.

Mercifully, Ama eventually calmed down. Though she would never closely bond with Holly or Willow, she eventually accepted them as members of her herd—not siblings, but perhaps distant cousins— and they quickly learned to keep their distance from her, a feat made easier by the fact that Ama's collar had a silver bell. Whenever Holly and Willow heard the telltale ringing, they darted off to the far side of the pasture. After a couple of weeks, the does seemed to have the dynamics of their relationship sorted out. Finally, we were able to leave them all in the field together.

According to Harry and Jill, Ama had been exposed on January 15. *Exposed*. That meant the day that pregnancy likely occurred, but somehow, it conjured images of a virulent virus or a pervert yanking down his shorts at a city park. It implied vulnerability, maybe even victimization, but once again, if I was going to be an actual farmer, I was going to have to toughen up. So I tried to focus on the numbers. In 145 to 153 days from that exposure date, give or take a few days, we could expect babies. According to my calculations, Ama should give birth in early June. So on June 4, day 145, we began our vigil.

Chapter Thirteen

WHEN GOATS ARE BORN, THEY dive into the world front legs first, poised to hit the ground. Their heads come next, nose, eyes, ears, the places where their horns will be, and then the rest: body, tail, back legs. Moments later, the doeling or buckling wobbles to its feet—stunned, amazed, ready to *begin*. Or at least that is the way it's supposed to happen.

We had read that most Nigerian dwarfs have a fairly easy time with labor and delivery, but David and I wanted to be prepared to assist Ama—just in case. We read everything we could find about goat pregnancy and labor and delivery. We studied diagrams of how the babies should be positioned, then studied more diagrams showing all the possible problematic postures—front legs back, elbows back, head back, breech. If the doe seemed to be having trouble, you were supposed to reach in and reposition the babies.

On paper, this seemed like an excellent idea—totally doable. The problem was that when it came to actual dicey situations, I had a history of collapsing under pressure. Once, when Aaron was a toddler, he had run into a wall and split open his forehead. Blood gushed everywhere—across the wall, into his blond hair, down his T-shirt, and all over me as I held him. David and I raced him to the emergency room. There, David held Aaron's hand and whispered comforting things while the doctor stitched his wound. I began to feel woozy and dizzy.

"You're doing great, sweetie," I told Aaron. "I have to leave," I told David.

Across the hall, I lay on the bathroom floor, my face pressed to the cold tile, my eyes closed to keep the room from spinning. When I finally felt better, I stood and splashed cool water on my face, then made my way back to the waiting area where David and Aaron sat reading *Highlights* magazine. Aaron, despite having a transparent bandage on his oozing gash and dried blood in his hair, was the very picture of tranquility.

"You can't just fall apart like that whenever something happens," David said on the way home.

"Of course I can," I said.

I blamed my wooziness on multiple things—my low blood pressure, my childhood diagnosis of epilepsy, etc.—but the fact was, I was just not any good in a crisis. Therefore, since I doubted I would be much help during the actual goat delivery, I vowed to do my part beforehand.

Because I had read that sometimes goats accidentally had their babies in their water buckets, we exchanged Ama's large bucket for a small Tupperware container, and I gathered the other necessities. At Walmart, I bought K-Y Jelly, adult pee pads, and a package of latex gloves, and David assembled a birthing kit—a plastic tub filled with all the aforementioned items plus iodine, towels, paper towels, trash bags, a computer printout of the various birthing positions, cotton balls, dental floss, etc. Having a birthing kit made me feel responsible, like I was doing something preparatory, preemptive, proactive, all those *p* words not normally associated with me.

Over the following days, we watched Ama almost as closely as we had watched the baby chicks. We made multiple trips back and forth to the barn as we looked for signs of impending labor. On the morning of June 5, day 146 after her initial exposure, Ama refused her breakfast and wouldn't leave her stall. This was definitely a change from her normal behavior, and refusing food was one of the indications of labor.

All the literature I had read said that you should feel a pregnant doe's tail ligaments to see if they were loose. Loose ligaments meant labor was near, so though I had no idea what "loose" versus "tight" felt like, I put my middle finger and thumb around the base of her tail. The ligaments *seemed* loose, but I wasn't sure, so I checked the angle of her teats. If the teats were pointed at a forty-five-degree angle, she would kid within the next twenty-four hours. It was practically guaranteed. I squatted beside Ama, turning my head this way and that until finally, I determined her teats were at something roughly like a forty-five-degree angle. It was as precise as I could be.

Certain that she would kid any moment, I returned to the house for the birthing supplies. I also brought the book I was reading, Leslie Jamison's *The Empathy Exams*. It would calm my nerves, I reasoned. Distract me. At the barn, I pulled a lawn chair into the entranceway and settled down beside Ama. As I read, I kept jumping up to check Ama's vulva, which was supposed to be changing—swelling, turning red, dripping fluid. As she paced around the barn, I cooed sympathetic things to her—*Good girl. You are so beautiful. You are going to be a great mama.* Finally, she stretched onto the straw, her hips spread wide—child's pose. Her breathing was heavy and loud, the air stale and thick.

Aaron's twenty-second birthday was eleven days away, and watching Ama's bulging, clumsy body, the way she shifted on the straw, searching for a comfortable position, reminded me of the hot, muggy summer years ago when I had been expecting Aaron. My legs and ankles were swollen, my belly round from my unborn son and the cannoli I ate after lunch each day. My diaphragm was smashed against my lungs. At night, I slept propped up on a stack of pillows, my stomach lurching and heaving like a giant water balloon.

Up until now, I had been excited about this moment, thrilled about seeing the kids and about what their births would mean—that after all this work, all the planning and hoping and dreaming, we might finally be able to have our own goat milk—but now, I panicked. The air in the barn felt too close. My heart began to race. My palms were damp, and I struggled to breathe. Frightened for Ama, worried that even after all our preparations, we weren't really prepared, I was now certain I wouldn't be able to handle any problems that might develop.

This was foolish. I was foolish. My formal education was useless. What I needed was practical knowledge, real-life experience, the type of know-how I had scorned when I was a teenager. In need of fresh air, I put down my book and walked out into the harsh sunlight.

Just beyond the barn, the hillside had exploded with roses in all shades of red and pink. As I stood admiring them, David pulled up in his truck. He had been to the store to get more birthing supplies—a rubber suction bulb and a stethoscope.

"I don't even know where a goat's heart is," he said. "But I'm going to Google it."

Google. What a poor substitute for experience, for the type of apprenticeship that happened naturally for kids who grew up on farms. At our high school, we had had two covered breezeways—the smokers' breezeway and the nonsmokers' breezeway. The smokers' breezeway led from the main building to the vocational wing, and many of the farm kids hung out there. They wore work boots and Wranglers and wide, round belt buckles. In between classes, they leaned against the railings, smoking Camels or dipping Skoal. My friends and I—the college-bound kids, the honors-class kids, the band kids—hung out on the other breezeway. We never smoked at school. We smoked on the weekends, and then only if we were drinking or stoned.

Looking back, I realize how ridiculous we were with our IZOD shirts and French jeans, our gold-bead necklaces, and our arrogance. If

I could go back and live it all over again, I would spend my whole day on the smokers' breezeway, asking all the questions I wish I knew the answers to now: *What's the best kind of hay for goats? How much grain does a pregnant doe need? How the hell do you know when a goat's tail ligaments are actually loose?*

Holly and Willow were out in the pasture, lying back to back, chewing their cuds. They seemed grateful for the break from Ama, glad to know that she wouldn't decide to claim the spot of grass they were sitting on. I called to them—*hey, sweet girls*—then headed back in the barn.

While Ama chewed on hay and scratched her nose on the barn wall, I knelt behind her to see if anything was happening. Her vulva was still tight, and there was no discharge. I sat back down and waited until eventually, the light began to fade. Finally, when the barn was so dark I could no longer read, I closed my book, shut all the goats in their stalls, and called it a night.

The next day, day 147, Pretzel and Hester walked down to the barn with me. Ama was unusually affectionate, a sure sign of imminent labor. As I knelt on the stall floor, she crawled onto my lap, then licked my arm all the way from my wrist to my elbow. I sat rubbing her head until David called for me. Outside the barn door, one of our hens, Terry, sat hunched over on a bed of straw in a dog crate.

For the past two days, Terry had hunkered by the coop door, not eating, not laying, not pooping. The other chickens had clustered around her, screaming and squawking, just like they did when Chicken

Seizure Salad had her episode. For her protection, David had moved Terry to the crate with her own food and water bowls. *The hospital*, David called it. A couple of times a day, he fed her electrolyte water from the rubber bulb that was supposed to be for suctioning the baby goats' noses. Now, he was crouched over a tub of warm water feeding her vegetable oil out of a teaspoon. My cheese thermometer was next to the tub.

"I need you to help me for a second," he said.

"Did you use my cheese thermometer?"

"Only before I put the chicken in."

"Jesus," I said.

Terry was missing feathers near her tail, and though we had never killed a chicken and never planned to, the scene itself was uncomfortably familiar. Add half an onion and some spices, and this tub was a Crock-Pot full of chicken and herbs. I filled and refilled the spoon while David held Terry and fed her the oil that was supposed to help her digestion. When he was satisfied she had had enough, he put her back in the crate, then headed into town in search of antibiotics.

Pretzel and Hester were lounging contentedly outside the goat pen, and I called to them as I went back into barn—*Good dogs!* Then I resumed my post beside Ama. It was a humid, lazy afternoon, and just when I was nodding off to sleep, I heard barking, which quickly became a frenzy of yipping and growling. Ama looked up. I looked up. But by the time I walked outside, it was too late to catch them. Hester was in front, Pretzel not far behind, his tiny legs flailing behind Hester's as they tore through the creek and up the mountain. I ran screaming after them, but they ignored me, and soon their frenetic yelps became more and more distant until finally, there was only silence.

They had run up the steepest part of the mountain, into the fifty acres that was nothing but thick brush and trees and rocks. There was nothing to do but wait for them to come home. I couldn't climb that far up the mountain by myself without getting lost, and even if I could find them, they would just run from me. I texted David—**Hester and Pretzel have run off!**—then headed back into the barn to sit with Ama. Every few minutes, I went outside and paced up and down the road. I listened and called for the dogs, alternately scolding and pleading for them to come back, but they were evidently too far away to hear me, or at least, I was too far away to hear them.

A couple of hours later, just when I was about to believe they were gone for good, when I was figuring out how I was going to tell David and the kids we had lost two *more* animals, they ambled down the mountain, tails wagging, tongues hanging out, fur covered in burrs and mud. By then, I had visualized their deaths so vividly and in so many different ways—sliced clean down the middle by a bear, shot by a hunter, attacked by a coyote—that their arrival wasn't even a relief. I was a tangle of nerves and adrenalin and frustration.

"Get in the house!" I yelled, pointing the way.

Pretzel looked at me, whined, and ambled toward the front door. Hester got down on her front legs, wagged, then took off again.

"You little shit!" I screamed after her.

But she didn't care. She was already long gone. Whatever she was chasing now—a fox, a deer, a rabbit—was on the opposite mountain, away from the highway, where the woods extended for miles. I was confident that she wouldn't get lost—she had an acute sense of smell—but I was not as confident she wouldn't get hurt. Finally, that evening, hours after she had first disappeared, I found her sitting on the front porch, her neck plastered with something dark, sticky, and rotten smelling. When I let her inside, she promptly passed out on her makeshift cushion—an old coffee sack stuffed with pillows. Then and only then did I allow myself to feel relieved.

I knew I shouldn't have a favorite dog. It was like having a favorite kid. Even if you had one, you weren't supposed to say it. And yet, Hester and I had been through so much, walked so many literal and figurative miles together, I couldn't help feeling a special kinship with her. I understood her fierce individualism, the fact that she both loved me and sometimes had a powerful need to strike out on her own, and there was something about her wild and restless spirit that seemed to soothe my own.

"Good dog," I told her while she slept.

She opened her eyes and wagged her tail once before passing out again.

The next day, day 148, Terry was still alive but barely. David, however, was still hopeful. He continued to feed her and give her antibiotics through the medicine dropper, but I began referring to *the hospital* as *hospice*. She was going to die, and perhaps because David had been trying so valiantly to save her, or perhaps because her impending death seemed to cast a shadow over Ama in her fragile condition, I was despondent. That afternoon, I crouched beside Terry's cage. She was a beautiful chicken, brown with golden-tipped wings. Her head was tucked deep into her chest, as if she were soundly sleeping.

"Hey, girl," I said. And despite every effort not to, every voice inside my head that told me this was childish and ridiculous and very *unfarmer-like*, I started to cry. "You've given us a lot of good eggs, and I want to thank you for that."

I hadn't planned to say it. It had just risen out of me, this sadness, this gratitude for Terry's short life. Back in my old life, I never thought twice about the chicken that laid my eggs, but now, every time I found an egg—in a nesting box, in the hay feeder, in a bed of straw in the barn—I felt the same sense of wonder and awe I felt the day our first hen laid an egg.

I knew Terry. I knew where she liked to sit on the roost, that she loved kale and shredded carrots and the ends of strawberries, that she liked to perch on the top of a dead tree limb on sunny days. Knowing the animal that had provided our breakfast on countless occasions had caused a quiet but definite shift in my being. It was a change I could not yet define or explain but something I nonetheless felt.

Terry didn't move at all, and for a second, I thought she was already dead, but then I could see the slightest movements in her back, a barely detectable rising and falling. Maybe she was just a chicken like any other of the millions of chickens that died every day in factory farms, their lives passing unnoticed. Or maybe she could hear me. Maybe she knew I was talking to her. I watched her quiet breathing for another moment, then headed into the barn.

David and I did not often share responsibilities. There were things *I* did (grocery shopping, cooking, laundry, walking the dogs) and things *he* did (everything else). Now, with the life-and-death drama happening at the barn, we each staked out our own areas. David's zone was outside the barn, next to Terry's crate. My area was inside the barn, beside Ama. While I watched Ama, he watched Terry, which worked well until he decided to prop open the barn door so he could watch Ama and the chicken at the same time.

"Stop!" I told him. "Leave it closed."

"Why?"

"It's bad luck for a pregnant goat to stare at a dying chicken."

I was kidding, in a way. But in another way, I was not. This close juxtaposition of birthing and dying was unsettling—disturbing, even. Plus, I was getting worried. It was now past time for Ama's babies to be born. She should have been in labor by now. Over the coming days, I spent almost all of my time following her around, checking her vulva for changes. It was round and puffy, like bubble wrap, which was a good sign that labor was approaching but not *the* sign that labor had begun.

And then Ama began doing something amazing. I had read that sometimes, in the days before they kid, expectant mothers "talk" to their unborn babies. I knew by now that goats were intelligent, sensitive beings. Still, that seemed a little far-fetched, so when Ama began twisting her head around and making quietly, motherly murmurings to her belly, I was astounded. She baaed so softly, so sweetly in tones so different from any I had heard her utter before that there was no mistaking that she was talking to her kids. What was she telling them? Was she reassuring them? Wishing them safe passage? Urging them to hurry? Perhaps she was simply confiding to them that she was stuck in the barn with a crazy lady who kept staring at her vulva.

I was now on chapter two of *The Empathy Exams*, "Devil's Bait." The chapter was about Morgellons disease, a disorder in which people believe they have things living under their skin, things like worms. Of course, the essay wasn't *really* about that. It was about empathy, about how compassion is more important than literal truth, a subject I pondered while gnats and flies and mosquitoes bit my face and arms and bare legs, and the hay and straw made me sneeze, and Ama's pungent pee made my eyes water. While I wanted to be empathetic with Ama, I'm not sure that what I felt was actually empathy. Perhaps it was more like mutual despair. We were both so very tired of waiting.

SPICY CROCK-POT CHICKEN
FOR CHICKEN LOVERS

- 1 to 2 teaspoons salt
- 2 teaspoons ground paprika
- 1 teaspoon ground cayenne pepper
- 1 teaspoon onion powder
- 1 teaspoon dried thyme
- 1 teaspoon ground black pepper
- ¼ teaspoon garlic powder
- 1 cup chopped onions
- 1 humanely raised large roasting chicken from someone else's farm

Combine spices. Massage into chicken. Put chopped onion into Crock-Pot. Add chicken and cover. Cook on low 4 to 6 hours.

Chapter Fourteen

WHEN SOMEONE YOU LOVE DIES, that person comes to you in spurts, in bleeps and flashes you never see coming until they are there. All that day in the barn, while Ama whispered to her unborn babies, my grandmother seemed so near, I almost believed I could reach out and touch her. Twice, I caught a glimpse of something in the corner of my eye, a shadow, a change in light, but when I whipped around, there was nothing there. It was a trick, a ruse, a ploy of my mind. But it was not until I heard the thunder rumbling over the hill and saw the first flash of lightning through the barn slats that I realized why.

Today was June 14, one week before the summer solstice, the first anniversary of my grandmother's death, a fact my body registered before my mind knew what was happening. All of my senses were on overdrive, tuned in to everything that was the same now as it was then—the delicate pink and white laurels dotting the mountainsides, the hot rain pounding the tin roof, the way my shirt clung to my chest like a wet rag. That night, after Ama was safely back in her stall, babbling and crooning to her babies, her vulva still unchanged, I lay awake for hours, and when I finally fell asleep, I had a dream that wasn't really a dream at all but a memory.

In my dream, it was summer, and I was at my grandmother's house. Through the open windows, the sweet scent of peonies mixed in the air with the acrid smoke from the paper plant over the hill. On the kitchen table, a fan whirred. My grandmother and I sat side-by-side. She was in a soft, pink armchair; I was in my grandfather's recliner, and I knew in the way of dreams, deeply, intuitively, that he was already dead. My grandmother chewed tobacco and spat into a Styrofoam cup. Tiny beads of sweat dotted her forehead, curled the soft hair at her temples. A thin, clear tube ran from her nose to the oxygen machine by her chair. The tank hummed. I rocked back and forth, my bare feet pulsing up and down on the rug, sweat pooling on my chest. Just outside the screen door, a ruby-throated hummingbird alit on the feeder, rapidly flickering his green-flecked wings, tiny, hot bursts of emerald light.

When I woke, my mind was muddled, hovering on the very edge of the real and the unreal, the past and the present. And as strange as it sounds, I thought of Terry. Perhaps I had been spending too much time in a dark barn scrutinizing a pregnant goat. Still, something about the chicken dying reminded me of my grandmother dying—the dull gray tint of Terry's beak, the way her face pitched forward, the way at first, she seemed to just be deeply sleeping, but then there was something even quieter than sleep—a raw, piercing stillness. In my old life, I had felt kinship and, of course, affection for my pets, but what I felt now was different, a deep sense that we were all connected, different parts of the same whole—Terry, Ama, my grandmother, David, my children, me—though what that whole was, I still did not know.

On day 149, I resumed my role as barn sentry and opened my book. I was now on the chapter on Nicaragua, which seemed appropriate given the heat. The solar-powered fan whirred and whizzed. Still, sweat poured off my forehead and onto my book, and Ama looked as uncomfortable as I remembered feeling in July 1994 when Eli was several days overdue.

Exhausted and miserable, I was nonetheless determined to take Aaron and Alex to the Fourth of July parade in downtown Brevard. Waddling along the sidewalk, heavy and round and sweating from every pore, I clasped each child by the hand and braved the cotton-candy-eating, lemonade-drinking, red-white-and-blue-clad crowd. And then a woman I knew from high school emerged from the throng.

"Oh my God!" she said, clutching my arm. "*You're pregnant.*"

Yes, I confirmed. I was, indeed, pregnant.

"When are you due?"

"A few days ago," I said.

"You look miserable," she said. "I'll tell you what you need to do. You need to go home to David and just *fuck like rabbits*. That does it every time."

Looking at Ama, remembering how oddly and immediately effective that remedy had been, I was sorry that was not an option for her. All day long, she paced and grunted and rubbed against the barn wall. That evening, Eli, who was home from college for the summer, broke out a bottle of, ironically, Nicaraguan rum—Flor de Caña— that a friend had given him. Using fresh pineapple and lots of ice, he whipped up a tall, cold pitcher of piña coladas. We divided the pitcher into two glasses, then headed down to the barn to put the animals up for the night.

Since Eli had only spent a year here before leaving for college, he was both fascinated by the goats and wary of them. For the other eighteen years of his life, he had been raised by parents who were completely different from the people David and I had become. The parents Eli knew wore business attire and grew basil and tomatoes at their quaint house in the country. The people now lugging around chickens and estimating the angles of goat teats must have seemed alien to him, almost as strange as the pregnant goat that toddled after us screaming for attention, head-butting the other goats, licking her lips and slamming her front paws onto our thighs. When she did this, it looked as if the babies were going to fall through her belly onto the ground, a feat my Flor-de-Caña-infused mind almost believed possible. After twenty minutes, Eli and I were out of rum and out of patience, our thighs covered with mud and scratches, so we put the girls in their stalls and shut the chickens—minus Terry—into the coop. Then we went back inside to make another batch of drinks.

By day 150, when Ama was still not in labor, I was deeply concerned. Maybe she had a false pregnancy. I had been reading about that online, about how a goat could believe she was pregnant when she was actually not. Her uterus would expand, and she would go into real labor before finally delivering an empty amniotic sac. I read all the discussion forums again—to myself and to David, who was also, at this point, worried that something was wrong. That evening, for reasons I cannot now explain, I watched a video of a pig giving birth. The sow lay on her side while baby after baby slid effortlessly from her silent, prone body. At the end, the videographer announced that she had fifteen piglets, eleven live babies. Below the video, people posted messages about the four dead babies. *Oh no! How sad.* And so on. It was unnerving.

The discussion forums I read said that most Nigerian dwarfs didn't go over 153 days, but someone had a pregnant doe that went to day 157. Someone else said you should never let them go over day 155 before performing a caesarean. Maybe that was right. Or maybe it wasn't. Once again, I wished I had a real, live human being to talk to, someone who had experienced this before. Since the information I had read about the teat angle was wrong—or perhaps *I* was wrong about the angle of the teat—I didn't know what to believe except that perhaps this was all a big mistake. I kept telling Ama everything was going to be okay, but the truth was, I had no idea how this was going to turn out. Ama could die. Her babies could die. They could all die.

Because we had somehow thought we could do this ourselves, we did not yet have a vet for our farm animals. After all, we had done pretty well taking care of the chickens. How much harder could goats be? But we were quickly discovering that not only were goats more complicated, our attachment to them was stronger. We were fond of our chickens, but they still seemed like farm animals. The goats, on the other hand, were more like pets.

So we began calling around, trying to find a vet who would come at night or on the weekend if Ama needed emergency care. We finally found two who did house calls and seemed to have good reputations. We added their phone numbers to the contacts in our phones, and though I should have felt somewhat relieved, that night, I dreamed a sheep gave birth to a lamb, but the lamb was not a real lamb. She was a tiny square, her head folded into her body, legs tucked underneath, an origami baby lamb. In the morning, I was certain: if Ama did not go into labor soon, I was going to go completely nuts.

Miraculously, though, Terry was still alive. David had been reading about all the possible home remedies for ailing chickens, and he decided she might have an obstruction in her throat. He took her from her cage and held her in one arm, massaging her chest and throat with the other hand. When he hung her upside down by her feet, Terry went limp.

"Oh no," he said. "She fainted."

He lifted her back up, and when her eyes fluttered open, he resumed rubbing her neck. I watched for a while, aware that we were in a strange state of limbo. We had a barn and farm animals, but that in itself didn't make us farmers. My ancestors had drawn clear distinctions between livestock and pets. They raised livestock for food, and whether or not they liked them was beside the point. They could not spend all day sitting at a barn rubbing a chicken's throat or playing midwife for an expectant milk doe. They had vegetables to can and water to haul and kids to feed, and an ailing chicken would have been quickly and efficiently dispatched and turned into something more useful, like chicken stew. But for David and me, the lines between pets and livestock, between animals and humans even, were fuzzy.

Ama still showed no signs of kidding. No pawing at the ground. No heavy panting. She ate hay and grain and weeds and head-butted Holly and Willow whenever they came within fifty feet of her. Every few minutes, she ran her enormous belly along the sides of the fence, then waited for me to rub her favorite spot—just between her horns. I squatted beside her and massaged her face and then her ears, sending positive energy intended to convey, *I'm here for you, girl. Just let me know when.*

———

Finally, on day 153, David did what he should have done from the beginning. He calculated Ama's due date himself rather than relying on my basic math skills. And when he did, he realized something important: I had the date wrong. I had asked Siri and counted myself, but either we both got the due date wrong or maybe I asked Siri the wrong question. In any case, I had made a mathematical error. It turned out that today was actually day 148 and the due date was still two days away. I had been so sure I had it right that I made him show me two different times, two different ways, but finally, I realized he was correct. It wasn't as if I needed more evidence of my incompetence, but there it was.

That same day, however, we had a small miracle in the form of Terry. For days, I had been telling David it would be better to go ahead and put an end to her misery, but I was forced to eat proverbial crow when around noon that day, she stood up and walked out of her hospice crate and rejoined the other chickens as if nothing had ever happened. Together, they scratched and fluffed and nibbled grain in the afternoon sun.

She would never lay eggs again, and though my ancestors would have scoffed at the idea of feeding a chicken that no longer produced eggs, we were emboldened by her progress, and David was beside himself with pride in his new animal husbandry skills. "I told you," he said when I marveled at her fine, gold-tipped feathers, at the especially spritely way she waltzed through the barnyard. She was not exactly restored to her former self, yet she was healed in some fundamental way that amazed and delighted her just as it amazed and delighted us.

That evening, after David and I put the goats in their stalls, we stood in the driveway, and for the first time in days, we breathed. In the midst of all the worry and uncertainty, here was a moment of tranquility, a moment when we accepted the crazy precariousness of it all—Ama's future, Terry's future, our future. Above us, the moon was full, the sky clear and vast. On nights like this, when it wasn't rainy or foggy or hazy, you could stand on the cabin rooftop and count the stars. The light bounced off the hillsides and the tin roofs on the henhouse and the barn and the cabin, like lights on a movie set or a busy runway, like somewhere where people were not waiting to be born or to die but instead dwelt in that moment in-between, that space where memory and reality and possibility collided.

On June 18, 2014, I drove into town to deliver some eggs to a friend. The errand would take less than an hour, so there was no reason to rush. Nothing at all was happening with Ama. Then, as soon as I got into town, David texted: Come home now.

I whipped into my friend's driveway, set three cartons of eggs by her back door, then raced home. In front of the barn, I stopped my car and bolted to the field, where Ama lay prone on the grass. David crouched beside her, and next to them both, a slippery gray, white, and black kid lay on a dog pee pad. The kid was wet and slimy, its eyes covered with a creamy goo, and Ama was furiously licking the tiny, squirming body. I watched, mesmerized, while David exchanged dirty pee pads for clean ones and suctioned out the kid's nose with the rubber bulb. Though I had made fun of him when he bought it, the bulb now seemed indispensable. How had I not known this?

Finally, the kid began to look like a kid—soft, fluffy fur, curious blue eyes. David lifted the kid's tail and looked closely: No vent. The kid was a boy—a beautiful, healthy boy. He baaed the tiniest baas, and while I was still trying to take it all in, to realize both the extraordinariness and the everydayness of this moment, Ama began moaning and pushing, her legs contracting as a second "bubble" emerged beneath her tail.

Quickly, with gloved hands, David produced a fresh pee pad and placed it underneath Ama's rear end. Moments later, the bubble burst, and a skinny white-and-black kid fell onto the sterile pad. David wiped the kid's face and cleared its airway while I tried to maneuver the firstborn kid to Ama's teat.

I had read that the cleansing ritual is an important part of the bonding process, the time when the new mother realizes this is her baby and she needs to care for it. A new mother who doesn't have this time with her kid might later reject it. I knew all of this, but I also knew that in order for the kids to have the best chance of survival, it was critical that they nurse soon after birth, preferably within the first hour. So from the moment I had arrived, I had been asking David what time the first kid was born. I wanted Ama to have enough time to clean him, but I also wanted to get him nursing. My best guess was we were about thirty minutes into the critical time frame. I squeezed Ama's teat to be sure she had a good milk flow and guided the kid's mouth to her. He fumbled about for a moment or two, like someone searching for a flashlight in the dark, and then he latched on. When I heard him swallow for the first time, I was immensely relieved. Now,

David slid the second kid up so Ama could see it. Again, Ama began cleaning, and David checked under the kid's tail. This time, there was a vent. She was a lovely doeling that more closely resembled a Holstein calf than a goat.

After much shifting and nudging and encouraging on our part and much licking and baaing on Ama's part, the doeling was soon clean and nursing as well. Despite all of our preparations and planning, Ama had not needed our assistance. She had done it all by herself. Nonetheless, we felt like heroes, as if we ourselves had done something astonishing. Ecstatic, relieved, exhausted, David and I pulled lawn chairs into the barnyard, and Eli, who had arrived on the scene just after the second kid was born, brought down a bottle opener and three bottles of Highland Brewing Gaelic Ale. We popped open the lids and toasted Ama, then watched as she fussed over the babies who were already standing and gazing contentedly from their mother to us.

Eventually, after much debate, we named the doeling Loretta and the wide-eyed buckling Conway—a pair of classic country kids. Ama and I had been partners in her pregnancy, but from the moment she delivered her kids safely into the world, she was no longer interested in me. Whatever hormone surges or instincts had caused her to seek my company and affection were gone, and she immediately reverted to her initial assessment—that David was a much better human companion than I was. Whenever I approached her, she ran, baaing and snorting, her hair raised. Whenever David approached her, she sidled up to him, batting her long lashes, tilting her head for him to rub the lovely black brushstrokes near the corners of her eyes.

And though she was generally a good mother to both her babies, from the moment they were born, Ama showed a strong preference for her son. When Conway cried, she nuzzled him to her teat, and he crouched down, tail wagging, drinking his fill. When Loretta tried to latch on to the other teat, however, Ama shook her away. Loretta stood beside her mother, her cries so high-pitched and insistent, we feared she was injured, punctured by the fence, gored by one of Ama's horns. Once we realized she was not mortally wounded, only hungry, David and I crouched down and grabbed Ama's collar, pushing Loretta from behind in the general direction of the teat. When Loretta's tail wagged, we knew she was drinking.

For the first two weeks, we left the babies with Ama all day, and at night, the three of them slept in a pile, each baby with its head on Ama's back. There was no electricity in the barn, only a solar-powered light that worked or didn't, depending on how much sun there had been that day. One evening, standing with David in the half-light watching the goats sleep—Holly and Willow curled up together in their stall, Ama and the babies in the stall beside them—I realized that if someone told me right then that I could go back ten years, have my old life back exactly as it was, a life where I never saw my husband, where our lives were always about *becoming* instead of *being*, I would have refused.

It was such a simple realization, yet it seemed momentous. Being poor means not having a lot of options other people have—*Should I pay at the pump for gas or pay cash in the store? Should I drive or fly to my destination? Should I get new brake pads like the mechanic recommends or just hope they hold out a while longer?* Now, even a hypothetical possibility emboldened me. Given the alternative of that life or this one, I would choose this one. And then, for once, instead of trying to fill in the rest of that thought—*but I really wish we had*—I tried to leave it just as it was: *I choose this.*

Prenatal Piña Coladas

- 1½ ounces coconut cream
- 1½ ounces pineapple juice
- A few slices fresh pineapple
- 2 ounces Flor de Caña rum
- 1 cup ice

Blend all ingredients in blender until smooth. Pour into tall, chilled glass. Drink in barn. Refuse to share with pregnant goat no matter how much she begs.

Chapter Fifteen

MY PARENTS STILL LIVED JUST across town in the same house I grew up in, and we saw them regularly. We took walks, had meals, celebrated birthdays and holidays, and whenever we added new animals to the farm, they came by to see them. My mother, especially, loved all animals, and she cooed over the chicks as they slept in the brooder, fed Holly and Ama licorice treats, cradled Willow in her arms. Still, living in a drafty, vermin-infested cabin was a fate that, through hard work and frugality, my parents had *escaped*. They would never have allowed themselves to end up in our situation, but if they had, they would have chosen any remedy over this one. They would have given their dogs away, sold their cat, moved to a modest, tidy, safe apartment in town like the one they lived in before I was born. In other words, they would have done something sensible.

My life now was so far removed from the life I had had growing up, from anyone else's I knew, in fact, that I moved deeper and deeper into the memories of my grandparents and great-grandparents, to their stories of survival and perseverance and connectedness to the land. Their spirits guided me, provided me solace and wisdom, and they came to me at the oddest times, when I was folding laundry or frying an egg, when I was walking down to the barn with my dogs each morning or shutting the goats in their stalls. They came to me when I was cooking dinner, when the kitchen was close and sticky, moisture droplets forming on the windows, the warmth rising and clinging to my face. They came not in a steady, logical progression but effervescent and shifting, all vapor and steam and heat.

My great-great-grandmother was Sarah Caroline, but everyone called her Callie, and when I imagined her, Callie was short and slender, with charcoal eyes and skin like burnt clay. Callie was part woman, part ghost. She was full-blooded Cherokee. She was the daughter of a slave. She was my great-grandmother's curly locks, my grandmother's strong arms. She was my mother's high cheekbones, my wandering, restless spirit. In the midst of my kitchen, among the jars of cumin and coriander, cinnamon and cloves, the baskets filled with spring onions and new potatoes, I conjured her, whispering her name over and over and over again—*Callie, Callie, Callie*—and when I finally came across a photo of her in a book of family history I inherited from my grandmother, I was shocked by the accuracy of my dreaming.

In the photo, Callie sat in front of a log cabin next to her husband, a baby girl on her knee, five older children clustered around her—three girls, two boys. Callie's eyes and hair were the color of coal and river silt, of obsidian and moonstone. Her eyebrows were thick and straight, her nose broad. Three of her children were dark like her, the other two lighter, like their father. I held the photo to the light. I put on my reading glasses. I tilted it to one angle and then another, searching for some sign of how she felt about the solemn, bearded man beside her. Did she love him? At night, when they were finally alone, when she loosened her hair from the tight bun and eased into bed, did he run his fingers through her smooth, silky hair? Did he whisper to her how beautiful she was, how loved? And did she touch the creases on his face, marvel at the broadness of his shoulders, at the hardness of his arms?

Try as I might, I could read nothing from Callie's face. Her lips were tight and closed, her expression impermeable. And yet there was something in her hands, a tenderness that reached out across the century and rendered me breathless. The baby in her lap, my great-grandmother, wore a long gown and leaned slightly forward—eager, expectant. Callie's left hand rested against her daughter's folded hands as if to hold her in place, as if her child might spring from her lap and fade into the ether, like a ghost.

⸻

One evening in early August, my parents came over for a family picnic on the front patio. Eli was still home for the summer, and Alex was visiting for the weekend. It was an idyllic Southern summer evening— warm but not hot, just breezy enough to keep the gnats and mosquitoes at bay. We popped open a couple of bottles of merlot and ate grilled chicken, vegetable kebabs, arugula salad with shaved fennel, parmesan, and walnuts, with blueberry cobbler and buttermilk pie. Afterward, we strolled down the road and picked daisies, which we fed to Conway and Loretta. Then we gathered eggs and shut the chickens into the coop for the night. Fireflies cast a soft, yellow glow over the blueberry bushes on the hillside as we walked back to the house.

Moments later, as we were once again sitting on the patio, sipping what was left of the wine and watching the moon rise over the waterfall, we heard a loud cracking sound, followed by a tremendous *splat*. All six of us were stunned into inertia until Eli screamed, "Oh shit!" followed by a command that was more sound than word, more sheer urgency than direction: "Move!"

Later, my mother would say she thought a bat had fallen on us. Alex thought part of the house had given way. David thought someone was throwing rocks at us. But then, there was no time to process our thoughts. Eli's instruction was so alarmingly insistent, we did not hesitate. Wine glass in hand, I jumped in the back seat of my Mountaineer, which was parked next to the patio. Alex and my mother ran down the driveway. David, my dad, and Eli leapt to the edge of the patio. From the car, I could see a tremendous black snake writhing on the porch. It was as wide as my hand and at least five feet long, maybe longer.

I was not a stranger to black snakes. I had grown up in a house surrounded by woods. As a kid, I had hiked and canoed. I had gone to summer camp. I was used to seeing black snakes at a distance—crossing a trail or crisscrossed around a tree limb. I knew they were harmless. They were good, helpful snakes. They ate mice and other rodents. But *still*. I huddled against the far car door, my knees pulled to my chest, my arms wrapped tightly around my knees, each arm clutching the opposite elbow.

"Oh God," I said to no one in particular. "Oh God, oh God, oh God."

And then I noticed the string of small, inert objects scattered across the rock. Still, it took a few minutes for me to put it all together. The patio was situated under two staggered overhangs, one for the second level of the house and another for the third. A defunct doorbell alarm, resembling a plastic megaphone, hung just beneath the third overhang. Usually, there were wasps' nests covering the alarm, but just a few days ago, I had noticed something new—a bird's nest. And then I understood what had happened. The snake had crawled underneath the roof to reach the nest and had fallen, dragging with it an entire nest of babies whose lifeless bodies now lay scattered across the patio.

It was a scene straight out of a Hitchcock film, a scene that instantly snapped me out of this place I had come to and back to where I was before: Our van repossessed. Our electricity cut off. The friends we had lost. The family members we had disappointed. The sound of the sledgehammer against my old garage door. A nest of mice in the walls. A copperhead writhing under my dead grandmother's china cabinet. No matter how hard I tried to put it all behind me, how far I believed I had come in embracing our new lives, they were always right there, just beneath the surface—all of our failures, all of our shortcomings. Perhaps they always would be.

Eli stood on the very edge of the patio. His arms were crossed, his watchful gaze trained on the snake. David and my dad hunched together for a moment, conferring, and then David ran around the corner of the house and rummaged around. He returned with a five-gallon plastic bucket, which he held sideways while my dad prodded the addled snake with a long stick.

My dad was in his midseventies. He wore loose khaki pants, trail shoes, and a cap, and as he danced nimbly about, dodging the snake, the snake coiled and drew its head back. For a moment, everything was still. My dad was still. David was still. Eli was still. The waterfall was still. No one said a word. No one breathed. I heard the blood pooling in my fingertips.

And then I became aware of a piercing screech coming from somewhere down the driveway. It was so haunted, so wild, so *not human*, it took me a moment to realize what it was. But then I knew: it was Alex.

In any real crisis, Alex was the calmest person in the room, but she did have one phobia: snakes. All her life, she had had nightmares about snakes. Even a photo or a dead snake by the side of the road sent her into hysterics. *Alex is twenty-five years old*, I told myself. *She'll be fine.* Now, the snake slowly twined around my father's outstretched stick until the snake and the stick were one dark shadow on the moonlit porch. In the distance, the wailing grew louder, more alarming. Part of me wanted to stay in that car forever, smashed up against the window, the window cool and damp against my cheek, the waterfall once again a pulse in the mountainside. But, just like all those years ago when she was the reason I had to pull myself together and keep going, my daughter needed me. So I slid over to the driver's side, the side opposite the patio, creaked open the door, and bolted down the driveway. Alex was crumpled over, trembling, her hands on her thighs. Her long, curly hair covered her face. My mother smoothed her hair, patted her back.

"You're okay," I told her.

But clearly, she was not. From what I could gather from Alex's disjointed report, the snake had narrowly missed her lap. It had whizzed past her, grazing her legs as it fell, the dead baby birds rolling between her feet.

"This is the worst thing that's ever happened to me!" Alex said.

"Oh, honey, no. No, it's not," my mother said, still patting her.

She meant to be comforting, I suppose, but her meaning was unclear. Was it a lesson in relativity? Did she mean having a black snake and a nest of doomed baby birds fall on you wasn't that bad compared to, say, being stung by a swarm of bees or accosted by a mother bear? Did she mean worse things had happened and that someday, this incident would take its rightful place behind other unfortunate happenings? Or perhaps, was she looking ahead to all the shocking, painful things that were bound to happen in the future, things we had no control of, things we could not even see coming?

Certainly, there were worse things, much worse things—cancer, car wrecks, drug addiction, suicide, natural disasters. Every day, people went broke and had to make adjustments, move to places much scarier than this—places that were actually dangerous. Some people had nowhere to live at all. They lived in cars or under bridges or in tents or makeshift lean-tos. They had no one other than themselves, no one they could call to coax a huge, angry black snake into a bucket for them. They were completely alone. And yet somehow, the shocking suddenness of this, the complete absurdity of it all, was still working its way through Alex's consciousness. Somehow, though, her frantic gasping and wheezing and crying made me calmer. Or at least convinced me that I needed to appear calmer.

"You're okay, honey," I said again.

For a moment, she was quieter, which I thought was a good sign, until I realized she was having trouble breathing.

"You're fine," I told her. "Perfectly fine. You need to just calm down. Just breathe."

Of course, she wasn't actually fine. But I knew a little something about not being fine, about how if you just kept going, taking one breath after another, putting one foot in front of the other, believing all along that it was possible for you to one day be fine again, that someday, things might actually be better. So I did my best to soothe her. I demonstrated how to breathe, slowly, deeply—in two, out two, in two, out two—and then the three of us—Mom, Alex, and I—huddled together in the driveway while Dad and David tried to come up with a strategy for humanely trapping the now-furious coiled snake.

Gradually, Alex seemed to grow calmer, her breaths longer, steadier, more sure. And then Eli called to us.

"All clear!"

The men had managed to capture the snake in the bucket, and they had pierced the bucket with air holes and covered it with a large, heavy rock. *Just in case*. The snake may have been injured after its fall, but if it lived through the night, David planned to relocate it the next morning. He put the bucket on the patio to the side of the house, out of sight. *Good*, we said. *Fine*. Still, we were shaken, and the incident had exhausted us all. My parents went home, and David, Alex, Eli, and I went to bed.

The next morning, David went outside first thing to check on the snake. I was reheating a mug of coffee in the microwave when he came back in. He stood in the doorway for a moment saying nothing, his eyes wide.

"What?" I asked. "*What?*"

"It's gone."

It was impossible, and yet it was apparent from the stunned look on David's face that it was true, and my very first thought was that if we ever wanted her to visit us again, we could not tell Alex.

"Shh!" I said.

But it was too late. She had heard. She came running down the stairs.

"Did he say that snake is gone?"

"Now, there is no need to freak out," I said.

"What the fuck?" Alex said.

Which pretty much summed up my feelings about the past two years: *What the fuck.* Just when I was becoming more comfortable here, just when I was starting to enjoy this place, a massive snake had fallen from the sky and landed practically on top of us. Nothing was the way I had planned. Nothing was the way it was supposed to be. The universe was out of sync. And now, apparently, that same snake had pushed a stone away and risen from a bucket, like Lazarus or Jesus. I couldn't decide which.

I filled a mug of coffee for Alex, and we sat at the kitchen counter, sipping coffee and watching David through the windows as he gathered wood and carried it into the shop. Every now and then, he stopped to gaze up the mountain, his eyes scanning the hillside. But he needn't have bothered. The snake was long gone, slithering, perhaps, along the creek bed, dodging salamanders and soothing sore muscles on the cool, smooth stones. Or perhaps it was winding along the Earlobe Trail, the feel of dirt on its belly glorious and thrilling and new.

Arugula Salad for a Snaky Picnic

This recipe is adapted from The New Blue Ridge Cookbook *by Elizabeth Wiegand.*

- 3 tablespoons extra-virgin olive oil
- 2 tablespoons balsamic vinegar
- 1 fennel bulb
- 1 large bunch arugula
- ¼ to ⅓ cup shaved Parmesan cheese
- A couple of handfuls of chopped, roasted walnuts

Whisk olive oil and vinegar together for dressing. Cut fronds from fennel bulb, and set fronds aside. Clean bulb thoroughly, and remove the end. Shave remaining bulb thinly with mandoline or cheese grater. Toss with dressing. Add arugula, cheese, and walnuts. Toss salad to distribute dressing evenly. Divide salad among four plates for serving. Serve reserved fennel fronds to your chickens, no plates required.

Chapter Sixteen

ACCORDING TO THE WEBSITE THE Prairie Homestead, one of my online go-to guides, when the goat babies were two weeks old, it was time to begin milking. I liked this particular website because, despite her religious bent, the farmer, Jill, talked a lot about the value of homesteading skills and returning to your roots, and though she and her husband raised animals for meat, she also believed in raising them humanely.

Other than our one failed attempt at milking Maple, neither David nor I had ever actually milked an animal. But Jill made it all seem simple and straightforward. According to her, we should put the babies in a separate stall at night, then milk Ama in the morning and return the babies to her for the remainder of the day. That way, the babies would get plenty of milk—milk that was far better for them than any powdered, store-bought substitute—and we would only have to milk once a day. Both cows and goats needed to be milked at pretty much the same time each day, but if we milked only in the mornings, we would have more flexibility in our schedules. We could still go out in the evenings without having to rush home to milk. This seemed like the perfect plan.

In early July, when Conway and Loretta were exactly two weeks old, David divided their stall in half with fencing. The first night we separated them, the babies and Ama howled and cried, and the kids' bleating was so mournful, I was tempted to let them back in with Ama. But we had read that this too was part of the process. Like babies learning to sleep in their cribs, they would learn their routine. It would get easier. And, for a while, it did.

Every evening, we fed the babies grain and hay in their section of the stall. At first, they nibbled disinterestedly on their food, but eventually, they figured out that these were things to look forward to, and they would run into their area and grab a piece of grain or hay and chew contentedly. At night, they slept curled together like kittens, against the fence. Ama slept with her body pressed against the babies through the divider. They could still see each other, smell each other, talk to each other, and sometimes I wondered if perhaps Ama enjoyed this brief break from her demanding offspring. *Mother's night out.*

Separating Ama and the kids was the easy part. The hard part was getting Ama to cooperate during milking. I had just assumed that Ama would *expect* to be milked, that she would see it like I did, a fair exchange for room and board. It turned out this was not exactly Ama's perspective. David and I had never had the same sleep schedule, and every day, for almost our entire married lives, I had gotten up and done the morning routine alone—taking care of the kids, letting the dogs out, making coffee, etc. Now, we woke at the same time, and while I had envisioned peaceful mornings watching the fog rise over the hollow with David while Ama happily ate her grain, the reality was more like a bizarre athletic event designed to test the endurance and emotional stamina of all the participants.

As in all other things, Ama preferred David to me, and when it came to milking, she seemed to somehow intuitively know which set of hands belonged to David and which to me. While she bucked and jostled both of us, she saved her most vicious kicks and thrusts for those times when I was crouched down, my head between her legs, trying to master the squeeze-and-roll-down technique. Granted, David was better at milking than I was. For one thing, he was more patient. For another, he seemed to instantly get the technique of massaging her tiny teats, a feat that required both dexterity and persistence. Still, the entire process was challenging. David had made a nice wooden milk stand, but it did not have a head grip, so though Ama jumped on the stand easily enough, the minute she started eating her grain, the clock started ticking. We had only a few minutes before she began kicking and jabbing us with her horns.

David sat in the chair on her right, his shoulder pressing into her side, just like Jill had indicated we should. However, Jill had demonstrated this technique on a Jersey cow, not on a Nigerian dwarf goat, so it was hard to gauge whether he was doing it exactly right. I stood on the other side, leaning into Ama so that she was wedged between David and me. While I held the sterilized mason jar, David wiped Ama's teats down, first with a washcloth, then with baby wipes. Then David put a lavender, hand-held human breast pump up to one teat. When the bottle was full, he handed it to me, and I emptied the contents into the mason jar while he left the milk funnel against Ama's teat.

The trick, we discovered, was for David to never lose contact with Ama's body. When that teat was completely empty, David and I switched places in a series of fluid movements. He glided around Ama's side, pivoting around her rear until he landed on her left side. I dipped under his arm, swung around, then positioned myself to block Ama's escape from the right. David had been a wrestler in high school, and his experience came in handy, since the whole process seemed a little like wrestling, a little like dancing, a little like giving a goat a massage.

If we ever forgot to use this technique or, say, slipped in the mud and lost contact with Ama's body, she took that as a cue that we were finished and bolted from the stand to the fence where Conway and Loretta stood bellowing—three goats yelling and hollering and bleating and trying to squeeze between the gate and the fence at the same time. Meanwhile, in a far corner of the pasture, Willow and Holly languidly nibbled dry leaves. David and I sighed and held up the mason jar, trying to determine, based on our weekly totals, whether we had enough milk to make a batch of cheese or yogurt or whether David needed to chase Ama down and carry her back to the milk stand.

Most mornings, though, using our hand-on-goat strategy, we got about a quart of milk, including a thick line of cream at the top. When we were finished, we let the babies out, and they rushed to Ama screaming *Mama, Mama!* Butting their heads hard into her teats, they lifted her back legs completely off the ground. As soon as the milk let down, they fell silent, their tails vigorously wagging, their mother slowly lowered to the earth.

This was our new routine, the way we started almost every day. However, one advantage to keeping the kids with the mother part of the time, according to Jill, was that we could occasionally leave the kids in the stall with Ama overnight and skip milking the next morning. Never one to adhere to a rigid schedule, I loved knowing I could take a day off without affecting Ama's milk supply, so one night a week, usually a Friday or Saturday, David and I planned a date night and left Conway and Loretta in with Ama.

Of course, we still had to go down to the barn to feed and water the animals and let them outside the next morning, but we could sleep a little later usual. David and I were thrilled with this arrangement since it gave us a brief reprieve. The babies were thrilled because they got to be with Ama. But it was hard to say whether or not Ama was thrilled. Perhaps *tolerant* was a better word. Sometimes in the evenings, Ama looked as tired and rundown as I remembered feeling when my kids were young, as exhausted as my mother looked in old family photos. Mothering was rewarding, but it was hard.

When I was in my twenties, I had three beautiful, healthy, boisterous, demanding children under the age of five and one stressed, overworked husband who was rarely home. Ama's calm resignation to her kids' incessant cravings reminded me how I had felt back then.

Though I adored my kids, I was often exhausted, mentally understimulated, emotionally spent, overwhelmed by my own offspring. *Who are these alien creatures? Why do they keep following me around asking for food and water, expecting me to open their juice boxes and the tops of their squeezable yogurts?* I sometimes wondered. *And where on earth is the grown-up who is supposed to be taking care of them?*

As Conway and Loretta tugged lustily at Ama's teats, I sympathized with her. Here her two kids were, hungry, fretful, in need of their mother's constant attention, and now David and I wanted something from her too. She must have sometimes felt a little like she was being crushed, the very breath sucked right out of her. I watched the three of them for a minute, the exquisite, eager babies, the young, high-spirited mom, and then I headed to the house to sterilize the milk.

Of course, I knew all about the virtues of unpasteurized milk. It tasted better. It was full of good bacteria. It was easier to digest. And so on. But we were so new to the milking process that I wasn't yet confident that it was safe to drink raw. Had we wiped Ama's teats down thoroughly? Did we get it in the refrigerator soon enough? At first, I strained the fresh milk, then sterilized it on the stove and dunked it into ice before refrigerating. Later, I got braver. As soon as we finished milking, I ran to the house, strained the milk, and iced it. Some days, David drank it immediately. Other mornings, I saved it until I had enough to make cheese—which, with only one Nigerian dwarf in milk, usually took several days. When Ama was feeling particularly obstinate, it could take even longer.

Since I had already learned to make ricotta and mozzarella, I had a few basic cheese-making supplies—mesophilic culture, thermophilic culture, vegetable rennet, etc. Now, I was ready to make soft, cultured goat cheese. I began by learning the basics, such as the difference between curds (the solid that forms during fermentation) and whey (the liquid). Before I started making cheese, I had heard those terms, but my experience with them had been limited to knowing that an arachnophobic girl named Miss Muffet enjoyed both of them. It turns out what I had needed all along was the visual representation cheese-making provided.

One of the things I loved most about making cheese was the waiting, the anticipation. Making cheese, even the simplest kinds, was not like running to the mall to buy a new pair of shoes or ordering a newly released book online that would arrive at your front door in two days. You had to get a goat, figure out how to mate it, help her through pregnancy and delivery, tend to her babies, figure out how to milk her, collect all the necessary ingredients and equipment for cheese-making, and then, after you had introduced the starter into the milk, you *still* had to wait more than a day to have cheese. It was the ultimate deferred gratification.

Once I learned to make soft goat cheese, I tried many different flavor combinations—Italian herbs, garlic and chives, olives and pimentos, honey and walnuts, cranberries and orange zest. David and I would stand in the kitchen, sampling the various mixtures as if we were at a formal tasting. Five kinds of cheese. Three kinds of crackers. Wine or beer to cleanse the palette. "A little too much garlic," we would say. Or "Not enough pepper." We were reclusive, hill-dwelling connoisseurs.

Since each batch of cheese yielded a considerable amount of whey, we soon had a huge supply of large mason jars full, lined up in the refrigerator. I used it in pies, as a base for soups, to cook beans and rice and oatmeal. I no longer bought chicken broth or vegetable broth and rarely bought milk from the store. Now, though we were by no means living completely off the land, with the dozen eggs a day we were collecting from our hens and the fresh goat cheese and the few vegetables we were able to grow, we were actually producing enough food to provide some of our meals. Despite the fact that I often had less than twenty dollars in the bank, that we drove cars that were falling apart, that we were struggling to pay for health insurance and dental care, that we were still deeply, hopelessly in debt to the government, we still ate better than most wealthy people I knew, and some days, sitting down to feast on sliced homegrown tomatoes sprinkled with fresh basil and goat cheese or cheesy vegetable quiche or goat cheese ice cream or cheesecake, I felt immeasurably rich.

We ate the goat cheese on everything—bagels and eggs and salads and pasta. And then I moved on to goat milk yogurt and *cajeta*, a delicious, golden, caramel sauce that transformed our ice cream and cakes and fruits. How was it possible that I had lived close to half a century and hadn't yet tried *cajeta*? Now, there were so many other things I wanted to make—butter, cream cheese, sour cream, goat milk soap, lotions, lip balms. I would never have to go to the store again.

And then one morning, with no apparent warning, Ama decided she was finished.

Whereas before she had, albeit begrudgingly, allowed us to milk for a while, now she refused to go onto the stand at all, even for her grain. She fixed her brown eyes at us, raise the hackles on her back, and double-dog dare us: *Make me get on that stand*. When David chased and cornered her and hoisted her onto the stand, she immediately butted and kicked. Though he had devised a wooden slat to keep her head still, one of us had to hold it in place. She quickly figured this out and repeatedly jabbed us with her horns. The minute we turned her loose, she was off and running.

When we did succeed in getting a little milk, she often kicked so hard, she threw dirt and debris into the jar. Sometimes, she knocked over the whole jar. Other times, though she clearly had some milk in her bag, we simply could not get any. And even though they were healthy and plump and almost old enough to be completely weaned, all the while, Conway and Loretta stood at the fence, screaming and egging her on.

"Stop that," I told them. "You need to share!"

The babies were eating hay and grain and browsing some now, and they were getting stronger, so much so that they were occasionally able to shove past the partition in the stall and get to Ama during the night. Some mornings, David and I would get up early, sterilize all of our milking equipment, bundle in layers of clothes, and head down to the barn only to find the babies happily nursing, drinking what I had now come to think of as *our* milk.

Eventually, the trek down to the barn no longer seemed worth the effort, so late that fall, we gave up milking Ama and considered our other options. Our plan had been to mix the milk from Holly, Willow, and Ama, thus yielding plenty of good, relatively high-fat milk for cheese. In order to have more milk, though, we needed pregnant does. Holly and Willow were both from strong milking lines and would each, at their peaks, be able to produce about a gallon of milk a day, half a gallon if we milked them only once a day.

Technically, both Holly and Willow were old enough to mate, and they were both within the acceptable weight range, but just barely. Both Saanens and LaManchas go into heat for only a few weeks out of the fall months, so if we missed our chance to mate them this year, we would have to wait another year. Still, just to be on the safe side, we decided to hold off until the next breeding season. We wanted to be certain the does were mature enough and healthy enough to carry and deliver their kids safely. And though Nigerians are fertile all year and we could have tried to breed Ama again, we decided to give her body a break as well. So we packed up our milking supplies and waited.

How to Milk a Stubborn Doe

The first hurdle is getting the goat onto the milk stand. Once she is on the stand, you're 90 percent done, but the first time or two this will likely involve a lot of coaxing and pulling and pleading. You may even need to act out hopping on the stand, just to show her how nice it is up there, how totally comfortable and *perfectly fine* it is.

Once she is finally in place, offer her plenty of grain. Then, while she eats, wash her teats and udder with a paper towel dipped in udder wash. I make my own wash by mixing a half tablespoon of bleach and a drop of Dawn dishwashing detergent with one cup of warm water. (Warm is optional here, but your doe will appreciate it. Remember your last gynecological exam. Warm gel is definitely preferable to cold.) After making sure that your hands are clean, position your thumb and forefinger at the top of the teat to close it off. Then firmly close your other fingers in a squeezing motion. You should never, ever yank or pull on the doe's teat.

Back in high school, I played the clarinet, and the first time I was successful in getting milk from the teat, I was reminded of my stint in the marching band, as this is pretty much the same motion you make on a clarinet as you move down the musical scale. The first few squirts should go into a strip cup (a cup with a screen on top) so that you can check the milk for any abnormalities, like blood. After this, milk into the pail or, if you prefer, a mason jar, which is actually my preferred method. That way, when the goat kicks, you have time to yank your hand away and save the milk from getting poop/mud/straw/hair in it. Sometimes, a particularly obstinate doe can be calmed by a little impromptu serenade, which you can deliver while still squeezing rhythmically. My favorite milking tunes are Charlie Rich's "The Most Beautiful Girl," Hank Williams's "Hey [Hay], Good Lookin'," and Bob Dylan's "Lay, Lady, Lay," which I change to "Hay, Lady, Hay" and which the girls seem to especially appreciate.

Chapter Seventeen

ONE DAY THAT SUMMER, I was at UNC Asheville teaching a high school writing workshop when David texted me. A helicopter was circling our roof, a helicopter with an insignia on the side—the highway patrol. It was so close, David could see the uniformed men inside.

We both knew why the helicopter was there. That first spring, we had planted a vegetable garden in the field near the bridge, but the only plants that produced anything were the herbs I had potted and set on our front porch, and even those were flimsy and sparse, not at all like the lovely plants I had grown at our old house.

Discouraged, I had tried to imagine how the original inhabitants of this place had survived. We knew from the remnants of the barn that they had raised animals and from the original garden plot that they had also raised vegetables. But how? We talked about trying to rent a garden plot somewhere else, perhaps in the field just over the hill from the house, but it seemed crazy to rent land when we had fifty-three acres at our disposal. Then, the next year, when the planting season rolled around, I had an idea. The tin roof of the cabin was a lovely, flat, sunny space, ideal for a rooftop garden.

"You're kidding," David said.

"Let's just try it."

He researched what type of plastic buckets to use and the proper ratio of dirt to compost to worms, and he spent hours hauling the dirt-filled containers to the roof. I had envisioned a couple of tomato plants and maybe some basil, but when he was finished, we had tomatoes, squash, bell peppers, mint, banana peppers, potatoes, and corn. From the yard, you could see the tomatoes bulging from the vines, the brown silks hanging from the corn husks.

At the time, we had joked about it. *Hope no one thinks we're growing weed up here.* It was hilarious, absurd. Besides, we rarely saw planes crossing over, much less helicopters. But that day at UNCA, I realized we were undergoing an aerial search, being sized up to see if we merited an all-out raid. It was both totally predictable and surreal, and as someone who had spent the better part of the last few years on the "wrong" side of the law, I felt an odd mixture of guilt and outrage. And then I started to panic, but I tried to appear calm while my students responded to the writing prompts I had given them: *Write about your earliest memory. Write about a time when you tried for something and failed. Write about your greatest fear.*

While my students worked, I texted David: Put the dogs up. Get them all inside.

I was most worried about Pretzel because of his habit of bolting directly toward cars, a tendency we likely encouraged when we stopped our cars and picked him up. "You wanna drive?" we said, and he rode the rest of the way to the house with his paws on the steering wheel. I also worried about Reba. In addition to occasionally trying to annihilate our other pets, she was also skittish and unpredictable with people. Once, she had lunged viciously at David's five-year-old niece. I could only imagine what she might do if a group of armed men barged into our house—and what they might do in return.

Besides, even after all our time here, almost three years now, the property still looked sketchy. The cracked porch window had not been repaired. Axes and chainsaws were propped by the barn. The coyote skull Hester had recently brought home was lying on the slab of tin covering the wood pile. An old copperhead skin was stretched across the front porch. In fact, we had long since stopped locking the doors because we figured that anyone brave enough to break into our house could just have whatever he wanted.

While I waited to hear from David, I thought of all these things. I also worried that he might panic, run into our bedroom, and pull our old rifle from its dusty leather case. Every time I gave my students a prompt, I instructed them to keep writing until I stopped them, and now they were writing furiously: *Write about the weirdest meal you've ever had. Write about your favorite teacher. Write about the strangest thing about you. Write about the first time you believed you were in love.*

While they wrote, I pictured the scene unfolding at home, both the scene that was actually happening and the scene that could happen if the cops got a search warrant and returned. Four months before, the home of a man who lived across the mountain from us had been raided. Police believed Bob had a moonshine still on his back porch, and in response, they sent in a team of officers from four law enforcement agencies—the sheriff's department, the police department, the North Carolina Alcohol Law Enforcement agency, and the U.S. Department of Homeland Security.

This show of force had arrived at his house at 6:00 on a Monday evening. As soon as the cops entered, Bob ran upstairs and grabbed a gun. He then stood on the stairs, and pointed a loaded rifle at the officers. One ALE special agent, a Homeland Security special agent, and two sheriff's deputies fired their weapons. Within moments, Bob was dead.

Now, I wondered whether he had had time to consider who among his friends and neighbors might have betrayed him. Perhaps it was someone who had sat on his back porch and drunk moonshine out of a mason jar and swapped tall tales with him. Perhaps it was a neighbor who didn't like the company he kept. Maybe it was a friend of a friend, someone he had never met.

In any case, his story was as familiar to me as the weeping of willow trees or the sharp scent of pines. It was the same old story generations of my family had told while gathered around dinner tables or on front porches, stories about running liquor across state lines, about dodging the law and outwitting the guys who would shoot first and ask questions later. Sitting in class, watching my students work, I saw it all as clearly as if I had been there—my neighbor standing on his staircase, the rifle aimed at the officers, his eyes blazing, his hands sure and steady.

Are they still there? I texted David.

Yes, he said. **Just above the tree line at the top of the waterfall.**

A moment later, David ran outside and stood at the base of the falls, his arms thrown open in a gesture of defiance: *What the hell are you doing? Leave us the fuck alone!*

Only he didn't actually say that. He just thought it. And I didn't know about that part of the saga until later that evening, when I was making avocado gazpacho with the corn from a neighbor's farm because our corn didn't get enough sun, even on the roof. While David reenacted the scene, I tried to imagine what the men in the helicopter must have thought, my husband's manic yelling, his unruly gray hair, his wild, unkempt beard.

Later, we learned that the highway patrol routinely did flyovers to scan for suspicious activity. If they found anything that met that criteria, they sent in a smaller helicopter, one that could get a closer view. An aerial search, apparently, did not require a warrant, and I suppose, to some people, we did look suspicious—an old, ramshackle cabin tucked back in the hills, a yard strewn with chunks of a tree trunk that needed to be chopped into manageable pieces, a chicken coop and barn pieced together with wooden pallets and salvaged tin. Like Bob, we were suspiciously Appalachian. *Rednecks. Yokels. Hillbillies.*

As the patrol helicopter hovered over the cabin, I thought of the simple dignity of the lives of my parents and grandparents and all the people who came before them, people of this region who had tried, sometimes for better, sometimes for worse, to eke a living off the land. Just weeks before, I had found, in a box of my grandmother's old cards and letters and photographs, a photograph of my great-grandmother, Lizzie, taken just before her wedding. In the photo, a dark-headed woman stood in a cabin doorway, one hand on her hip, the other by her side, her dress cinched tightly at her narrow waist. A handkerchief was tucked into the collar, and just below the waistline of her skirt was a small flaw—a tear, perhaps, or a patch. The woman was solemn, her lips full, her eyes deep coal, like the curly hair beneath her wide, straw hat. Next to Lizzie, the cabin boards gaped and yawned.

Lizzie's given name was Elizabeth, but as far back as anyone could remember, people had called her Lizzie, and when she married Weaver Haney on July 24, 1914, they were both so long from these Appalachian hills that they seem to have sprung from the oak trees, from the wide, meandering Pigeon River, from the very earth itself. Lizzie was just seventeen years old, Weaver only nineteen, but already, their histories were deeply intertwined. They knew most of the same people, had known each other's families most of their lives, but they also knew the land as intimately as a lover. They knew the places where it was soft and generous, the places where it was hard and unforgiving, the way the blight would come and wipe out a whole crop of tomatoes, the way a late frost or a dry summer could ruin a crop of beans or corn and leave families hungry, weak, and vulnerable to disease.

After Lizzie and Weaver married, they moved within shouting distance of both their parents' homes, near the country store his parents ran. Weaver built a log cabin with three rooms—a kitchen, a living area, and a bedroom—and a loft. The cabin was heated with a woodstove, which also provided the heat for cooking. There was an outhouse near the garden where they grew corn, beans, cucumbers, tomatoes, and potatoes, staples that would feed their family of twelve throughout the summer and through the long winter months. They also raised chickens and cows and pigs.

Lizzie had her first child when she was nineteen, and she had another child roughly every two years for the next twenty years—ten children born from 1916 to 1935. My grandmother, Adeline, was the fourth child, the second oldest girl. In addition to working beside her husband in the field, Lizzie cleaned house and canned vegetables and churned butter. She made her children's clothes, her own soap, her own cures for ailments of all kinds. She cooked massive cakes of cornbread and pots of pinto beans on top of the woodstove in the living room, and before her daughters were old enough to go to school, they too were lifting heavy skillets full of steaming cornbread, changing babies' diapers, gathering eggs, scrubbing floors.

It was not a life that allowed for much contemplation, but I often wondered what she had been thinking all those years when she was raising her babies, when she was wringing the necks of chickens and chopping and hauling firewood and plowing the fields alongside her husband and sons, when she was hacking black racer snakes to death with her hoe and boiling walnuts to dye her own clothes. Was she happy? Was she glad to have a husband and so many babies to love? Did she ever want to be something other than a wife and a mother, to wear something other than a homemade dress and a homemade apron? Did she ever wonder what the ocean sounded like or how a large city looked at night, all bustling and loud and full of light? Or was she simply too worn out to want anything at all?

These last months at the cabin, these questions had been taking shape in my subconscious, but now here they were, emerging in a vivid, visceral awareness. The knowledge my ancestors had was knowledge passed down from generation to generation, vital information that kept people alive—how to turn a breech calf, when to plant corn, how to roll and dry tobacco, how to wring a chicken's neck, how to salt and store hog meat, how to spray milk on green bean vines to keep off the beetles. Next to them, David and I were just two posers, two farmer wannabes pretending to be the real deal. Wandering among my working students, waiting for David to text me back, I saw that clearly for the first time.

"Keep working," I told them. "Keep going until I tell you to stop."

Write about a time someone you loved disappointed you. Write about a time you disappointed someone you love.

Finally, David texted me again: They're gone.

Keep the dogs up, I texted. All day. They might come back.

My students gathered in groups, sharing their responses to the prompts, telling each other what they loved, what they wanted to know more about. I moved from one group to another, mentally calcu-lating how long it would take the cops to get a search warrant, how long before they came tearing down our driveway, spewing dirt and gravel, sending our chickens flying into their coop, our goats kicking and galloping through the field. How easy it would be, I thought, to run upstairs and grab a gun. How counterintuitive, in fact, to just open the door and let them all in, all those men, all those guns.

Just stay calm, I texted David. **If they come back, you have to stay calm.**

On the day the officers shot our neighbor, two officers were treated for injuries received at the scene. One injury happened when an officer fell through a rotten step. Another officer had an "unexplained small wound to his elbow." In later news briefings, the sheriff would call the incident "incredibly tragic," as if some random event had taken this man's life, as if, by sending that massive show of force to get one man with one still, they had not set up a situation bound to beget violence.

At exactly noon, my students began packing up their notebooks, getting out their cell phones and their lunches. Today was my birth-day, and I had plans to go to lunch with my mother. It was too late to call her and cancel. She was already on her way. So I gathered my belongings and texted David one last time: **I'm leaving now. Remember to stay calm.**

I met my mother at the newly opened Sierra Nevada in Mills River to celebrate. I ordered an open-faced ricotta sandwich, Hop Hunter IPA, and blue-cheese cheesecake for dessert, and my mother and I talked about normal, everyday things, like how open-vat brewing differed from traditional brewing and how unusually dry the summer had been. And when we finished eating, I lingered, staring out the window, sipping my beer, missing my grandmother especially on this day we had so often spent together.

A few weeks before my grandmother died, after one of my overnight stays, we sat quietly at the kitchen table. While I drank coffee, she smashed a prune into sugary oatmeal, smeared Country Crock and Welch's grape jelly onto a slice of Sunbeam bread. With every bite, she took a different pill—a diuretic, a blood pressure pill, a thyroid pill. She was bent and tired, struggling to breathe. Beside her chair, an oxygen tank hummed. And yet, in the stillness of morning, the world to come just beyond her reach, her mind found a vivid spark.

"Do you remember that time we took you to Ruby Falls over in Tennessee?"

Maybe if she had asked me another time, when I had been washing dishes or helping her microwave lunch for her cat, I would not have remembered. But there was something about the quiet morning and the clarity in her voice that sent me tumbling back over forty years, and I was once again in a dark elevator shaft, my fingers clutching my grandfather's gray pants legs, his firm hand resting on my head, the air growing cooler and more damp as the elevator dipped beneath the earth.

"I remember," I told her.

She smiled and took a bite of her toast. Her eyes, once hazel, were milky white, and she stared beyond me to the robins gathering on the rock wall outside.

"There were hiking trails," she said. "And all sorts of exhibits. Do you remember?"

I tried to remember, to release the slippery fabric of my grandfather's pants and leave the elevator, but I was stuck there, four years old and terrified of the groaning, creaking elevator, of the darkness that seeped through my skin and settled in my bones.

"No," I said. "I wish I did, but I don't."

Months later, after she died, I tried again to remember, to find her there in the elevator, to remember what she had said and how she had said it, to recall if she had laughed or tried to comfort me, if she had been scared herself or enjoying the adventure, but as hard as I tried, I could not see her there. Still, I knew she was close by. I felt her presence. Perhaps she was in the dark back corner of the elevator, her arms folded demurely in front of her, her hands swishing the lint from my brother's shirtsleeve. Or maybe she was just above us, waiting to descend, her delicate fingertips poised above the "down" button, a blue vinyl bag dangling from one shoulder. Or perhaps she had gone down before us and was waiting by the water, her body light and shimmery against the dazzling falls.

Grief, it seemed, just kept finding me wherever I was, sweeping down and catching me unaware.

Post-Surveillance Gazpacho

This recipe is slightly adapted from Moosewood Restaurant's Gazpacho a la Guadalajara.

- 2 cups fresh corn, cut from the cob and boiled
- 4 cups tomato juice
- 1 cucumber, peeled and cubed
- 2 avocados, peeled, pitted, and cubed
- 4 tablespoons fresh lime juice
- 1 clove garlic, minced
- 1½ teaspoons ground cumin
- ¼ teaspoons ground cayenne pepper
- Salt
- Fresh cilantro for garnish

Combine all ingredients. Chill 1 to 2 hours before serving.

Chapter Eighteen

IN ORDER TO HAVE CHEESE, you must first have a pregnant goat. And in order to breed a goat, you must first know when your doe is in heat, and since does are usually only in heat for anywhere from six to seventy-two hours, you have to make sure that the buck and doe are together during that crucial time period, a feat that sounds easier than it actually is. Over the next year, while we waited for Holly and Willow to reach full maturity, David and I extensively researched heat cycles in goats. We read *Storey's* again. We read websites and discussion boards. We asked everyone we knew who had ever had a goat or who had ever thought about getting a goat.

A doe in heat may have a swollen vulva. She may have a discharge. She may be more affectionate or vocal than normal. However, like the temperature method of birth control in humans, this method is fallible. Sometimes, goats can have all of those signs but be in "false heat." Sometimes, they can actually be in heat and have few to none of those signs. However, if you put your doe in with a buck, and she "stands" for him to mount her, that is a pretty good sign that your doe is, in fact, fertile. In other words, the only way to know for sure that a doe is in heat is to put her in with a buck.

Assuming we did successfully manage to mate the girls, there would then be the issue of what to do with the babies. *Getting* baby animals was something at which David and I excelled. Getting *rid* of baby animals was not. Doelings should be fairly easy to sell, but bucklings often were not. *Storey's* guide had all sorts of suggestions about how to dispose of them: *Drown them. Butcher them.* And so on. I was sickened at the thought. But what if we ended up with all males, and we couldn't even *give* them away? What would we do then? We had wethered, or castrated, Conway to keep him as a pet, but we didn't have enough room for all the babies the girls could possibly produce.

The day we took Conway and Loretta to the vet to be disbudded, when they were just a week old, we had put them in a dog crate in the back of my car, and as we pulled out of the drive, Ama began a panicked, hysterical yowling. The kids, despondent, inconsolable, screamed back. When we returned that afternoon with the babies, still groggy from their anesthesia, they called to their mother, and as she answered them, they stumbled in the direction of her voice. Then they began head-butting her teats, wagging and flailing and crying in between gulps of milk. Their distress was real, and as I watched them, I thought of those nights when Aaron was a newborn, before we began letting him sleep in our bed. Every evening was traumatic, filled with his gut-wrenching wails.

"Just leave him in his crib. Let him cry himself to sleep," my mother and grandmother both told me.

But I couldn't do it for longer than five minutes. His desperate cries found me wherever I was, and soon, I was running to his crib and lifting him to my breast to soothe him. His face red and contorted, his hands balled into tiny, pink fists, he would nurse and sob, sob and nurse, the two urges intertwined, one indistinguishable from the other.

Of course, baby goats were not baby humans. They would eventually adjust to being separated from their mother, but I also really believed that, like dogs, goats had an emotional landscape, something that far surpassed simple instinct. I had seen too many examples of the goats' tenderness for us and for each other to believe differently.

One day, when Conway and Loretta's playful head-butting had become too rough, Willow had stood near them, watching. Loretta was often the last to get food. Ama still sometimes knocked her off a pallet or into the corner of the stall when she wanted to arrange a premium spot for Conway, and Holly frequently knocked her away from the food trough. She was on the bottom rung of the goat ladder. While Conway and Loretta sparred, Willow's eyes were keenly attentive, and it was clear she was assessing the situation. Finally, she decided that Conway was being too rough. Before Conway could butt Loretta again, Willow placed her body between them and slowly edged Conway away.

What was remarkable was not so much the fact that she intervened but that she evaluated the situation first, then made a conscious decision to do so. In all my years raising animals, I had never seen anything like it, and it was just one more piece of evidence to support what I already intuitively knew: goats are complex social beings. They are capable of feeling sadness, joy, and concern for their herdmates, which made the question of what to do with the does' kids even more complicated. It was a practical question, certainly, but for us, it was also an ethical issue. When would be the best time to take the kids from the mothers? And how could we ease that transition for both mother and kids? Finally, David and I settled those questions the way we resolved all difficult questions: we would cross that bridge when we came to it.

By fall, when Holly and Willow were a year and a half, we had decided that a stud service was the best option for impregnating our does. Stud services worked one of two ways. With "driveway breeding," which did not necessarily occur in a driveway, a doe in heat was visited by a ready and willing buck. The other option was to temporarily board the buck and doe together until the doe completed one or two heat cycles. Boarding was the pricier of the two options, and we really didn't want to leave the girls at another farm. Driveway breeding usually cost about fifty dollars per doe per session, and though it seemed a whole lot like prostituting our girls, we decided this was the best course of action.

We would find some handsome, smelly fellow and wait until the light was just right. Then we would put on some Barry White, pop open a bottle of wine, and put him in with our girls, and...voilà! *Goat cheese*. There was a certain *ick* factor here, the fact that if we chose one buck for more than one doe, the does would sort of be sister wives. But in the interest of creating excellent cheese, we were just going to have to get past that.

We wanted to find a pure Saanen buck to mate with Holly because we thought pure Saanen babies might be easier to sell and because we wanted to preserve her milking lines. For Willow, Ama, and, later, Loretta, we were hoping for a Nigerian dwarf buck. I asked everyone I knew—farmers, old-timers, vendors who sold goat cheese at the local market. No one did driveway breeding. They all bought and kept their own bucks to service their girls. *Service their girls.* This was how we talked now. So we began to consider buying our own buck, though all the goat guides and websites we read cautioned against it. *Bucks stink,* they said. *They can be aggressive. They do disgusting things like pee in their mouths. They will try to mount anything that moves or doesn't move.*

We also knew that bucks needed to be kept separately from does because having a buck in rut near a doe in milk causes the doe to produce hormones that could potentially taint the doe's milk, make it taste, well, *goaty.* Still, we had gotten the girls so that we would have milk, and if we didn't find a buck soon, we would go another year putting money into feed and fencing and bedding and vaccines and so on without getting anything in return. So finally, we began scanning Craigslist for bucks for sale, and one day in the early fall, we came across a beautiful American Dairy Goat Association (ADGA) registered Nigerian dwarf buck for only two hundred dollars.

The buck's name was Crescendo, and the owners lived on three hundred private acres in the midst of DuPont State Forest, a ten-thousand-acre tract of public land. Following our Google directions, David and I headed up the gravel road past the Guion Farm access to the forest. And then we kept going, past deer, wild turkey, the occasional hiker crossing the road. When we came to an intersection where the road headed into Henderson County, we realized we had gone too far and began to backtrack.

Finally, our GPS took us to an unmarked gate at the entrance to an unmarked road. The gate had multiple locks, but Todd, the goat's owner, had told us he would "dummy lock" the gate. It took David several minutes to figure out how to open it, but finally, he unlocked it. We pulled through, then refastened the gate and started up what initially looked like a road, only it wasn't really a road at all, more a two-lane dirt path filled with large rocks and roots and deep gullies.

I had never been off-roading before, but this must have been what it was like, and I fervently hoped my Mountaineer could withstand the trip. Finally, we came to a clearing. On the edge of the clearing was a dilapidated, rusty trailer that brought to mind every single television docudrama I had ever seen about people being kidnapped and held captive in dark, rat-infested sheds. Somehow, the thought of being imprisoned for years without any hope of escape seemed worse than being killed—infinitely more horrifying than being, say, hacked to death with a chainsaw. *Our gun*, I thought. *We should have brought a gun.* We did have Hester, but sliding and slipping around, clawing at the seat, she hardly looked intimidating.

"Turn around!" I told David. "We have to get out of here!"

None of these were particularly rational thoughts. The chances we were going to be kidnapped or murdered with a power tool were slim. The forest was normally one of the places where I felt safest. I biked and hiked out here all the time. Still, terrible things did occasionally happen in the woods—rapes and murders and people who suddenly went missing, never to be seen again.

"That's not it," David said. "That's not the place."

"Turn around!" I said again, but even as I said it, I knew there was nothing to do but go forward.

We were going deeper into the forest, and I wasn't sure that, even if we could turn around, we would be able to get back out. *Always tell someone where you are going.* That was rule #1 of being in the woods, a rule every hiker and biker around here knew. So rather belatedly, I tried to send Alex a text: **We are in DuPont looking at goats.** But the text wouldn't deliver. We had no service. Then, up ahead, where the road dead-ended, was another clearing. As we got closer, I could see a Hummer SUV caked in mud.

"This is it," David said as we pulled in parallel to the Hummer.

Just as I was about to suggest that we make a run for it while we still could, a man and woman emerged from a wooden structure to our right. It was not exactly a house, but it was not *not* a house either. It was more like a house-in-progress, a sort of upscale hunting shelter. David stopped the car. To our left was a playhouse with real windows that looked like something out of *Southern Living*, and next to that, a fenced area with Nigerian dwarf does and a Great Pyrenees. The dog barked frantically as the couple introduced themselves.

Todd and Debbie were young, in their late twenties or early thirties. Todd wore distressed True Religion jeans and a white T-shirt. Debbie wore Versace jeans, a T-shirt, and Coach sunglasses. The diamond on her hand was enormous. Todd stuck out his hand, and I shook it, and then David and Todd shook hands, and then Debbie and I shook hands, and it was such an odd combination of designer labels and purebred goats and prep-school manners meets serial-killer-on-the-run bungalow in the woods that I felt disoriented, as if I had gone bushwhacking and come out on Rodeo Drive.

"Wow. It's beautiful out here," I said. "How long have you guys been living here?"

David grimaced. He wanted to get on with the transaction. But something definitely did not feel right here, and though I was certainly not one to judge someone who might have run into a bit of financial trouble and needed to quickly leave town, I was trying to gauge the situation and determine whether or not we were going to be killed.

Todd seemed to be of David's mindset. He offered monosyllabic responses to my queries, but Debbie was more forthcoming. From our conversation, I gleaned that she and Todd were from Los Angeles. His uncle had purchased a few hundred acres here "for next to nothing" back in the eighties, long before this became a state forest. Todd and Debbie had "recently" moved out here, though I had a hard time pinning him down on how long ago that had actually been. Debbie agreed to move to the house sight unseen, and after they first moved in, they slept in a tent inside the house until the roof could be repaired. Now, his father had had a stroke, and they were moving back to California to care for him. All the goats had to go.

While Debbie and I talked, Todd was fidgety, nervous. He kept checking his phone messages and running back and forth to the house. David too was impatient. He meandered over to the bucks. They were kept in a small, separate enclosure to the side of the house—more like a dog lot than a goat pasture. Debbie, Todd, and I followed him.

"Do you ever see snakes up here?" I asked as we tromped through the tall grass.

"All the time," Todd said. "Copperheads. Rattlesnakes. You name it."

The bucks were heartily devouring a block of alfalfa hay, but when we squatted down next to the fence, they paused and looked up, then came over to greet us. Even through a metal fence, Crescendo's regal studliness was apparent. He had long tan and reddish-orange fur with streaks of white, eyes the color of straw, and a beard that was truly impressive. His bunkmate was polled and tricolored and beautiful as well, but he didn't have Crescendo's iconic, Billy Goat Gruff beard. David stuck his hand in to pet him and immediately yanked back his finger.

"He bit me!"

"He thinks you have a treat," Debbie said.

It wasn't a vicious bite, but even if it had been, it didn't matter. Crescendo was just so buckly. He was all boy, a man's man. David instantly loved him, and while I didn't adore him quite as much as David did—he was musky smelling, his beard tinged yellow with urine—I couldn't make an argument against getting him. He was, indeed, a beautiful buck, as far as bucks go.

"What do you think?" David asked.

"Sure," I said.

We needed time to build a space for him and to get the remaining one hundred dollars, and so, the decision made, David handed Todd a deposit, one hundred dollars in cash. Todd ran inside and scribbled out a receipt on a piece of scrap paper, and then the four of us lingered for a few more minutes while I talked to Debbie: Do you stay out here alone at night? Do you have a gun? The answers were: Yes, and yes, several.

"We have a gun too," I said, perhaps a little too urgently.

Todd gave me a look. David also gave me a look: *Stop. Please stop.* But before I could restrain myself, I was already clarifying. I didn't want them to think I was currently armed. Or maybe I did. Maybe I should leave the meaning ambiguous, but I was too nervous to be quiet.

"I mean, we keep guns at our cabin," I said.

All three of them—Todd, David, and Debbie—stared at me

awkwardly for a few seconds before agreeing. *Yes, yes. Out in the middle of nowhere like this, one might need a gun. You just never knew.* After we scheduled a time to come back to pay the balance and pick up Crescendo, we got in our car and waved goodbye to our new, somewhat shady friends and slipped and bumped our way back to the dummy-locked gate.

Crescendo was perfect—healthy and beautiful and a really good deal. He would make a wonderful sire for our girls. The problem was, we were short on cash. Really short. For days, we had been low on gas for the cars and on groceries, and if we had been being practical, we probably would have realized we just needed to spend our money on food. Instead, we were thinking long-term—about how to stop pouring goat food into animals who were not producing anything for us in return. Of course, we loved them. But they were farm animals, and farm animals are supposed to yield something, to contribute to their upkeep.

So the next morning, David called around until he found a buyer for his rifle, a family member who collected guns and who we knew was a responsible gun owner. Though the sale of the gun was legal, we did the exchange at a local park, which I was pretty certain was not legal, but it was a good halfway point between our houses. As David moved the rifle from the trunk of our car to the trunk of the buyer's car, I scanned the parking lot for cops. Then the three of us hung out and chatted for a few minutes before David pocketed the cash—enough for groceries and the amount due on one hopefully fertile buck.

There was something about the whole thing—the sellers, the deal, the gun trade—that felt sketchy, but we would have no other money for days. In the meantime, Crescendo's owners would be leaving town— if they hadn't already. So the next evening, while I was in a faculty meeting, David took the money we owed, in cash, and headed back to DuPont. That night, long after I was home, David pulled into the drive-way with Crescendo. He opened the hatch, and Crescendo stepped gracefully onto the gravel. David and I stood next to him, admiring the red and orange hues of his coat, his wildly epic beard.

"What are we going to name him?" David asked.

"Merle," I said.

And it was done. Though his mother was a blue-eyed beauty named Viviana and his father a stately buck named Sandstorm, he was just more a Merle sort of guy—shaggy, bearded, haggard. Plus, we just weren't Crescendo kind of people. Merle calmly and quietly followed David into the barn, where he ate some hay, sniffed around a bit, then delicately nibbled on an apple slice I offered him. The girls barely seemed to notice him.

Most websites we had read cautioned against indiscriminately leaving bucks and does together so that you knew when to expect babies. That way, you wouldn't sit around the barn drinking rum and waiting for goats to be born when, in fact, their due dates were nowhere near. So for now, Merle's area was separate from the girls' area, and until his stall was complete, he would sleep in the alcove of the barn, where he could admire the other goats but not make overt sexual advances toward them.

At first, Merle was quiet and affectionate and calm. However, twenty-four hours later, the barnyard turned into a high school classroom. Merle strutted around his section of the pasture, peeing on his beard and into his mouth, curling his lips, and making loud, gurgling sounds. He was a baboon—a goofy, goat baboon. And though he could not possibly have looked more ridiculous, the girls thought he was hotter than hot, a sexy, sweating, stinking football team captain.

The girls paraded past him, tails and heads held high—runway models. They started at one end of the fence, paused next to Merle, then continued another few feet before turning and walking slowly back. Merle loved them all. He ogled and goggled and drooled and peed. He was Hugh Hefner, the king of his very own doe kingdom. At first, he seemed to like Ama best. Then, he went ballistic when Holly sashayed past. Finally, Loretta did her runway walk, and he could barely contain himself. He tried to climb over the fence, squeeze under it, go straight through the metal.

"Isn't that just like a man," I said to David, "to prefer the younger woman?"

Whenever I disparaged Merle, David defended him. *He doesn't smell that bad. Actually, I think he smells pretty good. You just need to stand back when he pees.* And so on.

"He can't help it," David said. "It's just basic biology."

"I sure wish I had known this earlier," I said.

David rolled his eyes. *Here we go again.* But it did seem to me that until this very moment, I had lacked an understanding of some fundamental truths that farm kids must have grown up knowing—how a buck or bull or boar will instinctively and aggressively pursue any ready-and-willing female. Knowing that might have made the rejections and betrayals I experienced in my young dating years a whole lot easier to take.

Goat Cheese

- ½ gallon room-temperature goat's milk
- 1 drop double-strength liquid rennet
- ¼ cup nonchlorinated water
- ⅛ teaspoon mesophilic starter

Strain milk into a large mason jar or other nonmetallic container. Dissolve rennet in water, and add to the milk. Sprinkle in mesophilic starter, and gently stir. Cover, and let the whole mixture percolate for approximately 24 hours. After the curds have separated from the whey (the liquid), dump the whole mixture into butter muslin or double-layered cheese-cloth placed in a colander. Gather the ends of the cloth, tie the remaining cheese into a bundle, and hang for 3 to 4 hours to allow the whey to finish draining. Season with salt (I use about ½ teaspoon sea salt per batch) and herbs/vegetables/fruit, and refrigerate. (Be sure to save all of the leftover whey! There are tons of uses for whey, such as lemon whey pie on page 284.)

This cheese is wonderful plain or with flavor additions such as the following.

JALAPEÑO GARLIC

This is my husband's favorite. He spreads it over everything bagels instead of cream cheese.

- ½ jalapeño, seeded and minced
- ½ to 1 clove garlic, crushed

LEMON

This is amazing on ginger snaps.

- 1 teaspoon finely grated lemon rind*
- 1 teaspoon organic sugar

* Grated lemon rind is also excellent with fresh rosemary, chives, or dill.

GARDEN VEGETABLE

- ¼ red pepper, seeded and chopped
- ¼ green pepper, seeded and chopped
- ½ clove garlic, chopped
- 1 tablespoon finely chopped onion
- A handful of fresh basil, chopped
- 1 to 2 tablespoons shredded carrots

Chapter Nineteen

EVERY MORNING WHEN I WENT down to feed Merle, he had an erection. His penis closely resembled a very, very long hypodermic needle. On his way out of the barn, he gave a couple of hip thrusts, then dispersed his genetic material all over the barn floor.

"My goat cheese!" I said in dismay each time.

We had been warned about this—by every blogger and homesteading forum and farmer we knew. For some reason, though, maybe because Merle had been so sweet and clean and doglike when we first met him, this behavior still surprised me. And even though we had anticipated it, his stench was truly shocking. Sometimes, we could smell him half a mile away. Our eyes stung when we went into the barn. At first, we played a game: How far away from the barn can we smell Merle? The answers: From the driveway. From the beginning of the fence. From inside our closed cars as we drove past the barn.

At least I had expected Merle to smell bad. What I had not anticipated was that David insisted on petting Merle, giving him vigorous, enthusiastic head rubs and side hugs, way more than the little strokes on the nose that I gave him. When David came in from the barn, I could smell him upstairs. When he sat at his desk in the far corner of the great room, I could smell him all the way in the kitchen. Finally, he got tired of listening to me complain about the smell and began keeping a change of clothes downstairs—which helped a little, but not much.

Ama was the first girl to go on a "date" with Merle, which was really more like a conjugal visit. Our plan was to eventually have a completely separate pasture for the bucks, but for now, the girls and guys were separated only by a fence and a couple of gates. Ama had been enthusiastically wagging her tail and backing up to the fence and making all sorts of low, growling sounds in response to Merle's ridiculous displays, so we took this as a sign that the moment was right. David opened her gate and walked her into Merle's area. Then we sat in lawn chairs between the fences and watched.

Immediately, Ama and Merle began circling each other, yelping and howling and hooting in a baboon-like fashion until they were a merry-go-round, running around and around in circles, their sides pressed together. Then they separated, backed away, leapt into the air, and landed in a head-butt.

"She's going to hurt him," I told David.

"No, she's not."

Our chairs were pulled close to the fence, and we each sipped a mug of coffee. I felt creepy, voyeuristic, but according to all the expert advice we had read, we were supposed to watch and wait for the doe to "stand" for the buck to allow him to mount her. Then we were to count the number of "pokes." It was a decidedly unromantic term, but we had been told that three pokes were necessary to be sure the doe had a good chance of being pregnant. Three pokes or one hour together, whichever came first.

Once, Merle seemed to get a poke in, though Ama was edging slowly away at the time, so we weren't sure whether or not to count it.

"Was that standing?" we asked each other. "Did you see a poke?"

We couldn't be sure. We had also been told to look for her back to arch as a sign of successful mating, but that was not readily apparent either. Once again, we knew on an intellectual level what to look for, but on a much more important level—in reality—we had no idea what to expect. In any case, after this one episode, the two goats stood back and regarded each other from a distance. Then Merle turned his back on Ama and focused his full attention on his bucket of hay. They were done. David set his cup on his chair and opened the gate for Ama, who silently scurried out and into the girls' area. Altogether, the experience was anticlimactic and vaguely unsatisfying. We had not even finished our coffee.

One night in August, David and I were in the kitchen, drinking mojitos made from mint David grew on the roof, when a slender, pencil-like tail trailed from under the corner wall. I sat at a barstool at the counter, and David sat at the kitchen table with his back to the wall.

"Is that a snake going into the wall?" I asked. "I think that's a snake."

"Oh, yeah," David said, not even turning around. "It's ringneck season."

"What do you mean, 'It's ringneck season'?"

"I mean, I talked to the landlords, and they said they always had a problem with ringnecks this time of year."

Although I was astounded, incredulous even, I was not hysterical. Perhaps the rum numbed my reaction, or perhaps I was getting used to this place, to the unlikely events that all seemed to fall loosely under the term *adventure* nowadays. At least David had not said it was copperhead season. Ringnecks were, for the most part, harmless.

The scientific name for a ringneck is *Diadophis punctatus*. They are slim and fairly small, around a foot in length. Usually gray or black, they have slender bright bands around their necks, like collars. Ringneck dating involves a male rubbing his closed mouth along a female's body. Then, he bites the female around her neck ring and moves them both to an ideal position so he can insert his sperm into her vent. A love bite.

"What do you mean, you've talked to the landlords?" I said. "Have there been other snakes?"

"A few."

David downed his drink, then sauntered into the great room and returned carrying a broom and a small, beige trash can. Just then, the snake's tail disappeared into the gap between the floor and the wall.

We watched for a minute, waiting to see if it would come back out, and when it didn't, David sat back down.

I had not moved. The barstool I was sitting on was one of three we brought from the old house. At first, even though I wanted them, I had refused to bring the stools with us. It just seemed like bad form. The stools had been in the house when we purchased it. They came with the house, and since the house was no longer ours, these were not our stools. It was proper foreclosure etiquette. So my reasoning went. But then David said we had lost $150,000 in equity in the house and I should just take the goddamn stools if I wanted them. So I did.

"A few snakes?" I asked David. "How many is a few?"

"Four or five," he said. "They're harmless."

"You have found five snakes in this house?"

"Just in my area."

"Since when?"

"Oh, the last few days."

"You have found five snakes in this house over the last few days, and you didn't tell me? Why didn't you tell me?" I asked.

David smashed the mint leaves in the bottom of his glass with a spoon, then licked the sugar off the side of the glass.

"Why would I tell you that?" he said.

Because I'm your wife, I wanted to say. *Because I live here too, and I need to know what to be prepared for.* But if there was one thing I had learned over the past three years, it was that no matter how hard you tried to be prepared, what you most fretted and worried about, you were never really prepared. You prepared for one thing, and then another, totally unexpected thing happened. So I supposed David had a point. There were enough other things around here for me to lose sleep over. No need to add a harmless ringneck to the mix.

Ringneck Season Mojitos

- 6 ounces light rum
- 6 tablespoons fresh lime juice
- 4 tablespoons sugar
- Several mint sprigs
- Club soda
- Fresh lime

Combine rum, lime juice, sugar, and mint sprigs, crushing mint in liquid. Fill glass with club soda and ice, if desired. Garnish with fresh lime slices and more mint.

Chapter Twenty

By the end of September, we were desperate to find a bunkmate for Merle. Ideally, we wanted a Saanen that could also be a sire for Holly. Purebred Saanens would be easier to sell than Nigerian dwarf–Saanen crosses (or mini-Saanens). Plus, we had seen photos of crossbred Saanens online, and some were precious, but others were, well, odd looking. So David posted a wanted ad for a Saanen buck on Craigslist, and after several weeks, a woman finally responded. She had a pure, seven-month-old, ADGA-registered Saanen buck named Alf, the single offspring of their doe. Once again, we threw the dog crate in the back of my Mountaineer and set out to a tiny, rural community in the North Carolina Piedmont. After driving for almost three hours, David and I finally came to a winding gravel road lined on either side with cow pastures.

"Is this it?" David asked.

I held my phone, twisting and turning it, but the GPS was frozen, stuck on the last major road it actually recognized. I switched to a map and squinted to look at the road names.

"I think so," I said.

David tried to remember what exactly Amber, Alf's owner, had told him. Something about a white fence. Something about a deep curve.

"Did you not write any of that down?" I asked.

Clearly, he had not. Finally, we came to a white fence and a curve. A large No Trespassing sign was tacked to a tree.

"This is it," David said, heading up the steep drive.

At the crest of the hill, we came to a house, a small brick ranch. A youngish man in workout clothes was weed-eating along the front walkway. A German shepherd paced in a five-by-five pen in the yard, and a thin Saanen doe wandered loose, nibbling grass. David eased to a stop next to a large truck with a yellow state tag. The words Sheriff's Department were emblazoned in black letters on the side.

"Shit," David said. "He's a cop."

"Shit," I said.

Not all cops were bad. We knew that. But we had spent enough of the last few years on the wrong side of the law to have formed some negative impressions. It was like eating a big plate of spaghetti just before you came down with a bad stomach bug. You didn't necessarily blame the spaghetti, but then again, after vomiting chunks of tomato sauce and noodles all night, you sort of had an aversion to pasta after that.

Now, watching the lone doe wandering through the yard, the German shepherd barking frantically and lunging at the gate, I immediately wished we had not come. The doe was too thin, with only a German shepherd for a herdmate and no fenced area for grazing. David turned off the car, but he didn't get out. He looked at me, then back at the man who had glanced up at us then continued weed-eating.

"I don't know," I said.

"What do you mean, you don't know?"

"I just don't know about this."

"Do you want a buckling or not?" David asked. "This is the only one we're going to be able to get in time."

What I wanted was the perfect buckling, raised by a warm and fuzzy, liberal-minded family who believed in companion goats and secure fences. I wanted a goat that had been raised with a Great Pyrenees instead of a German shepherd, a goat who had an owner who was a little less paramilitary-esque. That's what I wanted, but it seemed our lives now were always about a compromise between what we really wanted and what we could actually get. The window for breeding Holly was closing. She had already been in heat for two days, and she might not go into heat again this season. We needed a buckling, and we needed it today.

So David hollered to the cop, who finally put down the weed-eater and came over to our car, and after a brief, somewhat cool exchange, the three of us—David, me, and the cop—determined we were at the wrong house. Amber was, indeed, the cop's wife, and Alf was, indeed, their goat, but the goat was at Amber's sister house, a mile or so away. Apparently, he had spent the last few weeks on one extended date with Amber's sister's doe. The cop was heading to the gym, which was near his sister-in-law's, and he offered for us to follow him to the correct location.

We caravanned down the driveway and through "town," such as it was, long stretches of roads with nothing but mobile homes and churches and dirt patches for front yards. Finally, we turned down yet another gravel road until we reached a small pond, then a bridge. To the right was a small pasture, and in front of the rambling log house, a group of people had gathered—Amber, Amber's sister, and Amber's three kids, including one sandy-haired toddler wearing nothing but a diaper, his feet completely caked in red mud. And romping through the grass—leaping up and down, head-butting, chasing, and nuzzling one another—were a young boy and a lanky Saanen buckling, two spirited buckling-boys.

"Oh no," David said as we pulled to a stop. "That's the kid."

On our way down, when we had called Amber to let her know we were running late, she had told us that was no problem whatsoever. It would give her time to get her son out of school so he could tell Alf goodbye. *Dear God*, we had said. *That's awful*. We had almost turned around right then and there but, we reasoned, if the goat was going to be sold, he might as well be sold to us. We had just hoped the goodbyes would be over before we arrived, that the child wouldn't have to watch us cart his pet away. But that was not to be. The scene that followed, therefore, was both expected and unexpected—the boy, about ten, lean as Alf, with freckles on the bridge of his nose, his jaw trembling, his eyes wet and round; the cop, now no longer a cop but a father, one arm slung around his son's shoulder, telling us all that Alf would be fine, the boy would be fine.

"It's just that they've played together every day since Alf was born," Amber explained. "He comes in from school and just runs to that goat."

Again, we hesitated. But I pictured the doe back at the other house, alone in the yard, an easy victim for predators, and here Alf was, running loose as well. Plus, he was thin—very thin—and I wondered if he had had enough to eat. David looked at me. I nodded, and he went back to the car for his wallet. Once the formalities were complete—the cash exchanged, the papers signed—the boy buried his face in Alf's soft fur and tenderly ran his palm over the goat's head. His entire being trembled—his lips, his bony shoulders, his pale, boy fingers. I put my arm around him.

"We're going to take good care of him," I said. "I promise."

The boy nodded but said nothing while David and the boy's father lifted Alf into the crate in the back of our car. As we pulled away, the boy and his mother stood in the drive, his face hidden in her T-shirt, her hand smoothing his hair. Abashed and close to tears myself, I looked away.

Later, of course, after the goat got sick, I would realize how wrong I was, how deeply flawed my thinking was, but in that moment, I truly believed that, in the long run, the buckling would be better off with us—surrounded by a protective fence and plenty of goat friends and fed a steady diet of hay and grain. By the time we hit the main road, I was sure of it. And by the time we saw the hazy blue outline of mountains, I had shaken off the image of the grieving boy, and Alf had a new name, a name that continued our somewhat hit-or-miss bluegrass and country music theme, and though we debated naming him Ralph after Ralph Stanley, because that rhymed with Alf and might be easier for him to learn, we figured goats didn't really know their names anyway. So we named him Waylon after Waylon Jennings. And as if to applaud the rightness of our choice, just as we turned off the interstate at the Flat Rock exit, my favorite Waylon Jennings tune came on the radio—"I'd Love to Lay You Down." David cranked it up, and I, certain that this was a good omen, sang along.

At home, we unloaded Waylon into his stall, then offered him grain and water. Then, before we even went inside the house, we decided to put him with Holly. It did not occur to us that we were asking too much of him, that a five-month-old goat that had just been ripped from his family, then dumped in a barn with strange goats might need a bit of time to get his bearings. Nor did we recall at that moment the lesson we had learned from immediately introducing Ama to the other goats. We just figured a date was a unique situation. What young, robust, fertile, heterosexual guy wouldn't want to hook up with a hot girl on his first night away from home?

Plus, a storm was imminent. Though there was no rain yet, dark clouds gathered at the tops of the ridges, and there was the low rumbling of not-too-distant thunder. David hustled Merle into his new stall, then opened Waylon's door into the yard. Waylon ambled cautiously out, head down. Then David opened Holly's gate and led her into the conjugal chamber. Standing just outside the fence, between the girls' pasture and the boys', giving them what we hoped was a respectable distance, we waited. Based on our experience with Ama and Merle, we fully expected them to rush at each other, to devour one another like a couple of ecstasy-popping teenagers. Instead, they stood several feet apart, completely silent, Holly bored and distracted, Waylon wide-eyed and overwhelmed.

The air was full of green smells—fresh cut hay and rain. From where David and I stood just outside the fence, I could see the rain coming. A giant, gray wave began at the house and moved down the driveway toward the field, then the barn. Goats hate rain more than just about anything, and as the torrential sheets headed our way, Waylon and Holly edged close to the barn, under the overhang, close to each other but not touching. Waylon gazed longingly toward the barn door. Holly stared expectantly at me. Clearly, we were done for the day.

"Maybe he's too young," I said.

David sighed and headed back into the pen. He managed to get the goats back into their respective stalls just in time. Lightning flashed between the pallet slats, and thunder shook the hollow. And then came the wind—terrific gusts that shook the oak trees and rattled the barn. Unless I wanted to make a run for it, I was going to be here for a while, so while David ran around, feeding the girls and doing repairs, I crouched next to Waylon.

"You're okay, buddy," I told him, rubbing his flank. "Everything is all right."

He looked away, his gaze directed at the barn wall. And then he stood and turned his back to me. The first time, I thought it was unintentional. Maybe he was just shifting positions. But then he did it again. And again. Whenever I moved to his front, he turned his back to me. Whenever I tried to pet him, he flinched and backed away. Not easily dissuaded, I offered him grain and hay and licorice treats, but every time I held out my hand, he clamped his jaws shut and looked away. The mere sight of the plastic licorice container caused all of the other goats to begin a frenetic clamoring, but the noise only seemed to make Waylon more quiet, more withdrawn.

Crouched in the far corner, his head against the doorframe, he was almost unrecognizable as the high-spirited buckling who had, just hours before, been joyfully head-butting his young friend. He wanted nothing to do with me or David, and it would be days before he allowed me to pet him, weeks before he would come over to greet me when I came into the barn. As we shut him into his stall that night, I thought of the boy who had witnessed his birth, who had chased him through tall grass and cradled him in his skinny boy arms, and I knew that Waylon must certainly have been thinking of him too.

The next morning, when Holly still seemed to be in heat, David and I decided to try her on another date with Waylon. We weren't too optimistic about the outcome, but we figured it couldn't hurt to try. We put them back in the pasture together and, once again, pulled up our chairs to watch. Instantly, the air felt different, charged with a quiet yet unmistakable energy.

At first, Waylon eyed Holly from afar, but his eyeing was no longer remote. It was eager, expectant. His ears went up. His entire body quivered. Like a bat honing in on a mouse, he cocked his head in Holly's direction. He leaned into the air and sniffed hard. Then out came the needlelike erection, and before I even saw him move, he was on top of her. I waited for her to try to throw him off, to dart toward the gate, but instead, she stood calmly and quietly, if not exactly enthusiastically, while he completed the act. It took three, five seconds, tops. And then, finally, there it was—a slight but definite arch of her spine.

"Bingo!" David said.

But I wanted to see a few more times just to be sure. After all, we had driven six hours round trip and spent our last bit of cash on this goat. I wanted to be guaranteed some goat cheese out of the deal. Fortunately, Waylon was happy to oblige. He completed the act four times within ten or fifteen minutes. In between lovemaking sessions, he stood with his head resting on Holly's back, a postcoital goat cuddle. And even more amazingly, our wild and unruly Holly let him do it. She cuddled him back. I got out my phone and snapped a million photos of them standing there together, his narrow white head resting in the crook of her back, her eyes, for once, soft and tranquil. All in all, it was decidedly different from Ama's manic mating with Merle, and when we finally took Holly back to her stall, she seemed already decidedly more maternal—older, wiser, more graceful and serene.

One morning a few days later, I started down to the barn and heard such an agonized yelling that I bolted down the drive and threw open the barn door. Loretta stood in the middle of her stall, screaming every bit as loudly as her mother had the day we got her. When I let her out of the barn, she ran to the fence, wagging her tail and positioning her posterior next to Merle's face, an act that sent Merle into a frenzy of sputtering and hollering and peeing and lip curling. He repeatedly threw himself at the fence. He tried to jump over, squeeze under, barrel through the wires. On the other side, Loretta attempted the same with equal vigor. And when it became apparent to them that they could not get to each other, Loretta let forth a shrill, tormented wail that continued for three straight days and three straight nights.

We planned to eventually move the bucks completely away from the girls, but for now, they were within sight during the day and within smelling distance of each other at all times, which meant that hormones were constantly flying in both the girls' dorm and the boys' dorm, which is how I had come to think of the different areas of the barn. Whenever Loretta began her wailing, about once every three weeks, we settled in for three days of lust so intense, it made our own dating years seem tame in comparison. It was as embarrassing as it was fascinating to watch. At the end of those three days, however, Loretta calmly walked back to her stall and joined her family, as if she had been under a spell and was suddenly released from its power.

Willow's heat cycles, however—like everything about Willow—
were more understated, more dignified. When I noticed her quietly
standing near the fence and wagging her tail one day, I was heading
out to go on a bike ride, but I texted David and asked him to put her
in with Merle. His report that night: she had stood. Merle had fulfilled
his role. Back arching may or may not have occurred.

"What do you mean it may or may not have occurred?" I asked.

"I just couldn't tell for sure," he said.

Over the next couple of weeks, Ama went into heat two more
times—or seemed to go into heat. She was routinely so loud and
demanding, it was hard to tell, so we put her back in with Merle two
more times, which meant that if she were pregnant, we wouldn't know
her exact due date for sure—again. David also wanted to put Holly
back in with Waylon, but I was certain, especially when she missed
her next heat cycle, that that one session had done the trick. Now, if
everything went as planned, we would have three pregnant does and a
slew of new kids by February.

Lemon Whey Pie

Filling

- 1½ cups whey, divided
- 1 cup sugar
- 3½ tablespoons cornstarch
- 3 egg yolks (save whites)
- 1½ tablespoons butter, melted
- ½ teaspoon salt
- ¼ cup fresh lemon juice

Preheat oven to 350 degrees. Bring 1 cup whey to boil in medium saucepan. In separate bowl, whisk sugar, cornstarch, and remaining ½ cup cold whey until it forms a smooth paste. Add paste mixture into the hot whey, stirring constantly until it thickens. In another small bowl, lightly beat egg yolks, and combine with butter, salt, and lemon juice. Pour a small amount of the hot whey mixture into egg yolk mixture, and stir. Add this mixture to the mixture in the saucepan and cook two minutes, stirring constantly.

MERINGUE

- 3 egg whites
- ¼ teaspoon cream of tartar
- ¼ teaspoon salt
- ½ teaspoon vanilla
- 6 tablespoons sugar

Beat egg whites, cream of tartar, salt, and vanilla in a bowl until foamy. Add sugar, one tablespoon at a time, beating thoroughly after each addition. Continue beating at medium-high speed until stiff, sharp peaks form.

TO ASSEMBLE

Pour filling into prebaked pie shell. Top with meringue, and smooth to seal edges along the pie crust. Bake in preheated oven at 350 degrees for 12 to 15 minutes.

Chapter Twenty-One

By LATE FALL, THE DACHSHUND calendar hanging in our kitchen began to look like a bizarre fertility clinic spreadsheet. In between my hair appointments and David's dentist appointments, I wrote "Lottie in heat," "Willow exposed to Merle," "Ama in heat," "Ama in heat?" "Ama in heat!" and so on. We also recorded the goat's weights and measurements, their birthdays, their history of worming and vaccines. This thing that had once been a new hobby, a distraction to help us forget everything we had lost, now seemed an integral part of our lives. Even though we didn't get paid in money, farming began to seem more and more like a job, and for the first time in our lives, David and I both loved going to work.

Instead of the corner office I had at the college—the one that smelled like coffee and floor wax, where students cried about their ex-lovers and argued about their grades while I sat in a black swivel chair, wearing REI dresses and flower-print bifocals from Whole Foods, trying achieve that perfect balance between being professional yet approachable, encouraging yet firm—now I worked in a barn. No matter how cold it was outside, the barn was warm and cozy, filled with the heat from so many bodies, and after my morning chores were done, I often lingered there, rubbing the goats' noses and drinking in their musky scent.

On those mornings, I often thought of my grandparents, of the sprawling farms from their childhoods that had been parceled out and divided among their many siblings, then finally sold for next to nothing in order to pay other expenses. My grandfather began work at Champion International in Canton in 1935 when he was eighteen years old. He only had a sixth-grade education, and he worked as a crane operator, lifting massive rolls of paper onto the loading dock for the train. The job paid well enough, but for a man who had grown up on a farm in Sandy Mush, who had spent his childhood baling hay and plowing fields, mill tasks—the dark confinement of the plant, the monotony of the work— was contrary to his nature. He craved fresh air and sunshine, something to do with his hands, he got to do that sort of work only twice in his lifetime, both times when he was laid off from Champion.

The first time, when he was not even twenty, he got a job in Houston digging pipelines. My grandmother got a job as a clerk in a general store. They had been there a year when my grandfather got the call to come back to work at Champion. He walked off his job and went straight to the general store.

"Come on," he told my grandmother. "We're going home."

The second time, when he was in his early twenties, he found work building the Blue Ridge Parkway as part of Roosevelt's Civil Conservation Corps. He had worked only one day when the foreman from Champion called to ask him to return to work. My grandmother took a taxi all the way from Canton to the parkway to give him the news. Years later, my grandfather still talked about how beautiful the parkway was that day, about the cool breeze off the mountains, the feel of the ax and pick in his hands, the sweaty, grueling work that was somehow purifying, and there must have been times when he regretted throwing down his tools and returning to the tedium of plant life. Still, he had a wife and two kids to support by then, and mill work was something he could depend on.

Then, one sultry summer day in 1946, when he was not yet thirty years old, my grandfather was sitting at the breakfast table one morning when he passed out cold. He had been drinking coffee, and he simply set down his mug, closed his eyes, and fell out of his chair. My grandmother was standing at the stove, frying sausage and scrambling eggs, and when she heard him hit the wood floor, she ran to him, shaking him and screaming his name while their two coal-headed babies looked on. My grandfather was so clammy and cool, so utterly still, she truly believed he was already gone. Nonetheless, she called for help, and while she sat on the floor with her husband, waiting for the doctor to arrive, something that had heretofore been just a fleeting shadow in her thoughts began to take form and shape, to grow into a horrifying and fully realized truth: her husband was an addict.

For the better part of two years, my grandfather had been popping handfuls of pain pills, moving groggily through one day and then the next. He kept pills on his nightstand, pills in his pants pocket, pills in his car. He didn't count them. He just took a "few" or "some," however many the occasion seemed to demand. By the time the doctor arrived that day, my grandmother had formulated her thoughts into words, and when she told the doctor where the remaining pills were and approximately how many he had taken, the doctor gave him an injection to "roust him up." By the time my grandfather regained consciousness, my grandmother had called her brother-in-law to report her husband's condition. Her brother-in-law, Bill, in turn, had called their father, and by the time my grandfather was back at work that evening, my great-grandfather was paying a visit to his son's dealer, the town doctor. I never knew my great-grandfather, but by all accounts, he was a formidable man, and whatever he said to the doctor must have been convincing because for the next sixty years, my grandfather was clean.

Standing in the barn one morning, my cheek resting against Willow's soft fur, I thought of how soul-zapping that sort of work must have been for a man who wanted nothing more than to be outside, a man who was smart and funny and savvy, who could have been anything he wanted to be, if only he had had an education and some money in the bank. My grandfather had been dead for five years when my grandmother told me about the pills, and now I knew why he had taken them. It came to me as simply and as surely as if he had told me himself, the whole story. It was as clear as the creek gurgling outside and the squawking of hens in the coop.

I knew how one day he had needed something to take the edge off the tedium, to float through yet another monotonous shift. How, once he started taking them, he didn't know how to stop. How he was twenty-seven years old with a wife and two young kids he adored, but that when he allowed himself to think, he saw his whole, long future stretching ahead of him. He saw himself, day after day, year after year, lifting bales of paper onto a crane and dumping them onto a loading dock. The whole idea must have filled him with a longing so intense, it was physically painful, and even when he finally accepted his lot in life, the yearning—not for another wife or different kids or a bigger house or nicer car, but for a day's work that left him feeling larger and more dignified instead of diminished and chipped away—must have stayed with him, the mysterious aches and pains a reminder of all that had passed him by.

All my life, I had had a safety net beneath me, people who had helped me get this far and who would be there again if I really needed them, if I were sick or one of my kids were sick, if I needed food or a temporary place to stay. We had never asked my parents or David's parents to bail us out of our tax situation. They were comfortable but not wealthy, and forking over the type of money we needed just wasn't feasible. They had given us plenty to get me started in life, and they had paid for plenty more along the way. We were lucky, way luckier than my grandparents had been, way luckier than many people who had lost their homes or who had never had homes to begin with. I knew that.

I also knew I was not made of the same stuff with which my grandfather had been made. I did not have his grit or determination, his selflessness, his wisdom and foresight. Perhaps, years ago, if I had known how bad things were going to turn out, I would have chosen another profession, worked longer and harder, been a better provider for my family. But now I had spent years training and working as a teacher and building my writing portfolio, and I held to the stubborn belief that the way out of this was not through abandoning my life's work but by digging in and working harder. Both of my grandparents had strongly encouraged my brother and me to get an education. They had celebrated our successes in school and in our careers, and I believed they would have encouraged me to keep going, to continue believing in work that fed both the body and the spirit, to achieve things that they had never had a chance to achieve.

Years before, when our children were in middle school and high school, David and I had taken our kids on a trip out West. In Utah, on our way to Salt Lake City, we had strolled along the rim of Bryce Canyon, admiring the cacti, the ponderosas, the magical, glowing hoodoos below. And then we came upon a grove of bristlecone pines, *Pinus longaeva*. They were twisted and stark, unimpressive, not at all like the magnificent white pines from home. But then we read the park service sign that told the story of these ancient pines. When the trunk of a bristlecone begins to decay, the tree, in an amazing feat of self-preservation, stretches its branches to the ground, forming a new trunk. It recreates itself. It is reborn. I had carried that image with me over the years, of the tired, mangled limbs untangling themselves and reaching for the ground. Hopeful. Tenacious.

What did it mean for me to be hopeful now? I wasn't sure. I only knew that though farming had changed David and me as human beings, made us kinder and gentler, more grateful for each other and for what we had, I still needed something else, something to grab on to, some other meaningful work. Up until this point, my teaching "career" had done little to improve our quality of life, and now I desperately needed to find something new, something beyond the farm that I could do to improve our financial situation.

So that December, I told the humanities division chair at the college that I would not be back the following semester. Though I would continue to lead writing workshops at other places, I was done with teaching freshman composition, finished with being a permanent adjunct. The whole affair was just too frustrating, too demoralizing, and it was doing nothing to truly improve our lives. I had been writing blog posts for the Huffington Post, and now I wrote about the plight of adjuncts, an emphatic protest to the practice of using adjuncts in place of full-time faculty, and early the next year, I began looking into low-residency master of fine arts (MFA) programs.

My bank balance was exactly $4.57. Taking out loans and going even further into debt was not the most practical solution to our problems, but I needed to do something different, something radical, and this was all I could think to do. It was a risky move. I could end up further in debt with no better career options. However, an MFA was considered a terminal degree in my field, and it might help me secure a better teaching position. Given our circumstances, it was really the only shot I had at a better job, and on a personal level, I thought that perhaps I had a story to tell, one that others might read if I could ever just get it right. When I was accepted to my top choice of programs, Vermont College of Fine Arts, I took out a government loan for the entire cost of tuition—minus a six-hundred-dollar scholarship. Then I took a deep breath and began.

I would be fifty before I finished the program. When I was in my twenties and even my thirties, fifty had been unimaginable—a lifetime away. I had so much to do before then. I had kids to raise, a career to tend to, so much to do and see and accomplish. But now, here I was on the cusp of fifty, and the only thing I really knew was how very much I did not know, how much I would never know.

"If you could go back to any age, any age at all," I asked my grandmother on my forty-fourth birthday, "what age would you choose?"

"Fifty-five," she said without hesitation.

She was ninety years old then, and her answer surprised me then as it did now. Why not seventeen or twenty-five or thirty-two? Why, if you could go back, wouldn't you go to a time when you had your whole life ahead of you, when you were young enough to alter the course of your future, to make better choices, be a better person? Perhaps she was simply being kind to me, choosing an age that was still ahead of me, giving me something to look forward to. Or perhaps this was one of the lessons she had learned in her long life: do not be too greedy, even in your wishing.

Goat's Milk Custard

This recipe is adapted from Guy Fieri's Goat Milk Crème Caramel recipe.

- ⅓ cup sugar
- 2 cups goat's milk
- ½ cup plus 1 tablespoon sugar
- 3 egg yolks, beaten
- 2 whole eggs, beaten
- ¼ teaspoon vanilla

Preheat oven to 350 degrees. Pour ⅓ cup sugar into a small saucepan, and heat slowly until the sugar melts and turns a dark brown. (Be careful not to burn!) Divide evenly among four ramekins.

Put milk and remaining sugar in a pan, and bring to a simmer. Combine egg yolks, whole eggs, and vanilla in a mixing bowl. Whisk until foamy. Temper by adding a small amount of the hot milk to the egg mixture. Slowly stir the egg mixture into the hot milk in the pan. Divide the mixture evenly among the four ramekins, and place in a roasting pan. Fill the pan with water until the ramekins are three-quarters covered. Bake 35 minutes or until the custards are set.

Chapter Twenty-Two

I WAS UPSTAIRS AT MY desk writing when David texted me: **Come down.** I normally did the morning routine at the barn, but this morning, it was raining, and I had convinced David to do it. I jumped up and ran downstairs, where David, still wearing his boots and barn coat, was standing by the door. Something was wrong.

"Waylon is acting funny."

"What do you mean, funny?"

"He's crying."

Crying seemed a fairly general symptom, indicative of any number of things, but it turned out Waylon was also standing at an odd angle, his rear legs spread, his body arching forward. Though we had never had a critically ill goat, I knew that goats were not like dogs. They didn't act ill one moment, then hop up and run around as if nothing had ever happened. The most pressing issue we had ever had was the previous winter when I was in Florida visiting my brother. Willow had gotten out of the pasture and eaten a few rhododendron leaves before David could stop her. Almost instantly, she had projec-tile vomited—spewing stomach acids and regurgitated rhododendron leaves all over David's jacket. But then, just as quickly, the toxins expelled, she recovered. Normally, though, whenever a goat was sick, it was cause for concern. A goat could go from fine to dead within a span of a few hours, so any signs of illness needed prompt attention. I threw on my shoes and followed David down to the barn.

Waylon, who had until this point been decidedly nonvocal, stood in his stall loudly bellowing. There was nothing obviously wrong with him, or rather, nothing that was obvious to us other than his odd stance. Concerned about the cost of taking him to the vet, we decided to wait a little while to see if he improved. Maybe he just had a bad case of indigestion. Maybe this would pass. In a couple of hours, when it became obvious his distress was not easing, David pulled up my Mountaineer, threw a tarp and straw down in the back, and led Waylon out to the car using Hester's leash. I jumped in the passenger seat.

The rain was by now torrential, and David smelled like a wet buck as of course did Waylon. The odor was nauseating and added to my growing sense of foreboding. This was not good—definitely not good. Waylon stood crying in the back of the car for the entire forty-minute drive. Periodically, I turned in my seat to face him.

"It's okay," I told him. "You're going to be okay."

But I was not at all sure he would be, and neither was he. His cries were agonized, his eyes wide and eerily bright. Finally, because my reassurances didn't seem to help, I turned back around and looked out the window. The rest of the way, David and I rode in silence, the only sounds Waylon's pitiful cries and the scratch-scratching of the wipers on the windshield.

We had been to Dr. Harris's office a couple of times before, once when we took Conway and Loretta to be disbudded and another time when Conway and Loretta were both a couple of months old. Loretta had had a bad cough, Conway a touch of a cough, so we had taken them both in, just to be sure. In our previous lives, we were accustomed to vets who looked a lot like hospital radiologists. They wore khaki pants and button-down oxfords and long, white lab coats. If we brought a dog in for a rabies shot, we could expect to pay for an office visit—around forty dollars—plus the shot. When we first met Dr. Harris, we felt like we were in a movie. Tall and broad-shouldered, clad in jeans, a loose flannel shirt, and cowboy boots, she was nothing like our previous vets. In fact, she was unlike anyone either of us had ever met. When she came in to examine Loretta, she had one arm was in a sling, a purply-black eye, and a nasty gash on her forehead.

"What happened?" I asked.

"Oh, this?" she said, touching just beneath the stitches on her face. "I had a run-in with an angry bull. He tried to crush me against the fence."

From that moment on, we adored her. She was both tough and tender, and when she readily diagnosed and treated Loretta's pneumonia, we could not have been more grateful.

When we got to Dr. Harris's office with Waylon, we pulled

around back, and David led Waylon in the rear entrance. Inside, David helped a vet technician, a slender blond woman wearing jeans and a T-shirt, settle Waylon into a kennel in the back room. The kennel was one of maybe eight or ten large cages, many of them filled with barking dogs. Unable to witness Waylon's suffering any longer, I retreated to the hallway while David and the technician stood next to Waylon's kennel.

"Has he been peeing?" the technician asked David after a moment.

"Of course," he said.

"Sure," I called from the hallway.

"Well, I'm just wondering," the technician said, "because it looks like he is straining to pee."

David stood in the doorway with his back to me. His jacket and hair were soaked. His pants and work boots were covered with straw and mud and spots of blood from where Waylon had recently lost a scur, a small bit of unattached horn that sometimes grows after disbudding. I wore muddy jeans, my grandfather's flannel shirt, and an old pair of hiking boots with soles so loose, they flapped up and down when I walked. I had not even combed my hair or brushed my teeth, and together, David and I looked disheveled, or perhaps worse than disheveled—like we had been lost for weeks in the wilderness. David looked from Waylon to the technician and back to Waylon. And what had seemed a deep mystery only moments before seemed so very obvious.

"Oh my God," he said. "You're right."

And right away, I knew that was bad—very bad. I had read all about how males, particularly wethered males, should not have too much grain because it can cause urinary calculi, or kidney stones. The stones can then block the urethra, and if the blockage is not somehow relieved, the bladder can rupture, quickly killing the goat.

"How much grain have you been feeding him?" the technician asked David.

David kept the goats supplied with hay, but I was the one who determined the amount of grain they were fed. According to the online guide I had used since we had gotten the goats—for feeding recommendations as well as pretty much everything else—young, unwethered males could have three cups of grain per day until they had reached one year of age. What I had discounted, but which I would later learn was extremely important, was that the guide also recommended giving bucks a regular dose of ammonium chloride, which helped break up any stones that might form. Because Waylon had looked so thin when we got him, I had been feeding him the same amount I had been feeding the does—three cups of grain in the morning along with a cup of beet pulp and a cup of sunflower seeds.

Now, David looked at me.

"Three cups a day," I said.

The technician was out in the hallway now. She gave me a long look.

"I'll let Dr. Harris know," she finally said.

And then she walked us toward the door, assuring us that Dr. Harris would call just as soon as she had examined Waylon.

Neither David nor I said much on the way home. What was

there to say? It was my fault Waylon was sick. It was obvious from the technician's questions, from her grim expression when I had told her how much grain Waylon had been getting, that I had been overfeeding him. I thought again, as I had so many times, of the day we had gotten Waylon, of the way he had mourned for the boy who had loved him and of the way the boy had mourned for him. I thought I had calculated the right amount of feed, but if there was one thing I had learned over the last few years, it was that, in farm life, good intentions were worth very little. When I had made a mistake in teaching, when I accidentally miscalculated a student's average or forgot to add enough spaces on my individual conference schedule, those mistakes were easily remedied. In farming, however, whatever mistakes you made had swift and certain consequences, both emotionally and financially.

Later that evening, we got a call from Dr. Harris. Waylon did, in fact, have a blockage, and we had two choices. She could try to place a catheter into his bladder to allow the urine to drain. Hopefully, then, the calculi would dissolve, and he would be able to urinate naturally. Or she could cut a hole in his side and attach his bladder to his side, creating a permanent way for urine to pass through the body. This latter procedure, though extreme, would be a permanent solution. However, he would constantly leak urine, and he would always smell like pee.

Because it seemed less extreme, David and I opted for the first solution. We hoped to use Waylon as a stud in the future to help offset the costs for his upkeep, and we worried that a urine-soaked goat might dissuade potential clients. We also hoped to still have the beautiful, pure-as-the-driven-snow goat we had brought home just weeks before. Those seemed like selfish reasons, but this procedure also seemed like the less invasive, the less difficult one for Waylon. We gave Dr. Harris the go-ahead for the surgery, and she called us less than an hour later. The procedure had gone well, and Waylon was comfortable. They would watch him for a few days before sending him home.

In the weeks since we had gotten him, Waylon had gradually become more affectionate, especially with David. He even allowed me to rub his head and the soft spot just above his nose. However, the next week, when Waylon returned home with a catheter, a bottle of antibiotics, and a container of ammonium chloride that we had been instructed to add to his water, his beautiful, golden eyes were glassy and we tried to pet him, he shied away. Perhaps he hadn't been here long enough to remember this was his home, or perhaps he still felt bad, or maybe the stay at the vet's had been traumatic for him. It was hard to know. We didn't really understand enough about goats to know exactly what was wrong or how to help him, but both David and I spent a lot of time talking to him and petting him, trying once again to reassure him and lift his spirits.

Dr. Harris had told us to look for signs that, in addition to passing urine through the catheter, Waylon was also peeing through his penis, so several times a day, David crouched on the ground next to him, his head next to Waylon's underbelly, looking for urine. At first, we only saw urine from the catheter, but gradually, in the coming days, tiny drops of pee began to flow from Waylon's penis. We were ecstatic.

He was going to be okay. We went out for barbecue (pork for David, tempeh for me) and local beer and toasted to Waylon's good health.

Finally, two weeks after the initial surgery, per the original plan, we took Waylon back to Dr. Harris's office and left him to have the catheter removed. This time, we were optimistic, eager for him to be back to "normal," but later that afternoon, the receptionist called. Waylon was no longer urinating from his penis, only the catheter. There was still a blockage. After a few days of "encouraging his urine flow," Dr. Harris felt that there was enough urine passing to remove the catheter, and Waylon once again returned home. This time, he was in better spirits. He head-butted with Merle, munched on the pine limbs David threw out for him, and whispered to Holly through the fence.

I loved watching the two of them "chatting," Waylon sticking his nose through the wires, Holly cooing back to him. Though Saanens tended to have only one kid at a time, Holly looked like she could easily have twelve kids in her belly. Waylon must have thought she was glowing. He never paid attention to any of the other does, only Holly, and I couldn't help believing that he knew or remembered or sensed—whatever goats do—that the two of them had a special bond.

After his illness, we no longer fed Waylon grain, just hay and beet pulp and sunflower seeds and the occasional fruit or vegetable peel, and though he still occasionally cried when he urinated, he was definitely eating and peeing and playing. And then, the morning after Christmas, David went down to the barn and found Waylon crying in his stall. Crouching on the ground next to him, David saw pee coming out his penis, but it was coming in dribbles, not in a steady flow.

Our children were all home for the holidays, and Dr. Harris's office was closed, so we decided just to watch Waylon that day. After all, there was *some* pee. Maybe he just needed to drink more. We added more ammonium chloride to his water, and all day long, David traipsed back and forth to the barn. Waylon cried intermittently, like he couldn't decide whether or not to be upset. David checked on him last around midnight. All the other goats were lying down, asleep, but Waylon was still standing in his stall. Finally, David decided there was nothing more to be done that night, and around 2:00 a.m., he finally fell asleep.

———

The next morning, I woke to find Piper, our Jack Russell, the dog my uncle Bill had given me, standing immobile, staring at his water bowl. His eyes were glassy and distant. Something was wrong, very wrong. Piper was now fourteen. Kate was twelve, and both Hester and Pretzel were pushing eleven. Kate had a weak sphincter muscle and took hormones to keep her bladder from leaking. Piper and Hester took arthritis medicine, glucosamine, and the occasional pain pill. Sometimes, after a hard day of mucking the barn or climbing onto the roof to repair it, David gave the dogs their medicines, then popped a glucosamine himself. We were all, it seemed, growing older.

I woke David, then Alex, and the three of us debated what to do.

We considered calling the vet, but due to the holiday, the office was still closed. The only option would be an emergency vet in Asheville, a forty-five-minute drive away. Besides the trauma of the travel for Piper, just walking in the door there would have cost us several hundred dollars, money we didn't have. And even if we had had the money, I wasn't sure that was the right course of action.

Years ago, we had had a fourteen-year-old corgi, Julie. She was very healthy and happy until a blood-borne disease left her needing repeated transfusions, a process our then-vet had encouraged. Never once did the vet suggest that we let her die peacefully, and never once did I consider that myself. I had thought it was my duty to keep Julie alive, but the way she had finally died—in a cage at the vet's office— had haunted me ever since. After that, I came to believe that my role was not to keep my animals alive but to, when the inevitable time came, let them leave this world quietly and tranquilly, surrounded by people and animals who loved them. It was, in fact, how I one day hoped to go, the very best death I could imagine.

Over the course of the morning, Piper became more responsive, but he was still breathing heavily. I gave him a pain pill from the supply our vet had given us to use in just such a crisis. Then I wrapped him in a warm blanket and sat next to him while he lay in a toy wagon David had converted into a dog bed. David had removed the wheels and piled layers of old towels onto the wagon bed, and Piper was nestled in the center. Alex and I sat next to him, rubbing his soft head, then the prickly fur on his back, telling him what a good boy he was, how very much we loved him. Through his fur, I could feel the sharp bones of his spine. His breathing was slow and labored, his eyes closed.

Mentally, I listed all the things I most loved about him—the way he walked by my heels down to the barn each morning, the enthusiasm with which he wrested a treat from my hand, nearly taking my fingers off, the way he never complained when I ate all the red and purple Skittles and left him all the green and yellow. I listed all the things I forgave him for—the time, years before, when he had viciously attacked our elderly border collie, the time he had bitten me between my thumb and forefinger, tearing the flesh so deeply, I could see the layers of tissue beneath.

And then I listed all the things I hoped he would forgive me for—for not taking him to the vet for regular checkups, for not continuing to take him on walks after he got old, for sometimes letting the cat lick my ice cream bowl instead of him. And I thought about all the funny things he had done, all the near-misses he had had with death, like the time he swallowed a nest of crickets that had been poisoned with insecticide, about how he was stubborn and bullheaded like his father, a sturdy Jack Russell named Rollo whose belly had been ripped clean open in a fight with a black bear.

And then, somewhere in the midst of my reverie, I realized David was standing in the doorway. He looked from Piper to me. For a moment, he didn't say anything.

"I've got to get Waylon to the vet," he finally said. "He's not peeing at all."

Which did not even seem possible. How unlikely was it that my oldest dog and my youngest goat would die on the same day? It was just so surreal. By that time, Aaron and Eli were awake, and while the boys made more coffee for us all, David loaded Waylon into the Mountaineer. He was gone a little over an hour when I got a text. **Meet me at the barn**, he said. **Alone.**

Piper was soundly sleeping, so I left him in the wagon, threw on my jacket, and headed down the driveway. It was unusually warm for December, with a soft, springlike breeze that carried Merle's scent through the air, like a bad perfume. I waited by the barn gate. Finally, David pulled in the drive and slowed to a stop. As he got out, I stuck my head in the door looking for Waylon, but he wasn't there. Then David's shoulders began to heave, and I simply assumed Waylon was dead. What else could it be? And as sad as I was, I knew that David, who had worked so hard to pull Waylon back from the brink of death, was devastated. I put my arms around him and hugged him hard while he cried, his beard wet and scratchy against my neck.

"You did everything you could," I said. "Everything anyone could possibly do."

Though I was sure that most farmers got used to seeing animals die, David and I never had. Over the last couple of years, we had lost a number of chickens, including Mella Yella and her sister and eventually, a year after David had so tenderly nursed her back to health, Terry. Most of these chickens just dropped dead one day, but a few lingered long enough to receive a few nights of special care in the "hospice" crate before quietly slipping away. We were always sad when we lost an animal, and we continued to be immensely grateful for the riches—emotional, spiritual, and physical—our animals brought us. Now, David nodded and cried until he was finally able to speak.

"She's going to try one more thing," he finally said.

"What?" I said.

I was now standing back, staring at David, trying to revise my understanding of what was happening. What was happening was that Waylon was not, in fact, dead—not yet. His ureter was badly damaged from the calculi, though, and his bladder was once again blocked, and Dr. Harris was going to attempt the radical hole-in-the-abdominal-wall procedure she had mentioned earlier. Given Waylon's weakened state, it was a long shot, but she would try.

The rest of the day was a blur. David and I did not see any of our kids very often, and it was rare for all three of them to be home at the same time. Alex had gotten us all tickets to see the new Star Wars movie as a belated gift for David's birthday, which had been a few weeks earlier, and that night we had planned to go to dinner, then to the movie. It was supposed to be a special evening for us all, a celebration. I felt like we should forge ahead, make Piper comfortable, then go on with our plans, but David and Aaron felt we should all stay home. Eli and Alex remained neutral on the matter. The problem was, no one could stop crying. All afternoon, David waited at his desk for the call from Dr. Harries, and I stayed upstairs near Piper so he would know I was there.

Piper seemed comfortable, not in pain, not panicky or scared, and finally, after much deliberation, we all decided on a compromise. We would go to the movie but not to dinner. I gave Piper another dose of pain medicine, then ensconced him in a pile of blankets and settled him in the bathroom, away from the other dogs. Our drive to the movie was quiet, melancholy, a mood not helped by the fact that, despite David's best efforts to clean and air out the car, the Mountaineer smelled unmistakably of buck.

We got our popcorn and our beer and settled in to watch a Star Wars movie, and about halfway through the movie, David's phone vibrated. He leapt up and ran into the hallway, and moments later, he sent a group text: **Waylon is okay.** The surgery had gone well, and Waylon could come home in a few days. David was ecstatic. I was, of course, pleased and happy that David was happy, but it was hard to be overly optimistic. Waylon had been through so much in such a short period of time, and it was hard to imagine that he would be happy and healthy once again.

And of course, I was worried about Piper, but I needn't have been. When we got home, he had thrown off all his blankets and was standing in the bathroom, barking for food. The next morning, he jumped up, ran outside, then followed me all the way to the barn and back. Still, David and I took him to our vet, who confirmed what we had suspected, that he had had a stroke, that he could have another one in the future. For now, though, he seemed to be on the mend.

The next day, David went to pick up Waylon, and when he got

back, I went down to the barn. For a moment, I couldn't believe this was the same goat we had sent to Dr. Harris's office just days before. He pranced into his stall and began munching on hay, then took a spin through the field, stopping to eat leaves and to whisper through the fence to Holly. His entire back end, once white, was now dark yellow from the urine constantly draining out the hole in his side, and he reeked, but then again, so did Merle. It was just that Merle's urine was all over his face rather than his back legs.

In the coming days, we began to focus on the future and to look forward to the births of the kids—Holly's, Willow's, and Ama's. We tried to envision what the kids would look like, what combination of colors and sizes they might be. Since Ama was brown, white, and black, and Merle was tan and white, the color combinations for their offspring were endless. Willow and Merle's kids would certainly be tan, maybe also white, but we wondered whose ears they would have, whether they would be long and floppy like Merle's or tiny like Willow's. And then we began to debate the color of Holly and Waylon's babies, which was ridiculous, since Holly and Waylon were identical, or at least they had been.

"I wonder if Holly's kids will be all-white like Holly or half-white, half-yellow, like Waylon," David said.

"That's funny," I said. "Very funny."

But joking was good. Joking meant that things were looking better, that we were on the upswing. One of the greatest surprises of this time, among all the others, was that Dr. Harris never charged us full price for any of Waylon's visits. Each time we went to pick him up, we looked at our bill and saw that, for one reason or another, we had received a discount—a substantial discount. When we asked the receptionist about it, she would offer an explanation that was never really clear, something about how it was because of all the trouble we had had. The bottom line was that Dr. Harris was just a kind, empathetic soul who took one look at David's bloodshot eyes and the buck that rode in the back of our car and decided we needed a break.

When you have gone through a sort of travesty of your own making, failure begins to feel like part of you. You get used to it. People around you expect you to fail, and you learn to expect it from yourself, to see it as almost comforting in its familiarity. You begin to believe you are destined to make a mess of things. But then there are those unexpected kindnesses, those moments when someone does something to make you believe that perhaps you are more than the sum of everything you have done wrong, that perhaps you are worth more than you think. Dr. Harris was one of those people, a person who looked at us and saw two people whose love for their animals made them better somehow, more gentle and more noble, and her presence in our lives made us begin to feel worthy again at last.

Pasta with Goat Cheese, Sun-Dried Tomatoes, and Broccoli

- ½ gallon whey
- 1 pound penne or bow tie pasta
- 1 crown of broccoli florets, chopped
- ½ to 1 bulb (not cloves) garlic, divided into cloves and crushed
- 2 to 4 tablespoons olive oil
- 2 tomatoes, chopped
- ½ cup chopped sun-dried tomatoes in oil, drained (reserve a tablespoon or two of oil)
- ½ cup Kalamata olives
- ½ cup chopped artichoke hearts in oil, drained
- ½ batch (about ½ cup) soft goat cheese, crumbled
- Salt and pepper to taste

Bring the whey to boil. Add pasta. Cook according to instructions, adding broccoli in the last 3 to 5 minutes of cooking. Drain. Sauté garlic in olive oil until fragrant. Add fresh tomatoes, and sauté for a minute or two. Stir in sun-dried tomatoes, olives, and artichoke hearts. Remove from heat, and add drained pasta and broccoli and goat cheese. Mix thoroughly. Season with salt and pepper to taste. If mixture seems too dry, add reserved oil from the sun-dried tomatoes. If you live in Asheville, serve this with Freak of Nature Double IPA from Wicked Weed Brewing because it is hoppy and refreshing and offsets the ton of garlic you are ingesting. If you live anywhere else in the world, serve it with a good merlot or something sparkling.

Chapter Twenty-Three

THE TERM *SPRING LAMB*, I have come to understand, is a euphemism. It actually means *dead-of-winter lamb* as, despite what the calendar says, goats, like sheep, give birth only on the most frigid nights of the year at some ungodly hour when wind is howling through the trees and sleet slicing through the barn slats. And if you are especially ill prepared to stay up all night—say, exhausted from a few nights of burning the midnight oil on your MFA packet or weak from too many meals of red wine and Starburst Minis—this is the time your doe will go into labor.

For three nights that March, David and I donned every warm thing we owned—long johns, two pairs of pants, three jackets, hats, two pairs of gloves, hand warmers, foot warmers, neck warmers—and traipsed down to the barn for what became hours of huddling in dim light on plastic chairs or crouching on the floor, our hands growing numb despite the gloves as we chatted about normal, everyday things, the sort of things most couples talked about over a nice dinner. We talked about David's work, about my work, about our human kids, about the unseasonably cold weather. Finally, we ran out of things to talk about and simply listened to the does' heavy breathing.

Holly's kids came first. One blustery midnight, she gave birth to two beautiful, healthy, snow-white babies, a buckling and a doeling. The delivery was essentially uneventful, and by two in the morning, we had cleaned the stall, and the kids were standing and nursing on their own. David and I fell into bed exhausted but thrilled. We had done it, the three of us—me, David, and Holly.

Then, six days later, I found Willow standing and staring blankly into the field—an early sign of labor. It was eleven in the morning. *Thank goodness.* The babies would be born by lunchtime, nursing steadily by midafternoon, and tucked in for the night at a decent hour. We had done this twice before now, so this should be a piece of cake. I moved Willow into her stall, put down fresh straw, and texted David, who was out seeing clients. **Hurry home**, I said. But there was no need for him to hurry. When he got home a couple of hours later, Willow was simply staring at the wall.

While David drank coffee to stay alert, I drank a bottle of hard cider to calm down, and we took turns running back and forth to the house to go to the bathroom and grab additional jackets and blankets. At dinnertime, I brought two slices of cold, leftover pizza down to the barn, which we ate with gloved hands. Finally, Willow lay down on the straw and began twisting and squirming. David went into her stall and lay beside her, and I moved my chair close enough to stroke her head. It was dark outside, and wind thrashed the sides of the barn so hard, I could not tell Willow's moans from the wind. Contractions wracked her body. Exhausted, she collapsed on my lap. I had read that one hour after a doe starts pushing, the babies should be born. If not, something was likely wrong. Now, Willow seemed to be pushing, but I wasn't sure.

"Was that pushing?" I asked David.

He didn't answer but crouched closer, rubbing her flank. After I was certain an hour had passed, I began to panic.

"We should call someone," I said. "Or take her somewhere."

"Who? Where?" David said. "There's no time."

He was right. Though I had both our vet and the emergency mobile vet numbers programmed into my phone, if something happened to Willow now, there would be no time to get her anywhere. Finally, David made a decision.

"Hand me a glove," he said.

He meant a latex glove, since he was stripping off his other gloves, and though I wasn't sure exactly what he planned to do, I considering stopping him, calling a time-out so we could reevaluate and reassess. But then, just as quickly, it occurred to me that there was no time to run back up to the house and Google this or browse once again through *Storey's Guide to Raising Dairy Goats* to catch any important information we might have missed. This was a test, a pop test, and we were either prepared or not. So I stood and rummaged through the birthing kit until I found the gloves.

"I need some lubricant," David said. "I'm just going to see if I can feel anything."

I found the off-brand K-Y Jelly and passed it over Willow's very still body. I crouched back down next to Willow, and when she raised her head, I kissed her muzzle. Her eyes were bleary and distant.

"You're a good girl," I told her while David reached inside her in search of anything he could pull. "The very, very best."

And then there was a gush of fluid, like someone had knocked over a bucket of water. In the other deliveries we had witnessed, this happened after the baby had emerged in the bubble, but now the bubble had ruptured inside Willow. I didn't know if this was okay or not, but she lifted her head and pushed again.

"Pass me a pee pad!" David said.

Determined to help, he once again stuck two fingers inside her birth canal. For a moment, he was silent, his face contorting as he tried to make sense of what he felt.

"Teeth!" he finally said. "I feel teeth!"

The baby's foot was not positioned properly. He was supposed to feel hooves. Willow, however, seemed invigorated. She raised up and began to push, then finally stood. David matched her movements like a quarterback, spotting her to make sure she didn't run into the barn wall. Finally, kneeling beside her and using one hand like forceps, he managed to reposition the kid. As Willow pushed, he pulled, and then I could see it, one wet, dark head and one hoof. And then she stopped again. She was just so tired. I could see it in her far-off look, in the way her back sagged and her head drooped.

"You can do it, girl!" I told her. "You are almost there."

Using just his index finger and his thumb, David maneuvered the kid's other hoof into diving position.

"Push, girl!" he told Willow with such tenderness and such desperation that I felt certain the kid was dead.

In that moment, though, I didn't care. I only cared about Willow. What if we had underestimated her strength and stamina? What if, after all we done to keep her strong and healthy and happy, this was the thing that killed her? What had seemed like a wonderful idea now seemed terribly selfish. I had prostituted her, then forced her to endure five months of pregnancy followed by the pain and trauma of giving birth just so I could make Guy Fieri's goat milk creme caramels. I would never do this again. Never. I laid my cheek against her cheek and closed my eyes. She was very, very still.

And then, she lifted her head and began to push.

"That's right," I told her. "Good girl!"

Finally, miraculously, the kid, aided by David, began to ease forward. At first, a wet, unidentifiable mass appeared at the opening of the birth canal. It seemed stuck, frozen in time. We were all silent— David, me, Willow, all the other goats in the barn. But then, gradually, a nose emerged. Then eyes. Then a hoof and a knee and another hoof, until finally, one slick, slimy kid slid onto the pad.

As I passed David a towel, the kid squirmed and kicked and

maaed and baaed. Together, Willow and David worked to clean him, David vigorously rubbing his face while Willow nuzzled and licked his lanky body until he was a beautiful, caramel brown. Within moments, he was standing.

"I think he's hungry," I said over his screams.

Some days on the farm, everything felt brand-new again, as if I were once again discovering that baby chicks can grow into miniature dinosaurs overnight or that goats are little escape artists with horns. There were other moments, though, when I realized that though we weren't experts on anything, we had learned a thing or two, such as the fact that if you pull a goat, it will instinctively back away. If you want a kid goat to nurse, you should gently push its bottom in the right direction. Now, I filled Willow's bowl with grain and beet pulp, and as she idled over to her bowl, David lifted the crying kid and nudged it toward Willow's teat. As the kid latched on and began guzzling milk, David lifted its tail to check the gender.

But I knew already. He just had the look of a buck—broader in the nose and face than a doe. We had hoped that Willow might have a doeling that we could milk later on, but now we were just relieved that he was here and healthy and even more relieved that she seemed to be recovering. She ate her food and drank her water, then curled on the straw beside her son. They were lovely and serene, the very picture of domestic bliss. They were also exhausted. While I stood by their stall watching them sleep, David went outside to do some chores in the barnyard. I was snapping photos on my cell phone and texting everyone I knew and acting like my own daughter had just given birth when Willow called out, a low groan. And then she stood.

"Something's happening!" I called to David.

He ran back into the barn and, just as he put on his gloves, a bubble appeared beneath her tail—another kid.

"Hand me a clean pad," he said.

He scooted the pad underneath Willow's tail, and seconds later, the kid dropped onto the clean surface. This kid was smaller than the first—and absolutely silent. David grabbed a clean towel and began rubbing its nose and mouth to clear its airway. And then Willow calmly began to help. She and David massaged the baby goat's head and belly and legs while the first kid, who would soon become Willie—a nod to both Willow and Willie Nelson—nursed. It was as if he had just run a marathon in south Florida in July. He could not get enough to drink. Finally, the second kid stretched, wobbled to its knees, and stood. It was brown with a white stripe down its nose and white splotches all over—a perfect blend of Merle and Willow. David pushed the tiny goat toward Willow's other teat, and while it nursed, I leaned over and lifted its tail. Underneath was one tiny slit—a vent.

"It's a girl!" I screamed, delirious with fatigue and excitement.

Both kids had long bodies, short legs, and tiny ears, and the doe, whom we would later name Merlene, was simply magical—a miniature camel or a plastic toy horse come to life. I felt wildly fortunate. Willow was alive and well, her babies safe and sound. And after everything, David and I were still here together, standing in a now-filthy barn stall, full of blood and mucus and all sorts of other unidentifiable bodily fluids, grinning broadly, as if we had just won the lottery or an all-expenses-paid trip to Paris or a new house with plenty of good insulation and a bona fide electric water heater. In that moment, I could think of absolutely nothing better than this, no place on earth I would rather be.

Cajeta

- ½ gallon goat's milk
- 2 cups sugar
- 1 cinnamon stick
- ½ teaspoon baking soda dissolved in 1 table-spoon water

Mate a beautiful LaMancha doe with an adorably haggard Nigerian dwarf buck. Wait 150 days. Sit in a freezing cold, dark barn with a laboring doe for eight hours or longer. Become sick and numb with worry as the doe's labor drags on and on. Make all sorts of pointless promises about how you will never put your doe through this again.

When the babies do finally arrive safely, feel enormous gratitude. Take eight million photos, and send them to all of your friends, family, colleagues, and people who inexplicably remain in your cell phone contact list despite the fact that you have long since forgotten why they are there. Post more photos on Facebook and Twitter and Instagram. Insist that all nearby friends and family visit. Check on kids obsessively, even though their mother is actually their mother, and you are just a bystander. Then, when the kids are two weeks old, when they have gotten all the colostrum they need and are strong and active and thriving, separate them from their mother at night so you can begin morning milking.

Once you have a half gallon of milk, bring the milk, sugar, and cinnamon stick to a simmer in a saucepan. Remove from heat, and stir in dissolved baking soda. Return to heat, and cook until thick and caramel colored, approximately one hour, stirring frequently. When mixture is the consistency of a thick caramel sauce, remove from heat, and store in refrigerator (make sure to remove the cinnamon stick). Serve over ice cream or pound cake with warm brie and crackers. Or, if you prefer, shamelessly eat it straight from the jar with a spoon.

Chapter Twenty-Four

I WAS WORKING UPSTAIRS AT my computer one evening that summer when I heard David exclaim loudly, then open the front door.

"Outside, Hester!" he said. "Outside!"

And then there was a loud hacking—the sound of metal beating against the laminate floor. For approximately two seconds, I considered running down to see if he needed my help but then just as quickly reconsidered. A few months before, I had stepped barefoot onto a wolf spider, and though wolf spiders are harmless, I had been hysterical for hours. Whatever this was, it was something at least as bad as a wolf spider, and I was pretty sure David did not want or need my help dealing with it. Moments later, he appeared in the doorway at the top of the stairs. His eyes were wide, his jeans splattered with blood.

"There was a fucking copperhead in the kitchen," he said.

"I figured," I said.

"Like two feet away from Hester!"

"That's bad," I said.

"Right by the refrigerator!"

He was breathing hard, his chest throbbing. He looked at me as if I hadn't heard, as if my ears were stopped up or my brain wasn't working properly.

"It was huge!" he said. "The biggest one yet."

I got it. I did. A massive copperhead had slithered across our kitchen floor, right where any of us could have easily stumbled upon it—me on my way to get a carton of Ben & Jerry's, or David on his way to stoke the boiler, or one of the dogs on his/her nightly kitchen patrol. Somehow, this was worse than a copperhead writhing beneath the china cabinet or a black snake crashing down onto the family picnic. Still, I found it hard to summon the same amount of horror I had felt with the first copperhead. Or the same depth of revulsion I had felt when I stepped on the wolf spider. Or the same degree of panic I had felt when wasps built a nest in our porch light and attacked me one morning before I had even had my coffee. I took my calm, lucid response as a sign of growth. David took it as a sign of psychosis.

"What is wrong with you?" he said. "Why aren't you flipping out? If ever there was a time to flip out, this is it!"

"I'm just not that surprised," I said. "I mean, I'm disgusted but not surprised."

It seemed that, in spite of myself, I had become accustomed, acclimated, habituated to life in the woods. In my old life, I had had the illusion of being in control, the illusion that things were okay, that my family and I were safe and secure. I no longer had such fantasies. Instead, I had learned to roll with the punches, to go with the flow, to—as one of my friends liked to say—bend with the wind. Wolf spiders and copperheads and critters of all kinds were a part of this life. I expected them, prepared for them. I shook out my boots before I put them on. I looked before sticking my hand in a dark cabinet. I used a flashlight when wandering around the cabin at night. Still, no matter how prepared I now was for the unexpected, there were surprises—such as the mammoth-sized possum David found scurrying up the barn wall one night.

I liked possums enough in theory—as a concept. I didn't want to hold one or own one as a pet, but we occasionally saw them in the woods or crossing the road at night, and I thought they were cute-ish. They had little pink noses and adorable, perky ears, and if you didn't look at their tails, they were really quite precious. Still, we had six kid goats then—Ama had delivered two more healthy kids just after Willow's kids were born—and they were all under two months old. Though we were pretty sure possums didn't eat baby goats, we weren't *100 percent sure*, so David ran out to Tractor Supply and bought a humane trap, baited it with peanut butter crackers, and set it in the barn. That night, when he went to check, the trap was empty, the possum clinging to the barn wall. After three successive nights of this, David had had enough.

"I think I can shoot it," he said over dinner on the fourth evening.

"What is wrong with you?" I said. "You are not going to shoot it! You are not."

This was my role, coming up with everything we *weren't* going to do with no plan for what we *were* going to do, and this strategy was wearing thin. David scowled.

"So what do you suggest?"

I faltered. He waited.

"Maybe we should bring the babies up here to the house," I finally said.

David seemed to scowl even more deeply, though his beard was so thick, it was hard to tell for sure.

"We're going to keep six baby goats in the house?" he said.

"Okay, so maybe not in the house. How about in the boiler room?"

David sighed, put his dirty plate in the sink, and sat back down to switch out his tennis shoes for his barn boots.

"What are you going to do?" I asked.

"I'm going to try to catch it."

"With your bare hands?"

"What are my other choices?" he asked.

He had a point.

"Wear your gloves!" I hollered after him as he headed outside.

Rabies was rare in possums, but it was possible. I was not sure how I knew this, but I did. A little while later, David returned with a report: no possums in sight. But later that night—much later—he checked again. I was in bed when he texted me: **Got it!** I hopped up and ran down to the driveway where he was standing next to a blue plastic tub.

"She was running up the wall," he said, "and I grabbed her by the tail."

Tiny holes dotted the tub lid, and I leaned down to peer into the dark, silent interior.

"It's awfully quiet," I said. "Are you sure she's okay?"

"Yes," David said.

"You didn't hurt her when you dragged her off the wall?"

"No, she's fine."

This was, in fact, not the first time we had had a discussion like this. Once, at the old house, our dogs had chased a possum into the wood pile, where we found it lying prone on a log. While David headed to the garage to get a shovel to bury it, I screamed for him to rescue it before the dogs killed it.

"It's dead," David had said.

"It's not dead! Have you not ever heard of 'playing possum'?"

And sure enough, after we had gathered all the dogs and gone inside, the possum had hopped up and headed back from whence it had come.

"I told you," I had told David. "*Playing possum*. It's a real thing."

Recently, I had read that in addition to the two primary stress responses—fight or flight—psychologists had named a third type of response: freeze. People freeze when they believe they cannot safely defeat the threat against them or outrun it. Instead, they become too afraid to act at all. They are paralyzed. It was a feeling with which I was all too familiar. So many times in my life that had been my response to fear, and I saw that now as clearly as I saw that possum playing dead on the pile of logs back at the old house. Now, perhaps we had another possum playing possum on our hands. Then again, maybe David had swung it too hard and jostled its little brains.

"I just think it's possible you hurt her," I said.

"I didn't hurt her."

"Well, let's take her up in the forest and let her out," I said.

I thought it sounded like a cool adventure, something fun to do at the end of the day. After the morning milking, I had spent most of the day working at my computer, typing up anecdotes about farm life. David, however, had worked all day doing repairs to the barn and fence. He had hammered and sawed and lugged and hauled until he was spent, and he was not so excited about a late-night excursion.

"At midnight? You want to go up in the forest at midnight?"

"Yes," I said. "Why not?"

David stared at me. My hair was wet from the shower, and I wore a short, black silk nightgown with a white lace bodice, my grandfather's flannel shirt, and a pair of Chacos caked in mud. David opened his mouth to say something, then closed it. He reached down and lifted the tub.

"Get the door for me," he said.

He heaved the container into the back seat of my car, then reached across and strapped it in, like a baby in a car seat.

"You drive," he said. "I'll ride in the back with the possum."

It was a line we would use from that night on. "You drive; I'll ride in the back with the possum," one of us would say, and the other one would spurt a mouthful of coffee or beer across the room. It was funny, yet it also seemed to encapsulate our situation in some essential way, to reduce it to its necessary parts. How crazy was this life we led, how weird and wacky and totally unexpected?

In a way, I wanted to ride next to the possum just so I could say I had once ridden next to a possum. But then I pictured it suddenly hopping up and manically flinging itself about the tub, and that's when I realized that I certainly did not want to ride beside a possum—even a confined one—so I climbed into the driver's seat, and David got into the back and rested his arm on the tub.

"Are you sure she can't get out?" I asked.

"I'm sure," he said. "Just focus on the road."

Constantly checking the rearview mirror, I drove slowly down the gravel drive and turned left onto the pavement. The road was dark and deserted, and though we passed a couple of houses, there were no lights anywhere. A quarter of a mile from our mailbox, we came to a place where the road cut through a wide field. On our right was a large crop of tomatoes. On our left was a vacant field.

"Here," David said. "Stop here."

"Here?"

"Yes! Stop!"

I slammed on the brakes and skidded onto the private gravel road leading to the empty field. At first, I thought the possum was trying to escape, that maybe David had been bitten, but when I glanced in the backseat, David was calmly unbuckling his seat belt and opening the door.

"Here?" I said. "You're going to dump her out here?"

"Why not? There's a great big field."

"Well, for one, it's private land. And for another, it's too close. She'll find her way back."

"No, she won't. There's that huge hill." David gestured behind us to the mountain where we had searched for Maple and Cinnamon, our runaway goats.

"She can climb that," I said.

"No, she can't."

"Yes, she can."

"No, she can't."

This was not going at all like I had anticipated. Sure, David was tired, and sure, this wasn't a night out at the symphony or the theater, but somehow, I had envisioned a romantic adventure with me in my silky negligee and David in his snug blue jeans and work jacket. We would wind through the forest along the Davidson River, past Looking Glass Falls where we had written the senior superlatives, past Sliding Glass Rock and Pink Beds and the Cradle of Forestry, all the way up to the parkway, where we would park and look across the Shining Rock Wilderness all the way to the pinnacle of Cold Mountain. We would marvel at the crisp, clear air, at the millions of stars overhead, at the tiny lights below us, and it would be exactly like when we were teenagers, only now we would be sober, and instead of me lying with my head on David's lap, he would be in the back with the possum, and I would be up front driving. Granted, it was not the perfect date, but it was certainly better than driving three-quarters of a mile and dumping an possum in our neighbor's field.

But it was too late to reset the mood, if it had ever been set to begin with. David had already dragged the tub out onto the grass, and he now stood with one hand on the lid.

"It's just a little anticlimactic," I said, right before he popped open the lid and turned the box on its side.

I squealed and jumped back inside the car. David opened the back door, threw in the bucket, then hopped up front. Together, we watched the possum's thick, rodent-like tail and her bright, beady eyes race across the tall grass and disappear into the brush on the far side of the field.

"Let's get out of here," David said when she was gone.

I hesitated. It seemed silly, I knew, but I felt an odd kinship with the possum. She had been evicted, expelled, ejected from her home, and while part of me hoped she would find her way back over the steep hillside, another part of me hoped that she would be happy here where there were plenty of mice and berries and snakes to eat, where she could romp unencumbered through the field, wiggling her little nose and making tiny possum handprints in the damp earth.

I looked once more in the direction she had fled before gunning the gas and heading back toward home.

Chapter Twenty-Five

THOUGH WE FELT LIKE WE had won the lottery when our six beautiful, healthy goats were born that summer, we did not *actually* win the lottery. However, by spring, we had reached a payment agreement with the state of North Carolina, and with our hefty monthly payments came a newfound freedom: our bank accounts were no longer levied, my wages no longer garnished. Finally, we could use our bank cards again. We could pay for gas at the pump, order a ninety-nine cent book from Amazon, reserve an airline ticket or hotel room when we traveled for work or school. Finally, we could envision a time when the state debt would be settled, when that was one less thing we had to worry about. Of course, we still owed the IRS a staggering amount that seemed no less insurmountable than it had four years ago. It was not cancer or heart disease or Alzheimer's, yet it was something we both thought about every day, a bitter, pungent haze that hovered over our lives. We lived through it, around it, in spite of it, but we were always aware of its presence.

We also lived with a slew of regrets—*what if we hads* and *what if we hadn'ts*: What if I had kept the full-time job at the university all those years ago? What if we hadn't sent our kids to private school? What if we kept our modest house in town rather than buying Denise and Jeff's house? What if we had had fewer dogs? What if we had talked sooner and more often and more honestly? What if I had majored in something other than English, something more lucrative?

I also often thought about Denise. As soon as our house had gone into foreclosure, I had begun avoiding places where I thought I might see her. I even drove to a grocery store in a neighboring town to reduce my chances of running into her. I just did not know what I would say if I saw her. I did not even know what I wanted to say.

For David, our relationship with Jeff and Denise had been primarily a financial one, but I had considered Denise a friend. Even though Denise and Jeff had experienced a net gain out of the deal by quickly reselling the house after foreclosing, I still wrestled with feelings of guilt and betrayal. Not one or the other, but both. Grief has a way of doing that—of forcing you to see everything more clearly. I had not been a good friend to Denise, nor had she been a good friend to me. Both of those things were true. They coexisted.

Through mutual friends, I heard that Denise's daughter had graduated from college and was in Europe and that her son had gotten his pilot's license, and I was glad that her family was happy and doing well. Still, I often dreamed of her. In my dreams, I would be strolling down the ice cream aisle in the grocery store when I would bump into her. Or I would be at a party, and there she would be, across the room, laughing with a group of friends, and her eyes would grow wide and wary as I approached, as the partygoers scattered and left us alone.

"I'm sorry for what happened," the dream me told her every time. "I didn't know it would turn out this way. I should have known, but I didn't."

Sometimes, I woke up then, enormously relieved to have said something—anything—but other times, I lingered just long enough to hear her answer.

"It's okay," she said each time.

Exonerating me. Absolving me.

———

One afternoon when the baby goats were a few months old, I was outside on the front porch making my first batch of goat milk soap. It was something I had always wanted to do, one of the reasons I had originally wanted goats, but until now, I had not been confident enough to try it on my own. The recipes I had seen were too complicated, too time consuming, too *science-y*. And then one day, while browsing online, I came across instructions for how to make soap in a Crock-Pot in under an hour. It sounded relatively simple, totally doable, not much more difficult, in fact, than making Crock-Pot pasta e fagioli. I was in.

The Crock-Pot was on a rickety, round glass table, which was not ideal but would have to do. I wore workout pants tucked into socks, tennis shoes, an old T-shirt, my grandfather's oldest flannel shirt, yellow rubber gloves, and safety goggles. Hester took one look at me and scooted under the picnic table.

"You're okay," I told her.

She wagged her tail weakly but stayed put. I dumped the olive and coconut oils into the Crock-Pot and turned it on low, then headed inside to weigh the goat's milk and the lye. This was the tricky part. I was very bad at measuring and weighing, at anything that required any level of precision or attention, and the whole process reminded me a lot more of high school chemistry class than anything I had done in recent years. And since high school chemistry class had not ended well for me, I was concerned. Though David had patiently explained to me how the scale worked—how to tell grams from ounces, how to weigh the measuring cup, then hit the home button to clear the scale before adding the ingredients—I was still nervous about using lye.

I located a gallon of vinegar, which would supposedly counteract the effects of any spilled lye, and reread the instructions—*always add lye to liquid. Lye to liquid. Lye to liquid.* I repeated it to myself over and over. I had recently seen *Crazy Love*, a movie about Burt Pugach, the New York attorney who was convicted of hiring hit men to throw lye on his estranged girlfriend, Linda Riss. Linda was permanently blinded and disfigured from the accident but ultimately reunited with Pugach after he got out of prison. The movie was deeply disturbing on many levels, and it was all I could think about as I poured the lye crystals into the glass mixing bowl full of partially frozen goat's milk. Walking outside so as to minimize the fumes in the kitchen, I held the mixing bowl at arm's length and stirred. When the goat milk was thawed and the lye incorporated, it looked a lot like snow cream—piping hot snow cream, that is.

I lifted the Crock-Pot lid and stirred the mixture into the melted oils. And then I got out my stick blender, stood way back, and began to pulse—short, tentative bursts at first, then more sustained movements. As the liquid began to thicken, I moved close to the table and watched as the mixture bubbled and fizzled and swelled. The stirring was meditative, soothing, like kneading bread dough. According to the directions I had printed from the internet, I was looking for a "trace," which meant that when you lifted the beater, there should be an indentation where the beater had been. A sort of beater road or alley-way, if you will.

After about ten minutes, the mixture began to look like butter-scotch pudding. It was smooth and heavy, and when I pulled out the beater and piled some of the mixture on top, it stayed, and it looked exactly like the photo on the website. This, I decided, was so much simpler than birthing a goat. There were no plan Bs and plan Cs and all manner of contingencies. You just followed one set of instructions, and if you did that right, you ended up with soap. Now, all I had to do was put the lid on the pot and leave it.

I took off my goggles and gloves and went inside to measure the essential oil, honey, and ground oats. Finally, after about fifty minutes, I went back outside and lifted the Crock-Pot lid. And there it was—my very first batch of soap. A warm shade of ivory or a very light caramel, it smelled woodsy, earthy. Quickly, I turned off the heat, stirred in the oil and honey and oats, and dumped the mixture into two loaf pans lined with parchment paper. And then I stood back to survey my work. The loaves were slightly lumpy and smelled a little like breakfast, but they were already beginning to harden, to settle into something that looked like real soap. I was amazed.

When I was growing up, my grandmother had often talked about her mother making soap in a pot over a fire in the yard, and perhaps because that seemed so laborious—so backbreaking and hard—or perhaps because I hadn't even known that soap was something that could be made at home instead of bought at the store, that image had stuck with me. Now, like my great-grandmother and her mother before her and her mother before her, I had done it. I had made my own soap. I felt like I had run an ultramarathon. I had scaled Everest. I had given birth to septuplets. I had flown solo around the world. I was a visionary, a true pioneer. No longer was I *returning* to my roots. I had *returned*. I was Louise Dickinson Rich and Louisa May Alcott, an Appalachian *Sarah, Plain and Tall*. Still, as independent and self-sufficient as I felt, I had a nagging sensation that I was not actually so down-home. Back in my great-grandmother's day, women did things like this because they had to, not because they wanted to, and if my great-grandmother had known I was whipping up soap in a Crock-Pot when I could just run down the road to Walmart and buy a pack of Ivory, she would have thought it a waste of time. And if she had known I was adding orange oil and organic oatmeal, she would have thought me beyond ridiculous.

For my great-grandmother, making soap had been grueling work, and if I tried hard enough, I could see her outside her humble cabin, a third the size of ours. I saw her chopping wood, starting a fire, lugging a huge, heavy pot, and setting it over the hot coals. I saw her adding a thick slab of lard to the pot and mixing lye with water she had drawn from the spring and hauled herself. I saw ten children playing a game of tag, their feet pounding the grass, their squeals echoing through the treetops. I saw her sweating and bone-tired, bent over the pot, stirring and stirring and stirring with a long stick she had cut and shaved, her gray hair swept into a tight bun, her hands red and chapped, her face drawn. I saw corn stalks rustling in the field, mice darting in and out of the half-runner beans, chickens running loose in the backyard.

And then I saw her pause and gaze across the valley to the mountains, at the trees flushing red and yellow and orange, at the deer and coyotes and black bear roaming the hillsides, at the trout and hellbenders and tadpoles swimming in the streams, the red-tailed hawks and the turkey vultures swarming overhead, and I saw the wrinkles at the edges of her eyes relax, the years fall away, and I knew then as certainly as if she had told me herself that her life, though hard, had its own magic, its own rewards.

David was down at the barn putting up the goats. I could hear Ama making the special sound she made to get his attention—the sort of hysterical, bloodcurdling scream you might expect if a goat were being slaughtered. She loved him that much. I grabbed myself a congratulatory bottle of Bold Rock hard cider and eased onto a chair on the porch. High above the waterfall, a hawk lighted on a tree branch. I watched him land before his visage disappeared in the misty spray of the falls.

Searching for the springhead one day, David had found a watershed about fifteen hundred feet above the cabin. There, in a mossy hollow, three springs emptied into a creek that gathered momentum as it flowed down the mountainside. I loved knowing that—that the waterfall was higher than I had ever imagined, that it sprang from the earth in a place where the soil was rich and loamy, that the part I could see from my porch was just a small fraction of the whole. Watching the sun dip behind the mountain and the moon rise high in the sky, I realized that the waterfall I saw in front of me was not the exact waterfall I would see tomorrow. It was continually reborn, renewed, restored.

What did it mean to be reborn, I wondered. How much did you have to leave behind? How much were you allowed to take? I wasn't sure I knew the answer to these questions, but what I did now know without a doubt was that I was not alone, that I had never been alone, that the people who came before me were still here, would always be here. And there, in the warm breeze, in the rustling trees, in the vast and endless sky, the ghosts of my grandparents gathered around me like stars.

———

My grandmother came to visit us at the cabin once, the autumn before she died. She was thin and frail, dependent on oxygen, a shadow of the woman who had raced down giant slides at the playground with Alex in her arms, carried Aaron on her sturdy hip, fed Eli green beans from a rubber-tipped spoon. She rarely left her home then, but she had wanted to see the cabin, so my brother, who was visiting from Florida, drove her over. My brother and David heaved her wheelchair onto the rocky front porch, and we all sat in the sun, watching the water pour down the mossy rocks. For a long time, my grandmother was silent, taking it all in.

"It's real pretty out here, Jennifer," she said at last. "Real pretty. I think you're going to like it out here."

And in that moment, I heard both what she said and what she didn't say, that she felt my sorrow over the foreclosure and my struggling marriage, that she wanted to comfort me, to reassure us both that I would be fine without her. As hard as I had tried to hide our circumstances from her, to pretend this foray into homesteading was one exciting adventure that we had planned all along, she had sensed the truth, and she had come to check on me for herself.

My grandmother understood loss. She understood hopelessness and poverty, the sort of wherewithal and gumption it took to live in a drafty old cabin in the woods. She also understood love and commitment and the value of family. She knew you could be happy with $4.57 in the bank if you were surrounded by people who loved you and people you loved. She knew you could make mistakes and get past them and that you could forgive the people you loved for doing the same. She was telling me that I could do this, that I would survive this, that I would be better because of this, and though it would be a while before I believed that myself, her words stayed with me long after her Toyota rumbled down the drive, kicking up dust and dirt and gravel in its wake. And later, when she was gone, truly gone, I would look back and remember how my grandmother had sat with me on the porch that day, her voice a soft and soothing echo through the hills.

Goat Milk Soap

The hardest parts about making goat milk soap are (1) milking the goat and (2) overcoming your fear of working with lye. The rest is a piece of cake. Once I got past my phobia of lye, I found soap making to be fun and relaxing. I loved all the smells and textures, the way the scents filled the entire house when the bars were curing. It was a lot like baking bread, and since I could no longer make anything as fussy as bread in our temperamental oven, soap making was a nice alternative.

I have tried various methods with varying degrees of success, but by far the easiest way I have found is a hot-processed method that uses a Crock-Pot. Though hot-processed soaps have a slightly rougher appearance and tend to be darker in color than cold-processed soaps, they are ready to use soon after making and thus fulfill my need for almost-instant gratification.

- 20 ounces olive oil
- 40 ounces coconut oil
- 18 ounces frozen goat's milk
- 9.56 ounces 100 percent pure lye

Melt the coconut oil in Crock-Pot turned to low. When coconut oil is completely melted, add olive oil.

Wearing protective gear and working in a well-ventilated area, slowly stir the lye into the frozen milk. (*Note: Always add lye to the milk, never the other way around.*) Once the lye has dissolved into the melted milk, slowly stir the lye/milk mixture into the oils in the Crock-Pot. Using a stick blender, blend in quick bursts for several minutes, until the mixture begins to "trace." At this point, the mixture should resemble a thick pudding (think butterscotch), and your blender should leave a "trace" or mark as you blend. You can test this by scooping out a spoonful of the mixture and plopping it on top of the remaining mixture. If it holds its shape, it's ready. Continue with either the cold or the hot soap-making process.

For cold-processed soap: Turn off the Crock-Pot, and stir in essential oils and other additions (such as oatmeal). Pour mixture into prepared molds. I use two standard glass loaf pans lined with wax paper. Smooth the mixture into the pan evenly. Let sit for 24 to 48 hours before unmolding and cutting into bars. (For a lighter-colored soap, you may put the molds in the refrigerator overnight. Remove the next day, and let sit for 24 to 48 hours before cutting.)

Place the cut bars a few inches apart so they can "breathe." Let sit for 4 to 6 weeks before using. I use old box tops lined with wax paper for this, and I try to turn my soaps once a week or so.

For hot-processed soap: Once the mixture has reached trace stage, put the lid on the Crock-Pot, and cook on low for approximately 50 minutes, or until a pH test strip reads 7 to 10. You may need to stir the mixture once or twice during the cooking process.

After the soap reaches the appropriate pH level, turn off the Crock-Pot, and stir in essential oils and other additions. Pour into prepared molds. Let rest 24 to 48 hours before unmolding and/or cutting into bars. This soap can be used right away but benefits from curing for a couple of weeks. I usually use one bar right away and save the rest.

Note: I use the hot-processed method for rustic, earthy scents such as sandalwood and the cold-processed for fruity, flowery scents such as lavender.

Reading Group Guide

1. Imagine you are with Jennifer and David when they see the cabin for the first time. What would your initial reaction be? What are the pros of living there? What are the cons?

2. Describe how Jennifer and David's relationship changed after discovering their financial situation. How did they recover? How did their relationship grow over the course of the book?

3. Why do you think Jennifer decided to take a teaching job out of state? What did that time away from the cabin and her husband teach her?

4. Jennifer feels a deep connection to her Appalachian roots and her ancestors who also lived off the land. How does that influence impact her daily life, even after her grandmother dies?

5. Being an educator while also living in the cabin, Jennifer sees the merits of both a formal education and a cultural education, where information is passed down from one generation to the next. How

does she benefit from both of these? How do you benefit from both in your own life?

6. Why do you think David adjusts so much more easily to life at the cabin than Jennifer?

7. Imagine you and a spouse, family member, or friend must make this move. Who do you think would have a better time adjusting? What challenges would the two of you face?

8. Throughout *Flat Broke with Two Goats*, cooking seems to be an outlet to help Jennifer process her family's new situation. What sort of influence does cooking or food have in your own life? Your family's life? What recipe from the book are you most eager to try?

9. Why do you think Jennifer and David decide to get goats even though neither of them have any prior experience raising farm animals? How did this decision change their marriage?

10. How does Jennifer come to terms with her own mistakes throughout the book? Do you think acknowledging these hard truths changed her character?

11. After reading about Jennifer's goat antics, what do you think

would be the best part of goat raising? What part would be the most difficult for you?

12. Jennifer finds that eating food she has grown or raised herself is a more rewarding experience. Have you ever felt this way? Describe a time that you have used something that you have either raised or created with your own two hands. What was that like?

13. From dealing with mice, snakes, and even the stray possum, Jennifer realizes that uninvited wildlife is unavoidable when you're living close to the land. If you were in Jennifer's shoes, how would you react to these unwanted houseguests? Is there an animal that you would be unable to deal with?

14. Jennifer and David name all of their animals, including their chickens. How does this reflect on the relationship they have with their animals? How would you define the difference between farm animals and pets?

15. After reading *Flat Broke with Two Goats*, what do you think would be the most appealing aspect of living off the land? What would be the most unappealing?

16. Overall, do you think moving to the cabin was a good move for Jennifer and her family? Why or why not?

A Conversation with the Author

When did you start writing *Flat Broke with Two Goats?*

I have always known I wanted to write some of my family stories, and I have been writing those in different ways for a long time. However, I really didn't begin to envision this particular book in this particular way until our home was foreclosed about five years ago. That incident was really the impetus for this book.

Are you and your husband still living in the cabin?

Yes.

Do you ever think you will move again?

Yes. Since we are renting our home, and this cabin is on land that has long been in someone else's family, I don't think staying here permanently will even be an option. However, we do plan to stay within this area, and when it's time for us to move, we will definitely look for another place where we enjoy the same sort of simple, close-to-nature lifestyle we enjoy now.

How many animals do you have now?

We have four dogs, a cat, and ten goats. We also still have chickens—somewhere around fifteen, but that number is constantly changing.

Let's talk about your goats, who, throughout the memoir, have some very distinct personalities. Do you have a favorite goat?

I love all our goats, but I would have to say that Willow is my favorite—though her doeling, Merlene, is a close second. Willow is just so gentle and intuitive, and she has these amazing, soulful eyes. I also think the fact that I was her de facto mom/herdmate for those weeks when she was young really helped solidify our bond. From what I understand, though, most La Manchas have sweet, easygoing temperaments, and I would love to eventually add a few more to our herd.

Does David have a favorite?

David has a strong sense of fairmindedness, so he would never admit *out loud* that he has a favorite, but he certainly does tend to give Ama a lot of extra attention!

Any new goat stories to share?

Well, we have had some challenges trying to get the girls pregnant this year. Waylon, our Saanen buck, has been impotent since his surgery, and when we tried to mate Willow with Merle again this fall, he was, despite considerable enthusiasm, unable to…ummm…complete the task. So it looks like we may have to find a couple of younger, more robust bucks to "service our girls" next fall. In the meantime, we are using milk and cheese that I froze last season. Anyone have an adorable, amorous Nigerian or Saanen buck for sale or lease?

What was the hardest adjustment you had to make when you moved to the cabin?

I suppose the hardest thing was adjusting to living in such close proximity to so many critters—venomous snakes, especially. And this may sound rather trivial, but the other hard thing has been not having a hot water heater. I never realized before how lucky I was to be able to hop in a hot shower with no advance planning. It has been a good lesson for me, though—to realize that many things I used to take for granted are really luxuries and to think about how many people in the world do not have those luxuries. That sort of awareness is good for the soul, and I truly do appreciate a hot shower now!

What was the easiest?

The easiest transition for me was giving up television. Our lives are just so much quieter and more peaceful, and it seems like I get so much more done when I don't have the option of sitting down and flipping through channels. Sometimes I feel a little left out of discussions about the latest hot television show, but this is a small price to pay for having so much extra time and space to read or write or just carry on a conversation with my husband.

We get to hear a lot about the uninvited wildlife who show up on your doorstep (or in your house, as it were). What is the worst experience you've had with an animal in the cabin?

Here in western North Carolina, we have two kind of venomous snakes—copperheads and rattlesnakes—and of those two, copperheads are the lesser of two evils. Still, a copperhead could easily kill one of our pets or make us very ill, and so that first copperhead we found inside the house terrified me. By the time we found the second copperhead, though, I was in a better frame of mind in general, so I was able to handle it a bit better.

The other animals we worry about—not for our safety but for the safety of our livestock—are coyotes and black bears. We have not yet seen a black bear on our property, but we know they are close by, and we have seen and heard plenty of evidence of coyotes. During the last kidding season, one of our across-the-way neighbors had a pack of coyotes crawl through a culvert into his goat pasture one night. His guard dogs killed the coyotes one by one and stacked up their bodies, so when he walked out to the pasture the next morning, he found a pile of dead coyotes! So stories like that are a bit alarming, especially since we don't have an official guard dog. However, our Lab, Hester, seems to have taken it upon herself to fulfill that role. Every night, after the goats are in the barn, she stands outside and repeatedly barks this really odd high-pitched bark. She does that for hours until we make her come inside for the night.

During this time, what did you learn about yourself that surprised you the most?

Oh, wow. I have learned so, so many things—practical things like that you should probably have a job that pays a living wage, and you should probably pay closer attention to your finances—as well as intangible things. My life before revolved around doing what I thought I *should* do or what I believed other people thought I should do, and I was so busy doing those things, I never really understood what I wanted. I didn't stop consider other possibilities or to listen to those parts of me that longed for a simpler life, for some deeper connection to the people I loved. So I think I have made some progress toward figuring out how to do that, how to create a life that is meaningful with the people I love.

Cooking is a major theme throughout *Flat Broke with Two Goats*. Do you have a favorite recipe right now?

I have recently gone back to teaching, and between that and writing, I have been so busy that I have kept my meal preparation fairly simple lately. Now, I often make a big batch of soup on Saturday or Sunday, and we eat that for days. Fortunately, neither of us minds having taco soup for three or four nights in a row!

What does your writing process look like?

I tend to approach writing like I approach most things in my life—in a fairly disjointed way without much of a plan! In general, I tend to draft a lot of material fairly quickly and then go back and edit and revise. Structure is always the hardest part for me (both in writing and in life), so when I know what I want to say, I sometimes ask someone I trust to help me assess whether my structure is working. Right now, for example, I am working on a collection of vignettes, and though I love the freedom and flexibility of writing in this form, I also find it challenging to organize all the various pieces. Lately, I have been turning to other authors who use the similar styles and techniques to see how they approach structure and how they have made coherent wholes out of seemingly disparate pieces.

What books or authors are your favorite?

There are so many books and authors I admire, but right now, Maggie Nelson's *Bluets* is at the top of my list. I just think it is so bold and beautiful and brilliant. I also really admire Cheryl Strayed (*Wild*) because she writes with such lovely, brutal honesty about her struggles and imperfections. I also love Jo Ann Beard's *The Boys of My Youth* and Marion Winik's *First Comes Love*. These women all tackle tough personal experiences with a frankness I tremendously admire. They are not afraid to go to hard places emotionally, and yet somehow in telling their stories, they elevate those painful experiences.

What do you want readers to take away from your story?

One of my closest friends has ovarian cancer, and I have often heard her speak of the "gift" of cancer. What she means is that the cancer, as horrific as it is, has deepened her relationships and sharpened her sense of what is important in her life. My financial crisis was not equivalent to a prolonged battle with a devastating form of cancer. However, our financial calamity forced me to reexamine my values and beliefs in a way I might never have done otherwise. If our home had never been foreclosed or the IRS had not come knocking on our doors, I would probably still be floundering around in the illusion of my upper-middle-class life. So I think that's the takeaway—or at least, I hope it is. I hope people walk away from my story knowing that they, too, have the power to reimagine their lives.

Acknowledgments

When I try to pinpoint the moment I began writing this book, I find it akin to trying to name the exact moment when I first knew I loved dogs or ice cream or the scent of lavender. I don't remember ever *not* liking those things. Likewise, I can't ever remember a time when I *wasn't* writing something, something that eventually led me to the words on these pages. This makes it ridiculously difficult to narrow down the list of those people who have helped me along my journey to the publication of this book. Nonetheless, I will try.

Many thanks to my agent, Suzy Evans, for fervently believing in my book from the get-go, for countless insights throughout this process and the willingness to ask me all the tough questions in all the nicest ways. Thanks also to all the wonderful, talented people at Sourcebooks but especially my editors, Anna Michels and Margaret Johnston, for their enthusiasm for this project and for their astute and gentle guidance along the way. Thanks also to the editors of *PANK*, SalonZine, Blue Mesa Review, Mason's Road, and *Lumina* who first published portions of this story in other forms. I am also immensely grateful to my mentors at Vermont College of Fine Arts—Connie May Fowler, Jacquelyn Mitchard, Robert Vivian, and Sue William

Silverman. They taught me to believe in the value of truth telling, and without their support and guidance, this book simply would not be.

I also owe a tremendous debt of gratitude to my friends who put up with all my crazy talk about writing a book about goats—especially Susan, whose love of quirkiness reaches a sort of reverence and who has never failed to make me laugh out loud while also making me think; Frannie, whose breathtaking storytelling continually emboldens me; Karen, who has served me food for the body and for the soul; Margaret, who has not yet given up trying to teach me to take things "little by little" and to "bend with the wind"; and April, whose grace, humor, wisdom, and courage inspire me daily. Though I have no blood sister, you are all sisters of my heart. Many, many thanks also go to Tommy Hays, one of my great heroes, both in writing and in life. Tommy, you were the first person to really believe in my work and one of my greatest champions along the way. I am forever grateful for your kindness and generosity.

Last, but certainly not least, I owe a tremendous debt of gratitude to my family, including my parents, who passed on to me their love of animals and nature and who supported me even when this whole idea of writing a book seemed a little far-fetched. I am also grateful for the love and support of my brother, Robert. Though you do not make an extended appearance in this book, you and Rodrigo appear in my life, where it counts.

For far too many reasons to name here, I am also unceasingly grateful for my three children. Your warm and funny and giving spirits fill me daily and make me know I have, indeed, done something right. You are the reasons any of this matters at all. And finally, I am profoundly grateful for my husband, whose name is not actually David but whose resourcefulness and tenacity and steadfastness have carried us this far. I love you more than Ama does—which is to say, an awful lot.

About the Author

Photo © Avery McGaha

Jennifer McGaha lives with her husband and menagerie of animals in the North Carolina mountains. She holds an MFA from Vermont College of Fine Arts, and her work has appeared in the Huffington Post, the Good Men Project, *PANK*, the *Chronicle of Higher Education*, Baltimore Fishbowl, Your Impossible Voice, the Brooklyner, *Switchback*, *Little Patuxent Review*, *Lumina*, and dozens of other magazines and journals. When she is not milking a goat or whipping up a batch of soap, she enjoys biking and hiking the trails and back roads of her native Appalachia.